MIND—
ITS MYSTERIES
AND CONTROL

MIND—ITS MYSTERIES AND CONTROL

Sri Swami Sivananda

Published by

THE DIVINE LIFE SOCIETY
P.O. SHIVANANDANAGAR—249 192
Tehri-Garhwal, Uttarakhand, Himalayas, India
www.sivanandaonline.org, www.dlshq.org

First Edition: 1935
Twenty-first Edition: 2023
[2,000 Copies]

ISBN 81-7052-006-1
ES 105

PRICE: ₹ 340/-

Published by Swami Padmanabhananda for
The Divine Life Society, Shivanandanagar, and printed
by him at the Yoga Vedanta Forest Academy Press,
P.O. Shivanandanagar, Distt. Tehri-Garhwal, Uttarakhand,
Himalayas, India
For online orders and Catalogue visit : dlsbooks.org

OM

1st July 1946

Beloved Dheerender!

Fear not. The mind is no doubt extremely turbulent. Through repeated attempts you can perfectly subdue it.

You are the master of the mind. By Abhyasa and Vairagya assert your mastery. Feel the power, bliss and splendour that result from perfect self-conquest.

Curb the mind ruthlessly. Annihilate desire. When desire dies mind is your slave. Become desireless and be victorious.

May you rest in your pristine freedom!

PRAYER

O Thou Invisible One! O Adorable One! O Supreme! Thou permeatest and penetratest this vast universe from the unlimited space down to the tiny blade of grass at my feet. Thou art the basis for all these names and forms. Thou art the apple of my eye, the Prema of my heart, the very Life of my life, the very Soul of my soul, the illuminator of my intellect and senses, the sweet Anahata music of my heart, and the substance of my physical, mental and causal frames.

I recognise Thee alone as the mighty Ruler of this universe and the Inner Controller (Antaryamin) of my three bodies. I prostrate again and again before Thee, my Lord! Thou art my sole refuge! I trust Thee alone, O ocean of mercy and love! Elevate, enlighten, guide and protect me. Remove obstacles from my spiritual path. Lift the veil of ignorance, O Thou Jagadguru! I cannot bear any longer even for a second, the miseries of this body, this life and this Samsara. Give Darsana quickly. O Prabho! I am pining. I am melting. Listen, listen to my fervent, Antarika prayer. Do not be cruel, my Lord. Thou art Dinabandhu. Thou art Adhama-Uddharaka. Thou art Patita Pavana (Purifier of the fallen).

Om Santih Santih Santih

PUBLISHERS' NOTE

To everyone striving for success in life, the invariable stumbling block proves to be the turbulent vagaries of the mind. An undisciplined mind makes a man slave and wrecks his life. Controlling and subduing it is the most vexing of problems to the earnest seeker of happiness. The vital importance of the subject, therefore, prompted H.H. Sri Swami Sivanandaji Maharaj to write this comprehensive work "MIND—ITS MYSTERIES AND CONTROL." It is meant to serve as a valuable guide to all aspirants and it is also of immense help to anyone in any walk of life. Being the outcome of personal experience of the revered author and written with a practical end in view, "MIND—ITS MYSTERIES AND CONTROL" is a treasure worthy to be possessed and studied constantly.

PREFACE

Happiness has for ever been the prime aim of every human being. All activities of man are directed towards acquiring the maximum happiness in life. But, through the wrong deluded notion that objects will give happiness, man searches for it outside. The result is that in spite of all his lifelong efforts, he gets disappointment only. Vexation and misery alone are to be seen everywhere. The real lasting happiness lies within man. Such happiness or Ananda is the Inner Self, the Antaratman. The very nature of Atman is pure Joy. This is never perceived because the mind is completely externalised. As long as the mind is restlessly wandering about amidst objects, ever fluctuating, excited, agitated and uncontrolled, this true joy cannot be realised and enjoyed. To control the restless mind and perfectly still all thoughts and cravings is the greatest problem of man. If he has subjugated the mind, he is the Emperor of emperors.

For gaining mastery over the mind, you have to know what it is, how it works, how it deceives you at every turn and by what methods it can be subdued. In this book, the subject has been dealt with; and the nature of the mind, the various forms that it assumes, the secret of its inner workings and the way to control it are fully and clearly explained. The previous editions were eagerly read and appreciated by thousands of aspirants who wrote to say how immensely they were helped by the instructions. The lessons and instructions are eminently practical and many helpful ideas and suggestions got during my meditations have been recorded and put down here. Very useful hints on concentration and meditation will be found in the book which, if faithfully followed, will bring success in a short time without fail.

I pray to every aspirant to study constantly the valuable instructions with care and follow the practical hints given in his Sadhana and daily life. It will doubtless enable you to gain control over your passions and cravings and to get established in Yoga. The Bhakta, the student of Vedanta, the Raja Yogin, the Karma Yogin—all will find this book an indispensable guide. The later stages of Yoga Sadhana are common in all the four paths and Dharana and Dhyana are quite impossible without first subduing the mind. All Sadhanas are, therefore, aimed at obtaining mastery over the mind. Hence it is that I have tried to present the ways and means of achieving this through simple, yet well-tried and effective methods. My efforts would be amply fulfilled if even a single earnest aspirant is helped on the spiritual path and attains the Goal.

May the Lord, the Antaryamin, the Supreme Indweller inspire all to attempt mind-control and Yoga! May He bestow success on the sincere aspirants that struggle to master the unruly mind! May you reach the Goal of Life, Immortality, Supreme Knowledge and Bliss!

Swami Sivananda

CONTENTS

(11)

Mind—Its Mysteries and Control

CHAPTER 1

WHAT IS MIND?

"He who knows the receptacle (Ayatana) verily becomes the receptacle of his people. Mind is verily the receptacle (of all our knowledge)."   *(Chhandogya Upanishad, V-i-5)*

That which separates you from God is mind. The wall that stands between you and God is mind. Pull the wall down through Om-Chintana or devotion and you will come face to face with God.

THE MIND—A MYSTERY

The vast majority of men know not the existence of the mind and its operations. Even the so-called educated persons know very little of the mind subjectively or of its nature and operations. They have only heard of a mind.

Western psychologists know something.

Western doctors know only a fragment of mind. The afferent nerves bring the sensations from the periphery or extremities of the spinal cord. The sensations then pass to the *medulla oblongata* at the back of the head, where the fibres decussate. From there, they pass on to the superior frontal gyrus or superior frontal convolution of the brain in the forehead, the supposed seat of the intellect or mind. The mind feels the sensations and sends motor impulses through the afferent nerves to the extremities—hands, legs, etc. It is a brain-function only for them. Mind, according to them, is only an excretion of the brain, like bile from liver. The doctors are still groping in utter darkness. Their minds need drastic flushing for the entry of Hindu philosophical ideas.

It is only the Yogins and those who practise meditation and introspection that know the existence of the mind, its nature, ways and subtle workings. They know also the various methods of subduing the mind.

Mind is one of the Ashta-Prakritis. "Earth, water, fire, air, ether, mind, reason and egoism—these constitute the eightfold division of My Nature" (Gita, VII-4).

Mind is nothing but Atma-Sakti. It is brain that wants rest (sleep), but not the mind. A Yogi who has controlled the mind never sleeps. He gets pure rest from meditation itself.

HOW THE MIND ORIGINATED

Mind is Atma-Sakti. It is through mind that Brahman manifests Himself as the differentiated universe with heterogeneous objects. Brahma thought, "There, indeed, are the worlds; I shall create the protectors of the worlds." He gathered the Purusha (Hiranyagarbha) from out of the waters only and fashioned him. He heated him by the heat of meditation. When he was thus heated, his heart burst out. From the heart, the mind came; from the mind the moon, the presiding deity of the mind. (Heart is the seat of the mind; so, the mind came out when the heart burst out. In Samadhi, the mind goes to its original seat, i.e., heart. In sleep also, it rests in the heart with a veil of ignorance between it and Brahman) (Aitareya Upanishad, 1-3-4).

COSMIC MIND AND INDIVIDUAL MIND

Hiranyagarbha, otherwise known as Karya Brahman and Sambhuti, is cosmic mind. He is the sum total (Samashti) of all the minds. The individual mind is connected with the cosmic mind. Cosmic mind, Hiranyagarbha, superconscious mind, infinite mind, universal mind are synonymous terms. Different authors have used different terms. Do not be puzzled. Do not be confused. It is Sabda-bheda only.

Hiranyagarbha is cosmic Prana also. He is the Sutratman (thread-like Self). He represents the electric, cosmic power-house. The different Jivas represent the different, small bulbs. Electricity from the power-house flows through the insulated copper wires into the bulbs. Similarly, the power from Hiranyagarbha flows into the Jivas.

The mind, being very subtle, is in close apposition or contact with other minds, though the human skull intervenes between them. As mind evolves, you come into conscious relation with the mental currents, with the minds of others—near and distant, living and dead. The individual mind of A, although separated from the mind-substance used by other individuals, B, C, D, E, X, Y, etc., by a thin wall of very finest kind of matter, is really in touch with the other apparently separated minds and with the universal mind of which it forms a part.

If A is a friend of B, A's mind is connected with B's mind. The minds of friends, relatives, brothers of A are attached to A's mind. Several minds are similarly linked to B's mind also. The minds of those who are attached to A's mind are, therefore, connected, in turn, with the minds of those who are hanging on B's mind. In this manner, one mind is in touch with all minds in the whole world. This is the Vibhu theory of mind of Raja Yoga.

MIND IN SANKHYA PHILOSOPHY

In Sankhya philosophy, Mahat is the term used to denote "cosmic mind" or "universal mind." It is the first principle that is derived from Avyakta. It is the first principle that is manifested out of the unmanifested Avyakta. The wheel of the bullock-cart rests on the spokes. The spokes rest on the nave. Even so, the mind rests on Prakriti and Prakriti rests on Brahman.

From Mahat comes Ahankara. From Sattvic Ahankara comes mind; from Rajasic Ahankara comes Prana; from Tamasic Ahankara, Tanmatras; from Tanmatras, gross elements; from gross elements, the gross universe. Mind is no other than Ahankara, the idea of 'I'. It is, indeed, difficult to eschew this idea of 'I'. Mind always attaches itself to something objective (Sthula). It cannot stand by itself. It is only this mind that asserts itself as 'I' in this body.

The idea of 'I' is the seed of the tree of mind. The sprout which first springs up from this seed of Ahankara is Buddhi. From this sprout, the ramifying branches called Sankalpas have their origin.

LINGA SARIRA AND ANTAVAHA SARIRA

Mind is the most important Tattva of Linga Sarira. Linga Sarira is the astral body or Sukshma Sarira that is linked to the physical body through physical Prana. It separates itself at death from the physical body and travels to Svarga or heaven. It is this body that does Avagamana (coming and going). This body melts in Videha Mukti (disembodied salvation).

There is a difference between Linga Sarira and Antarvaha Sarira. Linga Sarira is astral body with seventeen Tattvas, viz., five Karma-Indriyas, five Jnana-Indriyas, five Pranas, Mind and Buddhi. Antarvaha Sarira is very pure. It is full of Sattva. It is free from Rajas and Tamas. It is with this body that a Yogi passes from one body to another (Parakaya-Pravesa). Lila, through the grace of Sarasvati, came out of the physical body and travelled to higher worlds with this Antarvaha Sarira. You will find this in the Yogavasishtha. Sri Sankaracharya, Raja Vikramaditya, Hastamalaka and Tirumular had Antarvaha Sarira. With the help of this special kind of pure body, they passed into the bodies of other persons. A Yogi with Antarvaha Sarira has Sat-Sankalpa or Suddha Sankalpa.

MIND IS SUBTLE MATTER

Mind is not a gross thing, visible and tangible. Its existence is nowhere seen. Its magnitude cannot be measured. It does not require a space in which to exist.

Mind and matter are two aspects as subject and object of one and the same all-full Brahman, who is neither and yet includes both. Mind precedes matter. This is Vedantic theory. Matter precedes mind. This is scientific theory.

Mind can be said to be immaterial only in the sense that it has not the characteristics of ponderable matter. It is not, however, immaterial in the sense that Brahman (Pure Spirit) as such is. Mind is the subtle form of matter and hence the prompter of the body. Mind is made up of subtle, Sattvic, Apanchikrita (non-quintuplicated) Tanmatric matter. Mind is all electricity. According to the Chhandogya Upanishad, mind is formed out of the subtlest portion of food.

Mind is material. Mind is subtle matter. This discrimination is made on the principle that the soul is the only source of intelligence; it is self-evident; it shines by its own light. But the organs (mind and senses) derive their principle of activity and life from the soul. By themselves, they are lifeless. Hence the soul is always a subject and never an object. Manas can be an object of the soul. And it is a cardinal principle of Vedanta that that which is an object for a subject is non-intelligent (Jada). Even the principle of self-consciousness (Aham Pratyak-Vishayatva) or Ahankara is non-intelligent; it does not exist by its own light. It is the object of apperception to the soul.

THE MENTAL BODY

Just as the physical body is composed of solid, liquid and gaseous matter, so also the mind is made up of subtle matter of various grades of density with different rates of vibration. A Raja Yogi penetrates through different layers of mind by intense Sadhana.

The mental body varies much in different people. It is composed of coarse or finer matter, according to the needs of the more or less unfolded consciousness connected with it. In the educated, it is active and well-defined; in the undeveloped, it is cloudy and ill-defined.

There are several zones or slices in the mental body just as there are various compartments in the brain for particular types of thought. During intense anger, the whole mind is suffused with the black hue of malice and ill-will, which expresses itself in coils of thunderous blackness, from which fiery arrows of anger dart forth, seeking to injure the one for which the anger is felt.

TYPES OF MIND

Every man has a mental world of his own. Every man entirely differs from another man in mode of thinking, temperament, taste, mentality, physical characteristics, etc. Physically also a man differs from another man, although there might be slight resemblance. Observe carefully the nose, the ears, the lips, the eyes, the eyebrows, the arrangement of teeth, the shoulders, hands, fingers, toes, look, voice, gait, way of talking, etc., of different men. You will find vast differences between any two persons. Even the lines of the palm will differ. No two leaves are alike. Variety is the beauty of creation.

There are various types of mind. The Bengali type of mind is emotional and fit for devotion and art. The Madrasi type of mind is intellectual and clever in Mathematics. The Punjabi type of mind and Maharashtra type of mind are chivalrous. Bengal has produced emotional saints, Lord Gouranga or Chaitanya Mahaprabhu, Sri Ramakrishna Paramahamsa Deva, etc. Madras has produced intellectual philosophers like Sri Sankara and Sri Ramanuja. Punjab has produced Guru Nanak, Guru Govind Singh, etc. The Sadhana and path of Yoga vary according to the type of mind, temperament and capacity. Tastes also differ. The sight of a fish brings excessive joy to a Bengali. The sight of tamarind and chillies excites the glosso-pharyngeal nerve of a Madrasi. The sight of a Palmyra fruit excites the Jaffna Tamil of Ceylon and brings excessive joy. The sight of meat brings a peculiar joy to a meat-eater. Is this not a mystery that an object lies outside and saliva appears in the tongue at the sight of it? Because you have this experience daily in everyday life, you do not attach much importance to it. Mind is very mysterious. So is Maya, too.

Even an infinitely superior mind is yet a mind and of the same mould as any man's.

SIZE OF THE MENTAL BODY

Mind is atomic (Anu) according to the Nyaya School; is all-pervading (Vibhu) according to the Raja Yoga School of Maharshi Patanjali; is of middling size (same size as that of the body) according to the Vedantic School.

MENTAL AURA

Mind has got aura (mental aura or psychic aura). Aura is Tejas, brilliance or halo that emanates from the mind. The aura of those who have developed their minds is extremely effulgent. It can travel long distances and affect in a beneficial manner a large number of persons who come under its influence. The spiritual aura is more powerful than either the psychic or Pranic aura.

INFLUENCE OF STRONG MIND OVER WEAK MINDS

A strong mind has influence over weak minds. A hypnotist with a strong mind hypnotises a whole bunch or circle of boys of weak minds.

There are those among us who are much more sensitively organised than others. As an organism, their bodies are more finely and more sensitively constructed. These, generally speaking, are people who are always more or less affected by the mentalities of others with whom they come in contact, in whose company they are.

He who has purified his mind becomes a centre of force. All the lesser, impure, weak minds are unconsciously drawn towards the purified, greater mind, because they derive peace, power and strength from the greater, purified mind.

Mark the influence of a highly developed mind over a less developed mind. It is impossible to describe what it is like to be in the presence of a Master or developed adept. To sit in his presence, though he hardly speaks a word, is to feel a thrilling sensation so much as to feel new inspirations touching one mentally. It will be an extraordinary experience.

If you want to drink water at a tap, you will have to bend your body. Even so, a lower mind will have to bend (to be humble) before a developed mind if it longs to imbibe its virtues. The thought itself must be calm and unruffled. Then only you can draw inspirations. In such conditions only benign influences can be thrown down into the lower mind from the higher. In such calm, mental states, you can hold communion with God. Planning, angry and depressed moods—all disturb the mind and act as stumbling blocks to God-realisation.

MIND IS EVER CHANGING

Mind is nothing but a collection of Samskaras. It is nothing but a bundle of habits. It is nothing but a collection of desires arising from contact with different objects. It is also a collection of feelings aroused by worldly botherations. It is a collection of ideas gathered from different objects. Now, these desires, ideas and feelings constantly change. Some of the old desires and feelings are constantly departing from their storehouse, the mind, and new ones are replacing them.

This constant change does not in any way interfere with the harmony of mental operations. Only some of the old desires, ideas and feelings depart. Those that remain work in healthy co-operation and concord with the new arrivals. The new arrivals are strongly magnetised by the old ones. They both work in harmony and this harmony sustains the identity of the mental existence.

Mind is not only made daily, but always made. Every minute, it changes its colours and shape like a chameleon. It is very Chanchala (wavering) and Asthira (unsteady)—(Gita, VI, 26). Mind is constantly changing. You are gaining new experiences daily. Your beliefs and conscience of 1932 and the faculty which judges right from wrong will change in 1942. The mind evolves through experience. The world is the best teacher or Guru.

According to the state of his knowledge, man's conscience is built up and changes from time to time with the correction of his views, in the light of further knowledge gained subsequently. Conscience is one's own convictions arrived at either instinctively or by reasoning. The conscience of a child or a savage is entirely different from the conscience of a fully grown civilised man and, even amongst civilised men, knowledge varies so much that their consciences direct different lines of conduct. The conscience of a Sattvic man considerably differs from that of a Rajasic man. The conscience of a Sattvic man is very, very clean and pure.

FOURFOLD MIND OR ANTAHKARANA CHATUSHTAYA

Antahkarana is a term used by the Vedantins to include mind, Buddhi, Chitta and Ahankara. When used in a broad sense, it means the internal instrument. 'Antah' means internal; 'Karana' means instrument. It is the inner instrument (as distinguished from the term Bahya Karana, outer instrument or the senses or Indriyas) through which you sense, perceive, think and reason out.

Ahankara is derived from Prithvi-Tanmatra. (Tanmatras are Sukshma Bhutas or subtle elements. The five gross elements are derived from the Tanmatras.) Chitta is derived from Jala-Tanmatra; Buddhi from Agni-Tanmatra; mind from Vayu-Tanmatra; heart from Akasa-Tanmatra.

Mind is Chetana (intelligent) when compared with the senses. It is Jada (non-intelligent) when compared with Buddhi. Sankhya Buddhi or Buddhi in Sankhya Philosophy is will and intellect combined. Some put Chitta under mind, Ahankara under Buddhi.

Manas, Buddhi, Chitta and Ahankara are only Vritti-bhedas or functional aspects of the mind. The Manas has all things for its objects and extends through the past, present and future; it is one only, but has various functions. You are a Judge when you exercise your judicial powers in the court. You are a cook when you work in the kitchen. You are a president of an association when you sit in the chair in that capacity. You are the same man, but you function differently and you are called by different names according to those different functions. Similarly, when the mind does Sankalpa-Vikalpa (will-thought and doubt), it is called Mind; when it discriminates and decides, it is Buddhi; when it self-arrogates, it is Ahankara; when it is the storehouse of Samskaras and seat of memory, it is Chitta; also when it does Dharana and Anusandhana.

Who gave coolness to water, warmth to fire, motion to air?

These qualities are their very nature. Even so, mind has got its Svabhava of running towards objects, Buddhi of determining, Ahankara of self-assertion and self-identification, Chitta of thinking (Smriti) of those objects which are identified by Ahankara.

When the mind is at work, Buddhi and Ahankara work simultaneously along with the mind. Mind, Buddhi and Ahankara work in healthy co-operation. Mind makes Sankalpa-Vikalpa. It thinks whether a certain thing is good or bad. Buddhi comes for determination. It is Buddhi which discriminates the Vishaya (Nischyatmika, Vyavasayatmika).

The Svarupa of mind is thought only. Mind is Sankalpa-Vikalpatmaka. It is Vyakaranatmaka when it forwards the decisions of Buddhi, the messages from Buddhi, to the organs of action for execution. Mind selects, attends and rejects.

FUNCTIONS OF MIND

Sensation, thought and volition are the threefold functions of the mind. Cognition, desire, volition are the three mental processes.

Mind has three states, viz., active, passive and neutral. Mind always wants variety and new sensations. It is disgusted with monotony.

Law of Association, Law of Continuity and Law of Relativity are the three principal laws of the mind.

These are the characteristics of the mind, viz., change (Parinama), activity (Cheshta), suppression (Nirodha), ideation in action (Sakti), physical life (Jivana), characterisation (Dharma).

Thinking, planning, feeling, knowing are the various activities that are going on in the mind. Sometimes you plan. Sometimes you feel. Sometimes you try to know. Sometimes you think seriously. Sometimes you will (volition). Volition brings all the mental faculties into play. You must be able to know by introspection what exactly is going on at different times in the mind.

ASPECTS OF MIND

Conscious mind or objective mind, subconscious mind or subjective mind (Chitta) and superconscious mind are three aspects of the mind. You see, hear and read with the objective mind.

Sensational mind, rational mind and intuitive mind are three aspects of mind according to another classification of Western philosophers.

Heart is the seat of four Tattvas—Prana, Mind, Ahankara and Atman. According to Vedanta, the seat of mind is the heart. Ajna Chakra, which consists of two lotuses and which is tentatively situated in the space between the two eyebrows, is the seat of mind according to the Hatha Yoga School.

SEAT OF MIND

Mind has various faculties and centres and operates through corresponding physical centres in the brain. Mind, Buddhi and understanding are in the Linga Sarira; but they operate through corresponding centres in the physical brain. The brain is not mind as the Westerners think. Mind has its seat in the physical brain. It gains experiences of this physical universe through the vibrations of the brain.

A king, though he has complete sway over his whole territory, though the whole kingdom belongs to him, has got special places for his residence. He has got a splendid palace in the capital and another beautiful, palatial building in Mussoorie or Mount Abu for his stay in summer. Even so, the mind, though it is all-pervading throughout the body, has got three places to reside in during the three states—Jagrat, Svapna and Sushupti. The seat of mind in deep sleep is heart. In dream, the seat of the mind is neck. In waking state, the seat of the mind is the right eye or Ajna Chakra. Just mark what you do in Alochana (deep thinking). You hold your finger on the chin, turn the neck to the right side, turn the gaze towards the space between the two eyebrows and then begin to think seriously on the problem in hand. This goes to show that the seat of the mind is the Ajna Chakra.

MIND IS NOT ATMAN

In the West, the psychologists make a serious mistake in saying that consciousness is a function and attribute of the mind. It is Chit or Atman only that is Pure Consciousness Itself. Mind borrows its light from time to time from its source—Atman, the Light of lights or the Sun of suns and glitters temporarily like consciousness, like the golden gilt in brass. Mind borrows its light and power from Brahman, the source (Yoni), just as the iron-rod borrows its heat and effulgence from fire. Mind is Jada or non-intelligent, but appears to be intelligent by borrowing light from Brahman, just as water exposed to the sun borrows heat from the sun.

Mind can do only one thing at a time. It is finite (Parichhinna). It is Jada. It is the effect (Karya) of Sattva Guna. It is Vinasi (perishable). It is Chanchala (ever-fluctuating). It is a bundle of ideas, Samskaras, habits, impulses and emotions. It borrows light from the Adhishthana (the underlying substratum), Brahman. You can control the mind. The thinker is different from thought. There is no functioning of the mind in deep sleep. You always say, "My mind", as if mind is one of your instruments just like your walking-stick or umbrella. Therefore, mind is not the self-shining Atman.

Even in cases of delirium or in cases where there is paralysis of the mental functions, where a man loses his memory and other faculties partly or wholly, 'He' remains. The 'I' exists (*Aham Asmi*). The mind seems to be as much your property and outside of you as the limbs, the dress worn or the building you dwell in. Therefore, mind is different from 'I'.

Mind gropes in darkness. It forgets every moment. It is changing every second. If food is withdrawn for a couple of days, it cannot think properly. There is no functioning of the mind during deep sleep. It is full of impurities, Vasanas and Trishnas (cravings). It gets puzzled during anger. In fear, it trembles. In shock, it sinks. How can you take the mind, then, as the pure Self?

Manas is an organ of sensation and thought. This instrument must be under the control of someone who uses it. The Jiva or human soul is not the director of the mind, because we see that ordinary men cannot control their minds. They are simply swayed hither and thither by petty Raga-Dvesha, emotion and fear. Therefore, there must exist some other Being, who is Director of the mind. Who is that Being? He is the Manasah pati (Lord of mind), Antaryamin, Kutastha Brahman.

Just as you see the tree in front of you, there must be somebody to see and know what is going on in the mind of

Jivas. That somebody is Kutastha. Kutastha is Brahman Himself. There is a tumbler in front of you. It cannot see itself. An instrument, eye and a seer are needed. If you say that the tumbler can see itself, then there will be Karmakartritvabhava-virodha. It is a logical absurdity. Therefore, you have to admit that there is a silent Sakshi of the mind, who is eternal, unchanging, eternal knower, always the knowing subject. He is witnessing the motives and modifications that arise in the minds of Jivas.

Isvara or Saguna Brahman (Personal God) has full consciousness of Nirguna Brahman. That is His Svarupa-Lakshana. At the same time, he has full cosmic consciousness. He knows what is going on in every mind.

Consciousness *per se* or the Absolute Consciousness is common in all. This pure consciousness is one. It is Kutastha Chaitanya. All the workings of the mind, all modifications that arise in the minds of all are presented to the one common consciousness which is the witness of the mental Vrittis. Even though consciousness is one, when Rama is stung by a scorpion, only Rama feels and not his friend Krishna who is standing near him. Antahkarana or mind is different in every individual. It is Antahkarana that limits a man who is, in reality, identical with the Brahman or Supreme Soul! This identity is realised when the Avarana or veil of ignorance is removed.

The mind is an object of perception for Brahman. Atman directly cognises all the phenomena of the mind, viz., desire, imagination, doubt, belief, disbelief, shame, intelligence, fear, etc. He remains Himself quite unattached and unaffected like the omnipresent ether, like the crystal which reflects different coloured objects, like the sun.

ATMAN—THE SOURCE FOR THE MIND

Manas, which expands through Sankalpas and Vikalpas, is generated with Brahman as its cause. The form which the endless Atman (Supreme Spirit) assumes through Sankalpa is Manas (mind). It first turned its back to discrimination and hence entangled itself in the folds of Vasanas of objects. The underlying substratum, Adhishthana of the mind, the source or basis for mind is Atman or Brahman or Absolute Consciousness. The Power of powers who gives power to the mind, the Light of lights who sheds light on the mind, the Seer of seers

222 they

who witnesses the motives of and movements in the mind, the Support of supports on which the mind rests in sleep is BRAHMAN.

"*Om Keneshitam Patati Preshitam Manah*—Willed and directed by whom does the mind go towards its desired objects?" (Kenopanishad). To that Power of powers I bow with folded hands. That Power of powers I am (*Soham, Sivoham*).

That Secondless Supreme Being who resides in the chambers of your hearts as Antaryamin or Inner Ruler or Controller or Sutradhara or Sakshi (silent Witness), Antaratman (Inner Self), who has no beginning, middle or end, who is the source of this world, the Vedas, body, mind, Indriyas and Prana, who is all-pervading, who is unchanging, who is One Homogeneous Essence (Ekarasa), who exists in the past, present and future, who is self-existent (Svayambhu), who is independent (Svatantra) and who is self-luminous (Svayam-jyotis) is God or Atman or Brahman or Purusha or Chaitanya or Bhagavan or Purushottama.

During dream, you are splendid, effulgent light. Where does it come from? From Atman. The light that is present in the dream clearly indicates that Atman is self-luminous (Svayamjyotis, Svaprakasha).

God is Truth. God is Love. God is Light of lights. God is Peace. God is Knowledge. God is the embodiment of Bliss. God is Sat-Chit-Ananda—Existence Absolute, Knowledge Absolute and Bliss Absolute. God is Eternity. God is Immortality. God is Infinity. God is Avinasi, Supreme Vastu. God is All-pervading Essence or Substance. God is the only Sara Vastu. God is Infinite Beauty.

Bhagavan is a synonymous term for God. He who has the six attributes, viz., Jnana (wisdom), Vairagya (dispassion), Yasas (fame), Aisvarya (divine powers), Sri (wealth) and Dharma (righteousness) in their fullest measure is Bhagavan.

According to Vayu Purana, "Omniscience, satisfaction, eternal knowledge, independence, constant presence of power, infinity of power—these six are said to be the aspects (Angas) of the Great Lord."

Sarvajnatva (omniscience, knowledge of all the worlds, their Jivas and their Karmas), Sarvesvaratva (supreme rulership of all, the power of dispensing the fruits of all Jivas), Sarvantaryamitva (inner control of all names and forms and all

Indriyas and minds), Sarvakaranatva (causality for the creation, preservation and destruction of all), Sarvaniyantritva (doing everything without failure of Niyama), Sarvakartritva (the doing of all actions), Sarvasaktimatva (omnipotence), Svatantratva (absolute independence) are the eight attributes of God.

"Knowledge, desireless, power of control, purificatory action, truth, forgiveness, endurance, creation, the Knowledge of the Self, and being the substratum of all activities—these ten unchangeable (Avyaya) qualities always live in the Great Source of all Good."

Srishti (creation), Sthiti (preservation), Samhara (destruction), Tirodhana (veiling) and Anugraha (blessing) are the five kinds of action (Panchakrityas) of God.

God is the Niyamaka (ruler), Antaryamin (knower of the heart) and Preraka (prompter) also. He helps the Sadhakas in a variety of ways, viz., through dreams, the Inner Voice, by talking through the mouths of others in daily conversations and advice from friends.

Nitya Sukha (eternal bliss), Parama Santi (supreme peace), Nitya Tripti (eternal satisfaction), infinite happiness, Akhanda Sukha (unbroken joy) can be had only in God. Attain this God-consciousness or Self-realisation or Darshana of God through Ananya Bhakti or Vichara. This is the goal of life. This is your highest duty. All other duties are secondary.

The essence of Indriyas is the mind; the essence of mind is Buddhi; the essence of Buddhi is Ahankara; the essence of Ahankara is Jiva (the individual soul). Brahman or Suddha Chaitanya is the womb or Yoni or Adhishthana or substratum for everything. He is the Sakshi or witness of everything.

Atman is the proprietor of a big firm, this mental factory. Buddhi is the manager. Mind is the head clerk. The head clerk has got two functions to perform. He gets direct orders from the manager and he has to supervise the workmen also. Even so, the mind has got two functions. It has connections with the Buddhi, the manager and Karma-Indriyas, the workers.

Mind is more internal than speech. Buddhi (intellect) is more internal than the mind. Ahankara is more internal than Buddhi. Jiva Chaitanya (Abhasa, reflected intelligence) is more internal than Ahankara. Atman or Kutastha is more internal than the Jiva Chaitanya. There is nothing internal to Atman. It is Paripurna (All-Full).

When, by analysing your own mind, you come face to face with something which is never destroyed, something which is by its own nature eternally pure, perfect, self-luminous and unchanging, you will no longer be miserable, no more unhappy.

One Essence only exists. It is One without a second (*Ekameva Advitiyam Brahma*). It is Ananta, spotless, ever pure and Paripurna. Meditate upon It without fluctuation of mind and free yourself from all pains with true calmness of mind. Being quite unreal, Ahankara will perish through efforts.

PROOF FOR THE EXISTENCE OF MIND

What is the nature of the Atman or Brahman? It is Sat-Chit-Ananda. Atman is Vyapaka. Then, what is it that limits the individual soul's vision? It is only mind. This fact proves the existence of an internal instrument, the mind.

In the commentary on the Brihadaranyaka, Sri Sankara gives two proofs of the existence of Manas.

One is that it is Manas which renders all knowledge through senses possible. It is called Sarva Karma Vishaya Yoga. Sense-knowledge is the product of the connection between the mind and the sensory organs. That is why there is no simultaneity of the knowledge of the impressions received through the various sensory organs. People say, "My mind was elsewhere. I did not see that." The impossibility of this simultaneity of knowledge through various sensory organs is an indication of the existence of the mind.

The soul is a constant factor. Between the Atman and the organs of senses, a connecting link is necessary. We have to acknowledge the existence of an internal organ (Mind), through whose attention and non-attention, perception takes place. If we do not admit the internal organ, there would result either perpetual perception or perpetual non-perception—the former when there is a conjunction of Atman, the sense (Indriya) and the object (Vishaya), the three constituting the instruments of perception. If, on the conjunction of these three causes, the effect did not follow, there would take place perpetual non-perception. But, neither is the case. We have, therefore, to acknowledge the existence of an internal organ on whose attention (Avadhana) and non-attention (Anavadhana) perception and non-perception take place. This is the argument for the existence of Antahkarana or mind.

The other proof is the capacity for judgment which we possess. Somebody whom we cannot see touches us; and, we infer the person. Now, mere touch cannot make us aware of this fact. The faculty by which we make such an inference is Manas.

SPECIAL KNOWLEDGE THAT DIFFERENTIATES MAN FROM ANIMAL

An animal is not able to "know itself." It has only physical consciousness. It has no self-consciousness. An animal feels the discomfort and pain. It is not able to analyse its own mental states. A man not only "knows", but he "knows that he knows." This is either mental consciousness or self-consciousness. The man not only "feels" or "senses" things, but he has words to express his feelings and sensations. He can vividly describe his feelings. He may think of himself as experiencing them. He can separate himself from the sensation of feeling. He is able to think, "I feel; I hear; I see; I smell; I taste; I desire; I act; I enjoy," "I know this book," "I know also that I know this book." This is self-consciousness peculiar to human beings only.

In the Police Station, the Chaprasi (peon) strikes ten at the gate. The sound vibrates and passes into the ears of men and animals. The animals also hear ten times the beating. But the man counts them and knows through his Buddhi, "Now it is ten o'clock." He has got this Visesha Jnana (special knowledge); whereas animals have got Samanya Jnana (ordinary knowledge). It is this special knowledge that differentiates a man from an animal. Ahara (food), Nidra (sleep), Bhaya (fear) and Maithuna (copulation) are common to both. Through this Visesha Jnana he knows right from wrong, good from bad, what to do (Kartavya) and what not to do (Akartavya).

THE FOUR SOURCES OF KNOWLEDGE

Inspiration, revelation, insight, intuition, ecstasy, divine sight and Paramananda state are the seven planes of knowledge. There are four sources of knowledge, viz., instinct, reason, intuition and super-intuition or Brahma-Jnana.

Instinct

When an ant crawls on your right arm, the left arm automatically moves towards the right arm to drive away the ant. The mind does not reason there. When you see a scorpion in front of your leg, you withdraw your leg automatically. This is termed instinctive or automatic movement. As you cross a street, how instinctively you move your body to save yourself from the cars! There is no Vritti in such mechanical movement.

Instinct is found in animals and birds. In birds, the ego does not interfere with the free divine flow and divine play. Hence the work done by them through their instincts is more perfect than that done by human beings. Have you not noticed the excellent work done by birds in their building of wonderful nests?

Reason

Reason is higher than instinct and is found only in human beings. It collects facts, generalises, reasons out from cause to effect, from effect to cause (*a priori* and *a posteriori* methods of reasoning), from premises to conclusions, from propositions to proofs. It concludes, decides and comes to judgment. It takes you safely to the door of intuition and leaves you there.

Belief, reasoning, knowledge and faith are the four important psychic processes. First you have belief in a doctor. You go to him for diagnosis and treatment. He makes a thorough examination and then prescribes certain medicines. You take them. You reason out: "Such and such is the disease. The doctor has given me Iron and Iodide. Iron will improve my blood. The Iodide will stimulate the lymphatics and absorb the exudation and growth in the liver. So I should take it." Then the disease is cured, by a course of these drugs, in a month. Then you get knowledge of and perfect faith in the efficacy of the medicine and the proficiency of the doctor. Then you recommend to your friends this doctor and his drugs.

Intuition

Intuition is spiritual Anubhava. Knowledge through functioning of Karana-Sarira is intuition. Sri Aurobindo calls it super-mind or supramental consciousness. There is direct perception of truth (Pratyaksha) or immediate knowledge through Samadhi. You know things by a flash. Professor Bergson preached about intuition in France to make the people understand that there is another higher source of knowledge than intellect. In intuition, there is no reasoning process at all. It is Pratyaksha. Intuition transcends reason, but does not contradict it. Intellect takes a man to the door of intuition and returns back. Intuition is Divyadrishti. It is Jnana-Chakshus. Spiritual flashes and glimpses of truth come through intuition. Inspiration, revelation, spiritual insight come through intuition.

Atma-Jnana

Atma-Jnana is above intuition. It transcends the Karana-Sarira. It is the highest form of Knowledge. It is the only Reality.

CHAPTER 2

MIND AND BODY

BODY, THE MOULD FOR MIND'S ENJOYMENT

The body with its organs is no other than the mind. The physical body is the outward manifestation of the mind. Mind is the subtle form of this physical body. The mind contemplating upon the body becomes the body itself and then, enmeshed in it, is afflicted by it. All the bodies have their seat in the mind only. Should the mind be paralysed, then the body will not evince our intelligence. Without water, can a garden exist? It is the mind which transacts all business and is the highest of the bodies. Mental actions are the real actions. The mind performs all actions very speedily in the Linga Sarira and fluctuates thereby. But, the gross body knows not anything and is inert. Even should this gross body be dissolved, the mind will assume fresh bodies to its liking very quickly. This physical body is the mould, as it were, made by the mind for its own enjoyment, for its outpouring of its energy and thereby gaining different experiences of this world through the five avenues or channels of knowledge, the five Jnana-Indriyas (organs of knowledge or perception).

THOUGHTS MAKE THE BODY

The actions of the mind alone are indeed actions; not so much those of the body. The body is really our thoughts, moods, convictions and emotions objectivised, made visible to the naked eyes. It is a point worthy to note with care that every cell in the body suffers or grows, receives a life-impulse or a death-impulse, from every thought that enters the mind, for you tend to grow into the image of that which you think about most.

When the mind is turned to a particular thought and dwells on it, a definite vibration of matter is set up and often more of this vibration is caused, the more does it tend to repeat itself to become a habit, to become automatic. The body follows the mind and imitates its changes. If you concentrate your thought, the eyes become fixed.

(33)

Every change in thought makes a vibration in your mental body and this, when transmitted to the physical body, causes activity in the nervous matter of your brain. This activity in the nervous cells causes many electrical and chemical changes in them. It is thought-activity which causes these changes.

FACE: AN INDEX OF MIND

Mind is the subtle form of this physical body. The physical body is the outward manifestation of the mind. So when the mind is rough, the body is rough too. As a man of rough appearance generally cannot invoke love and mercy of others, so a rough-minded man cannot invoke love and mercy of anybody. Mind very conspicuously reflects on the face its various states which a man of intelligence can very easily read. Face is an index of the mind, just as the tongue is an index of the stomach.

The body follows the mind. If the mind thinks of falling from a height, the body prepares itself immediately and shows external signs. Fear, anxiety, grief, cheerfulness, hilarity, anger—all produce their various impressions on the face.

The eyes which represent the windows of the soul bespeak of the condition and state of the mind. There is a telegraphic instrument in the eyes to transmit the messages or thoughts of treachery, cunningness, fraud, pure love, compassion, devotion, depression, gloom, hatred, cheerfulness, peace, harmony, health, power, strength and beauty.

If you have the faculty to read the eyes of others, you can read the mind at once. You can read the uppermost thought or dominant thought of a man if you are careful to mark the signs in his face, conversation and behaviour. It needs a little pluck, acumen, training, intelligence and experience.

Your thoughts, sentiments, modes and emotions produce their strong impressions on the face. The face is like an advertisement board wherein is advertised what is going on inside the mind. In face, you can hardly hide your thoughts. You may foolishly think that you have kept up your thoughts in secret. Thoughts of lust, greed, jealousy, anger, revenge, hatred, etc., at once produce their deep impressions on your face. The face is a faithful recorder and a sensitive registering apparatus to register and record all the thoughts that are running in your mind. The face is a polished mirror to indicate the nature of the mind and its contents at a particular time.

He who thinks that he can hide his thoughts is a dunce of the first water. His position is like that of the ostrich which, when chased by the hunters, hides its head underneath the sand and imagines that it cannot be seen by anyone.

Your face is like a gramophone record or plate. Whatever you think is at once written on your face. Every vicious thought serves as a chisel or needle to write down the thoughts on your countenance. Your faces are covered with the scars and wounds which are made by the vicious thoughts of hatred, anger, lust, jealousy, revenge, etc. From the nature of the scar in your face, I can at once read your state of mind. I can at once diagnose your disease of the mind.

MUTUAL INFLUENCE BETWEEN MIND AND BODY

The mind is intimately connected with the body. The mind acts upon the body and the body reacts upon the mind. Mind has influence over the body. A pure, healthy mind means a healthy body. Grief in the mind weakens the body. Body influences the mind also in its turn. If the body is strong and healthy, the mind also becomes healthy and strong. If the body is sick, the mind also becomes sick. A pain in the stomach causes depression in the mind.

BAD THOUGHTS, THE PRIMARY CAUSE OF DISEASE

The primary cause of diseases which afflict the body is bad thoughts. Whatever you hold in your mind will be produced in the physical body. Any ill-feeling or bitterness towards another person will at once affect the body and produce some kind of disease in the body. Intense passion, hatred, longstanding bitter jealousy, corroding anxiety, fits of hot temper actually destroy the cells of the body and induce disease of the heart, liver, kidneys, spleen and stomach. Violent fits of hot temper do serious damage to the brain cells, throw poisonous chemical products into the blood, produce general shock and depression and suppress the secretion of gastric juice, bile and other digestive juices in the alimentary canal, drain away your energy, vitality, induce premature old age and shorten life.

When the mind is agitated, then this body also is agitated. Wherever the body goes, the mind follows. When both the body and mind are agitated, the Prana flows in a wrong direction. Instead of pervading the whole body steadily and equally, it will vibrate at an unequal rate (unrhythmically). Then the food is not digested properly. Diseases originate. If the primary cause is removed, then all diseases will disappear.

The pains that afflict the physical body are called secondary diseases, whilst the Vasanas that affect the mind are termed mental or primary diseases. If bad thoughts are destroyed, all bodily diseases will vanish. Purity of mind means healthy body. Therefore, be careful in your thinking, in the selection of your thoughts. Always entertain noble, sublime, loving and kind thoughts. You will have harmony, health and beauty.

A LAMENTABLE PRACTICE

It is lamentable, indeed, to note that most of the doctors in the world, particularly the allopaths, do more harm than good to their patients. They exaggerate the nature of the disease to their patients. They fill their minds with imaginary fears of all sorts. They do not know the power of suggestions and their influences on the minds of their patients. As greed is ingrained in their minds, as the desire to become rich is deep-rooted in their minds, they try their level best to extract from their patients as much money as they can. If they say to their patients, "This disease is nothing. I will make you all right within a couple of hours," who is going to pay them amply? They give wrong suggestions to their patients: "This is a terrible disease. This is an incurable disease. A dangerous poison, a dangerous microbe is lurking in your lungs." The poor patient spends sleepless nights on account of imaginary fear, on account of wrong suggestion given by the doctor. Every moment he thinks: "I may die at any moment. The doctor has said that my disease is dangerous and incurable." He drags a cheerless existence. The worry and anxiety and fear destroy millions of red blood-corpuscles daily. The doctor gives the wrong suggestions to glorify his skill, dexterity in the profession also.

THE ROOT OF ALL EVILS

The erroneous imagination that you are the body is the root of all evils. Through wrong thinking, you identify yourself with the body. Dehadhyasa arises. You are attached to the body. This is Abhimana. Then, Mamata (mineness) arises. You identify yourself with your wife, children, house, etc. It is identification or attachment that brings about bondage, misery and pain. You never wept when millions of Germans died in the war. Why? Because, there was no identification and attachment. But, you weep profusely when your son dies, on account of attachment. The word 'My' produces wonderful influence in the mind. Note the difference in effects produced in the mind when you hear the two sentences: 'Horse is dead' and 'My horse is dead.'

PAIN IS IN MIND ONLY

Pain is evident so long as you connect yourself with the mind. There is no pain in sleep. If there is an inflammatory swelling on your back with throbbing pain, you do not experience any pain at night when you are asleep. Only when the mind is connected with the diseased part through nerves and thinking, you begin to experience pain. There is no pain when the mind is disconnected from the body by the administration of chloroform. During moments of great joy, the severe pain entirely ceases, as the mind is taken away from the body, from the seat of the pain. If you can consciously withdraw the mind from the diseased part by concentrating it on God or any other attractive object, you will not experience any pain even when you are wide awake. If you have a powerful will and strong Titiksha (power of endurance), then also you will not experience any pain. By constant thinking of any trouble or disease, you only augment your pain and suffering. Pain is in mind. Atman or spirit is Anandasvarupa (full of bliss).

CONQUER THE MIND TO CONTROL THE BODY

With the majority of mankind, the mind is greatly under the control of the body. Their minds being very little developed, they live on Annamaya Kosha mostly. Develop the Vijnanamaya Kosha and, through Vijnanamaya Kosha (Buddhi), control the Manomaya Kosha (mind). The Vijnanamaya kosha is developed by abstract thinking and reasoning, by systematic tion, Brahma-Chintana, study of the Upanishads, Yogavasishtha and Brahma Sutras.

When you have controlled the mind, you have perfect control over the body. The body is only a shadow of the mind. It is the mould prepared by the mind for its expression. The body becomes your slave when you have conquered the mind.

CHAPTER 3

MIND, PRANA AND KUNDALINI

PRANA—THE OUTER COAT OF MIND

There are two principal Tattvas in the universe, viz., mind and Prana. Wherever there is Prana, there is mind also. Even in the external movement of breath beyond the nose, the mind is mixed with the external breath. Prana (energy) is the outer overcoat for the mind. Prana digests the food, turns it into chyle and blood and sends it to the brain and mind. The mind is then able to think and do Brahma-Vichara (enquiry into Brahman). The life of the mind is kept up through the vibration of the subtle psychic Prana which gives rise to the formation of thought.

Prana is gross. Mind is subtle. Mind is formed out of the conglomerate Sattvic essence of the five Tanmatras; whereas, Prana is formed out of the sum total of Rajasic essence of the five Tanmatras. That is the reason why mind is more Sukshma than the Prana.

The Pranamaya Kosha (vital sheath) is more subtle than the physical body. It overlaps the Annamaya Kosha (physical sheath) and is more extensive than it. Manomaya Kosha is more subtle than the Pranamaya Kosha and more extensive than the vital sheath. You have to touch the body of another man to have a physical influence over him. Whereas you can stand at a distance and by mere 'passes' you can impart your Prana to him; because, Prana (vital) is more subtle than the body. You can influence a man mentally through thought even though he lives a thousand miles away from you, because mental force is more subtle than Prana.

INTER-DEPENDENCE OF MIND AND PRANA

Prana and mind stand to one another in the relationship of the supporter and the supported. Both these are only like the flower and its odour or a sesamum seed and the oil in it. If either of them is slain, then the other also will cease to exist. If the mind and Prana cease to exist, then thoughts will not arise at all. The destruction of both will confer Moksha on all.

Ekagrata (one-pointedness) and Nirodha (controlled state) are two Avasthas of the mind. Spanda (subtle or Sukshma) and Nirodha are two Avasthas of the Prana. When the mind becomes one-pointed, Spanda Avastha of the Prana comes by itself. If the mind is purified with true Sattva Guna, the Prana will be distributed freely throughout the body. The food will be digested thoroughly.

MIND, PRANA AND VIRYA

Mind, Prana and Virya (semen) are under one Sambandha (connection). If you can control any one of these three, the other two are controlled by themselves, quite easily. Hatha Yogins try to control the Prana. Raja Yogins try to control the mind. Jnana Yogins start their Sadhana with Buddhi and will.

BENEFITS OF PRANAYAMA

By Pranayama (control of Prana or restraint of breath), you can also increase the mental energy and develop thought-control and thought-culture. This will help concentration and meditation. This will make the mind steady. This will remove Rajas (passion) and Tamas (inertia). This will burn the dross in the mind.

By Pranayama, the mind gradually moves from the gross to the subtle. It, therefore, exercises a wholesome check upon sexual irritation. When some evil thought disturbs your mind, at once take to Padmasana or Siddhasana and do Pranayama. The thought will leave you immediately.

THE SUPERIORITY OF PRANA OVER MIND

The sight is more internal than speech as the sight generally informs without contradiction. Similarly, the hearing than the sight, as the eye may convey false impressions, e.g., the mother of pearl as silver, but the ear never hears a non-existing sound. Similarly, the ear only exercises its functions with the aid of the mind's attention and, similarly, the mind depends on the Prana or life. Prana is, therefore, Brahman, the Innermost of all.

"Forsooth, mind departed from the body. It returned after a year's absence and enquired of the organs: 'How did you survive my separation?' 'In the same way', replied the organs, 'in which an infant not possessing the power of reflection breathes through the agency of his respiratory organs, speaks through the organ of speech, sees by his eyes, hears by his ears.' Mind resumed its place. Then did mind say unto Prana, 'The quality of containing all, which belonged to me, is due to thee.' The function of mind belongs to Prana; from Prana or life proceed all." (Chhandogya Upanishad, V-xiv-15). This parable illustrates the superiority of life (Prana) over mind and other organs. In reality, there was no dispute of any kind.

MIND AND KUNDALINI

Kundalini, the serpent-like coiled power that lies dormant with 3 $\frac{1}{2}$ coils with the face downwards in the Muladhara Chakra, the basal lotus at the end of the spinal column, is connected with Prana and Prana is connected with the mind.

Even a Vedantin (student of the path of Jnana) can get Jnana-Nishtha (superconscious state) only through the awakening of Kundalini Sakti. No superconscious state or Samadhi is possible without the awakening of this primordial energy, whether it is in Raja Yoga, Bhakti Yoga or Jnana Yoga.

Kundalini Sakti can only be aroused when the mind is actually free from passions and desires. Sakti-Chalana or Asvani Mudra, Tadana, Pracharana—all help in awakening the Kundalini. Mahabheda helps in taking the Kundalini higher up. When the Kundalini Sakti is awakened, the mind enters, along with Prana and Jiva, the Sushumna and all perceptions are in the mental space (Chidakasa). After Kundalini is awakened, Prana passes upwards through Sushumna or Brahma Nadi within the spinal cord, along with mind and Agni. The Yogin is freed from physical consciousness. You are shut out from the external objective world. As soon as Kundalini is awakened for the first time, a Yogin gets these six kinds of experiences which last for a short time, viz., Ananda (spiritual bliss), Kampana (tremor of various parts of the body), Udbhava (rising above the ground from his Asana), Ghurni (intoxication divine—the body moves in a circle), Nidra (sleep) and Murchha (fainting). After awakening the Kundalini, you will have to take it up to Sahasrara in the top of the head.

When this Kundalini moves from Chakra to Chakra (from centre to centre), layer after layer of the mind opens up. The Yogin experiences different kinds of bliss (Ananda) at each new centre. He gets different experiences also as well as different powers. He gets control over the five elements. He perceives the universe in its subtle or causal form. He gets full knowledge of the types of various kinds of the causal plane. When Kundalini reaches the Sahasrara Chakra, you are in the Chidakasa (knowledge space).

CHAPTER 4

MIND AND FOOD

"Aharasuddhau Sattvasuddhih
Sattvasuddhau Dhruva Smritih
Smritilabhe Sarvagrantheenam Vipramokshah."

"When the food is pure, the whole nature becomes pure; when the nature becomes pure, the memory becomes firm; and when a man is in possession of a firm memory, all the ties are severed." *(Chhandogya Upanishad, VII-xxvi-2)*

MIND IS MADE OF FOOD

Mind is manufactured out of the food that we take. Subtlest part of food reaches upward to the heart and thence entering the arteries called the 'Hita', and thereby bringing into existence the aggregate of the organs of speech and being changed into the form of the mind, it increases the mind. And thus, the mind, being increased by food, is material and not eternal as held by the Vaiseshikas.

The Upanishadic philosophers believed that the mind depends upon the food for its formation. "The food that we take is transformed in three different ways: the gross or the heaviest part of it becomes the excrement; that of medium density is transformed into flesh and the finest part goes to form the mind." (Chhandogya Upanishad, VI-v-1). "Just as in the churning of curd, its fine particles rise up and are transformed into butter, so when food is consumed, the subtlest part rises up and is transformed into mind." (Chhandogya Upanishad, VI-vi-1 & 2). Later, even in the days of the Bhagavad-Gita, we find that the three different mental temperaments—the Sattvic, the Rajasic and the Tamasic—were supposed to be due to the three different kinds of food that we eat. (Bhagavad-Gita, XVII-8 & 10).

QUALITY OF MIND DEPENDS UPON QUALITY OF FOOD

Food has a direct and intimate connection with the mind and plays a vital part in the make-up of the mind. Sattvic diet calms

(42)

the mind. Rajasic diet excites the mind. Mark the difference in nature between a tiger which lives on flesh and a cow which lives on grass. Food exercises important influence on the mind. You see it clearly every day. It is very difficult to control the mind after a heavy, sumptuous, indigestible, rich meal. The mind runs, wanders and jumps like a monkey all the time. Alcohol causes tremendous excitement in the mind.

Food plays an important role in meditation. For purposes of meditation, the food must be light, Sattvic and nutritious. The body is Annamaya (made up of food). Bhairavi Chakra is in Annamaya Kosha. Bhairavi Chakra is Maya. Light Sattvic food, such as fruits, milk, etc., takes you to Vishnu Chakra and thence to Nirvikalpa state quite easily.

When the quality of the mind depends upon the quality of the food taken, it is natural to insist in the interest of the highest morality upon a kind of Sattvic regimen of diet for those aspirants who lead a contemplative life and householders who are attempting to lead a spiritual life in the world. It was because Narada had his impurity destroyed that the venerable Sanatkumara pointed out to him the way beyond darkness. The way which leads up beyond darkness, therefore, must be sought for in the purity of food, which involves in its train, the purity of mind.

HARMFUL FOODS

Different foods produce different effects in different compartments of the brain. Spiced dishes, sour things, black gram, onions, garlic, tea, wine, fish, meat, mustard oil, etc., excite passions and emotions and should, therefore, be avoided. They should be particularly avoided by a Sadhaka. A Jijnasu (spiritual aspirant) should strictly give up meat, fish and alcoholic drinks as these make the mind coarse and produce excitement in the mind. Heavy food brings Tandri (drowsiness) and Alasya (laziness). Tea should be given up. It destroys Virya. Sugar must be taken in moderation. It is better if it is given up.

FOOD ITEMS HELPFUL IN MEDITATION

Milk, fruits, almonds, sugar-candy, butter, green oats, Bengal oats (Chana) soaked in water overnight, bread, etc., are all helpful in meditation. Thed, a kind of Kandamula found in abundance in Brahmapuri, Vasishtha Guha and other parts of the Himalayas, is very Sattvic. It helps meditation. My friend and spiritual brother Swami Purushottamanandaji used to live on that for some days when he was at Vasishtha Guha, fourteen miles from the reputed Rishikesh. Sunthi-Sevana (taking powder of dried ginger) is very good for aspirants. It can be taken along with milk. It refreshes the mind and helps digestion. Yogins take it very often. Triphala water also is taken by Yogins. It removes constipation, cools the system and stops wet-dreams. Myrobalan or Haritaki (Harad of the yellow kind) can be chewed by Yogic practitioners very often. It preserves semen and checks nocturnal discharges. Potatoes boiled without salt or roasted in fire are very good.

A NOTE OF CAUTION

Evolution is better than revolution. Do not make sudden changes in anything, particularly in food. Let the change be gradual. The system should accommodate it without any hitch. *Natura non facil saltum* (nature never moves by leaps).

A Raja Yogin who wants to control the mind must be able to avoid the two extremes, viz., luxury and severe Tamasic Tapas. Too much fasting brings about extreme weakness. You cannot do any Sadhana. You cannot think. You cannot ratiocinate. Take any food that suits you. Do not make much fuss about it. Any food that is readily available and that agrees with your system is harmless.

WHEN FOOD CAN BE DISPENSED WITH

Food is only a mass of energy. Water supplies energy to the body. Air also furnishes energy. You can live without food for very many days, but you cannot live without air even for some minutes. Oxygen is even more important. What is wanted to support the body is energy. If you can supply the energy from any other source, you can dispense with food entirely. Yogins keep up the body without food by drinking nectar. This nectar flows through a hole in the palate. It dribbles and nourishes the body. A Jnani can draw energy directly from his pure, irresistible will and support the body without food. If you know the process of drawing the energy from the cosmic energy or solar energy, you can maintain the body with this energy alone for any length of time and can dispense with food.

THE SECRET OF MADHUKARI BHIKSHA

The mind is made out of the subtle essence of food. So it is attached to those persons from whom it receives the food. If you live with a friend for a couple of months and take food with him, your mind gets attached to that friend who feeds you. That is the reason why a Sannyasin lives on Madhukari Bhiksha from three to five houses, avoids attachment and travels from village to village. He is not allowed to stay for more than a day in a village during his Parivrajaka (wandering itinerant) life. The mind of a Paramahamsa who thus lives on alms is as clean as the Ganga water and is absolutely free from attachment of any kind. ATTACHMENT BRINGS BONDAGE. Attachment is death. Attachment is the root of all evils.

CHAPTER 5

THE THREE AVASTHAS

Mind has got three Avasthas, viz., Jagrat (waking state), Svapna (dreaming state) and Sushupti (deep sleep state).

JAGRAT AVASTHA (WAKING STATE)

The individual soul (Jiva) is called awake as long as it is connected with the various external objects by means of the modifications of the mind—which thus constitute limiting adjuncts of the soul—apprehends those external objects and identifies itself with the gross body which is one of those external objects. During waking state, the mind occupies the brain.

SVAPNA AVASTHA (DREAMING STATE)

When the mind enters the Hita Nadi, which proceeds from the heart and surrounds the great membrane round the heart, which is as thin as a hair divided into thousand parts and is filled with the minute essence of various colours of white, black, yellow and red, the individual soul or Jiva (ego) experiences the state of dream (Svapna Avastha).

In dream, the senses are thrown off just as you throw off your suit when going to bed. In dream state, the senses are quiet and absorbed in the mind. Mind alone plays during dream. The mind alone operates in a free and unfettered manner. There is no land, no sea, no horse, no elephant in dream; but mind creates everything out of its own body, out of the materials supplied from waking consciousness. The mind itself assumes the various forms of bee, flower, mountain, elephant, horse, river, etc. It is the subject. It is the object as well. The seer and the seen are one.

The objects perceived in dreams are revivals of impressions received in waking state and have an external reality only to the dreamer. When modified by the impressions which the external objects have left, the Jiva sees dreams. Perception takes place through the internal organ called Manas; so it is called "inner perception."

Every man has his own subjective mental world and his own dream-creatures. The dream-creatures of a young lady are her husband and new-born babe. Her mind has two strong mental images, viz., those of her husband and baby. The mental images are strengthened by constant thinking. The dream-creatures of a doctor are his patients, while those of a barrister are his clients.

There is temperamental difference. Some rarely get dreams. A Jnani who has Knowledge of the Self will not have any dream.

THE DIFFERENCE BETWEEN JAGRAT AND SVAPNA

The difference between the waking and the dreaming states consists in this, that in the waking condition the mind depends on the outward impressions, while in the dreaming state, it creates its own impressions and enjoys them. It uses, of course, the materials of the waking hours.

In Jagrat state, the objects exist independent of the mind. So, every day you see the same objects as soon as you wake up from sleep. But in dreams, the objects of dream exist only so long as there is mind, so long as the dream lasts, because the dream-creatures are manufactured out of mind only. In dream, mind itself creates the dream-creatures out of the materials supplied by waking experiences with some modifications. When mind drops down to waking state, all dream-objects vanish.

WAKING STATE, A LONG DREAM

You dream that you are a king. You enjoy various kinds of royal pleasures. As soon as you wake up, everything vanishes. But, you do not feel for the loss because you know that the dream-creatures are all false. Similarly, even in the waking consciousness if you are well established in the idea that the world is a false illusion, you will not get any pain. When you know the real Tattva (Brahman), the waking consciousness also will become quite false like a dream. Jagrat state is only a long dream (Dirgha Svapna). The state of waking consciousness does not exist either in dream or sleep. Therefore, it is illusory. Reality always exists in all conditions or states. Wake up and realise, my child!

SVAPNA-JAGRAT

Manorajya (building castles in the air), recollection of the events and things of dream, recollection of things long past in the waking state are all Svapna-Jagrat (dreaming in the waking state).

SUSHUPTI AVASTHA (DEEP SLEEP STATE)

When the mind enters the Puritat Nadi, the state of deep sleep sets in. In Dridha Sushupti (dreamless sleep), you have a cessation of empirical consciousness. There is no play of the mind in this Avastha (state). There is neither Raga nor Dvesha (attraction or repulsion, like or dislike). The mind gets Laya into its cause. Manolaya (involution of the mind) takes place. There is no play of the Indriyas (organs, senses) too.

This state of profound sleep is not a complete non-being or negative, for such a hypothesis conflicts with the later recollections of a happy repose of sleep. The self continues to exist, though it is bereft of all experiences. The consciousness is continuous. You feel you have existed even during sleep as soon as you are awake. You feel that you exist always. Vedantins build their philosophy around this Sushupti Avastha. This stage gives them the clue to the non-dual state (Advaitic state). A careful study of the three states—Jagrat, Svapna and Sushupti (waking, dreaming and deep sleep)—is of immense practical use for the clear understanding of the Vedanta.

Says Ajata Satru to Gargya in Brihadaranyaka Upanishad (II-i-16): "Where was the spirit whose nature is like knowledge at the time when one profoundly sleeps? When the spirit whose nature is like knowledge thus profoundly slept, then the ether in the midst of the heart, drawing in, together with the knowledge of the senses, slept therein in the ether. When the spirit draws in that (knowledge of the senses), then he sleeps indeed. Thus, life is drawn in, speech is drawn in, the eye is drawn in, the ear is drawn in and the mind is drawn in."

When, on the cessation of the two limiting adjuncts (i.e., the subtle and the gross bodies) and the consequent absence of the modifications due to the adjuncts, the Jiva is in the state of deep sleep, merged in the self as it were, then it is said to be asleep. "When a man sleeps here, then my dear, he becomes united with the Sat; he is gone to his own self. Therefore, they say of him, 'He sleeps (Svapiti), because he is gone to his own (Svamapiti)'." (Chhandogya Upanishad).

Sankara observes that the phenomena of duality caused by the action of the mind are present in the waking and dreaming states only, but absent in deep sleep state. In waking and dreaming states, there is the play of the thoughts (and the simultaneous occurrence of names and forms) and hence the world as well. In dreamless sleep, there are no thoughts; and hence, there is no world too. We taste the nature of absolute bliss in dreamless sleep, where a man is cut off from the distracting world. It is the mind (lower Manas) that creates differences, distinctions, duality and separateness. If this mind is destroyed by increasing the Sattva and Ahangraha Upasana, then you will feel oneness everywhere (Sarvatmabhava). This needs continuous and strenuous efforts on the part of the Sadhakas.

DEGREE OF CONSCIOUSNESS IN THE THREE STATES

In sleep, some action or other is always going on in your mental or vital being; things happen there and they govern waking consciousness. For instance, some are very anxious to perfect themselves and make a great effort in this direction during the day. They go to sleep and when they rise the next day, they find no trace of the gains of their previous day's efforts; they have to traverse the same ground once again. This means that the effort, and whatever achievement there was, belonged to the mere superficial or wakeful parts of the being, but there were deeper and dormant parts that were not touched. In sleep, you fell into the grip of these unconscious regions and they opened and swallowed all that you had laboriously built up in your conscious hours.

Be conscious. Be conscious of the night as well as of the day. First, you will have to get consciousness, afterwards control. Such of you as remember your dreams may have had this experience that sometimes, even while dreaming, you knew it was a dream; you knew that it was an experience that did not belong to the material world. Once you know, you can act there in the same way as in the material world. Even in the dreaming state, you can exercise your conscious will and change the whole course of your dream experience. And, as you become more and more conscious, you will begin to have the same control over your being at night as you have during the daytime, perhaps even more. For, at night, you are free from slavery to the mechanism of the body. The control over the processes of the body-consciousness is more difficult, since they are more rigid, less amenable to change than are the mental or the vital processes. At night, the mental and vital parts of your being, especially the vital ones, are very active. During the day, they are under check; the physical consciousness automatically replaces their free play and expression. In sleep, this check is removed and they come out with their natural and free movements.

SUSHUPTI AND ADVAITA NISHTHA DISTINGUISHED

In sleep, the mind is in a subtle state. The Vrittis have also assumed a subtle state. But, in Advaita (Vedantic) Nishtha, there is no mind. There is no universe. The world sinks down in Brahman (Prapanchopasamam) —(Vide Mandukya Upanishad, II-1).

THE SUPREME SELF IN THE THREE AVASTHAS

The Supreme Self which has four forms, is inside the bodies of all living beings and is known by the names Visva, Taijasa, Prajna and Turiya. The seat of the Visva is the right eye; within the Manas dwells Taijasa (*Manasyantastu Taijasah*—Gaudapada's Karika on the Mandukya Upanishad), while Prajna resides in the ether of the heart. The objects of enjoyment are of three kinds—gross, subtle and bliss itself. Satisfaction is also threefold.

Jagaritasthano Bahishprajnah Saptanga Ekonavimsati-mukhah Sthulabhuk Vaisvanarah Prathamah Padah—The first foot of Omkara is Vaisvanara, whose region is the waking state, who has objective consciousness, who has seven limbs[1] and nineteen mouths[2] and who enjoys gross objects." (Mandukya Upanishad, I-3). The objective mind or conscious mind plays in the waking state.

"*Svapnasthano'ntahprajnah Saptanga Ekonavimsati-mukhah Praviviktabhuk Taijaso Dvitiyah Padah*—The second foot of Omkara is the Taijasa, whose region is dream, who has subjective consciousness, who has seven limbs and nineteen

1   The seven limbs are: (i) Heaven (is His head), (ii) Sun (is His eye), (iii) Wind (is His breath), (iv) Akasa (is His waist), (v) Water (is His pelvis), (vi) Fire (is His mouth) and (vii) Earth (is His feet).

2   The nineteen mouths are: Five Jnana-Indriyas, five Karma-Indriyas, five Pranas and four Antahkaranas (Manas, Buddhi, Chitta and Ahankara.

mouths and who enjoys subtle objects." (Mandukya Upanishad, I-4). Taijasa is the reflected Chaitanya or consciousness associated with the dream state. Taijasa is the enjoyer of the subtle world. The subjective mind and false ego play in dreams.

"*Yatra Supto Na Kanchana Kamam Kamayate Na Kanchana Svapnam Pasyati Tat Sushuptam Sushuptasthana Ekeebhutah Prajnanaghana Evanandamayo Hyanandabhuk Chetomukhah Prajnastritiyah Padah*—The third foot of Omkara is the Prajna, whose region is deep sleep, in whom all melt into one, who is a mass of knowledge, who is full of bliss, who enjoys bliss and who is the door (to the two states of consciousness—waking and dreaming). That is the state of deep sleep wherein the sleeper does not desire anything and does not see any dream." (Mandukya Upanishad, I-5). The mind with the Vasanas rests in deep sleep in Mukhya Prana (chief vital air) in the heart. Mukhya Prana means Brahman. All the Vrittis assume a Sukshma state.

THE THREE GUNAS

GUNAS AND VRITTIS

The mind has three Gunas, viz., Sattva (light, bliss, goodness), Rajas (passion, motion) and Tamas (inertia, darkness). There are three Vrittis in the mind corresponding to the three Gunas. Santa Vritti (peace) comes out of Sattva Guna, Ghora Vritti from Rajo Guna and Mudha Vritti from Tamo Guna. Equilibrium or balance is Santa Vritti; anger is Ghora Vritti; laziness (Alasya), carelessness (Pramada) and drowsiness (Tandri) are Mudha Vrittis.

CHARACTERISTICS OF SATTVA GUNA

Sattva Guna is purity. It is Prakasa (illumination, light). Sattva Guna is a force favourable for the attainment of Moksha. Daivi Sampat—virtues such as fearlessness, purity of heart, etc.,—will confer liberation on you. The effect of Sattva Guna is Brahmavichara (enquiry or search for Truth; differentiation between Sat and Asat, what is real and what is unreal).

A Sattvic mind is always steady. It finds delight internally. It may stick to one place indefinitely. It keeps friendship with persons for a long, long time. It can read the Gita or the Yogavasishtha any number of days. It can live on Dal-roti for years together without any grumbling.

During Sattvic moments, when there is preponderance of pure Sattva in the mind, you are in touch with the Divine Source owing to the cleanness of the mind-mirror. You will get inspiration. You will compose beautiful poetry, etc. Preserve those inspired writings. Jot them down in your notebook.

Sattvapatti is a state of mind wherein the mind is full of Sattva or purity. There is purity of thought (Bhava-Samsuddhi) and purity of heart (Sattva-Samsuddhi). It is the fourth Jnana-Bhumika or fourth stage of Jnana.

CHARACTERISTICS OF RAJO GUNA

Rajo Guna is a hostile force to pull you down into Samsara.

Asuri Sampat—vices like Dambha, Darpa, Krodha, etc.—will drag you down into hell. A mind endowed with Sattva Guna will make a man still and inactive, while a mind with Rajo Guna will make him restless. It will not allow him to sit idle and will force him to work.

The Rajasic mind always wants new sensations and variety. It likes certain persons, objects and places now and, after some time, it becomes disgusted with them and wants new persons for company, new vegetables to eat, new books to read and new places to see (finds pleasure in sightseeing).

The mind of Rajasic type wants always company and talk. These are the two defects which distract the mind much. Avoid company. Live alone. Observe Mouna. You will get peace of mind. Most of the pain comes from bad company. Be careful in the selection of your companions. You will rarely find a good, sincere friend. Never take a friend into your close confidence without testing him for a long time. There is no company or talk in Brahman who is Asanga and Asabda.

The Rajasic mind has a tendency to look into the defects of others. It also remembers the bad deeds or wrongs done by others and forgets easily their good acts. These two tendencies intensify hatred and cause frequent disturbance in the mind.

A mind which is devoid of Sattva Guna will not be good enough to consider others' happiness as its own and will, therefore, be ever reeling. Again, as this mind has not the complacency to rejoice at another's virtues, there is no internal contentment. Then, as it does not consider others' sufferings as its own, there arises in it no compassion for them.

It is the Rajasic mind that splits, separates, divides and deceptively shows plurality (Nanatva). The sun is one. The moon is one. Akasa is one. The idea behind languages is one. The feeling of sincerity is one. There is no inside or outside. Husband and wife become one in heart. Intimate friends are one in heart. Matter is one. Energy is one. Sattvic mind is one. It unifies. Cosmic Mahat is one. Karma (law of cause and effect) is one. Dharma is one. Religion is one. Truth is one. Brahman is one. *Ekameva Advitiyam Brahma* (Brahman is one without a second).

Intense Rajas takes Sattvic turn. Dacoit Ratnakar became the sage Valmiki. Jagai and Madhai, who were intensely Rajasic and who pelted stones at Lord Gouranga, became his first disciples.

IMPORTANCE OF SATTVA GUNA

The real peace of mind does not come from outside. It is produced in the same mind when the mind is controlled and its thoughts are checked. You must put forth great efforts to check the passions and desires. Then alone will your aptitude for activity be subdued and you will be at rest and your thoughts will be stilled. Develop, therefore, Sattva Guna by Japa, Vichara, Satsanga, meditation, light Sattvic food, Tapas and Svadhyaya.

An ordinary worldly-minded man can hardly hear the inner voice of Atman. He cannot get pure thoughts or Vichara (enquiry into Self) also. Every Sattvic (pure) thought emanates from Sattvic Buddhi (pure intellect). In the case of worldlings, all thoughts proceed from the mind only. He who does Nishkama Karma Yoga (selfless service) and has purity of the mind, begins to entertain thoughts of God and meditation. Generally, the mind raises various sorts of curious, fantastic thoughts. It deludes all. It may pretend to do Vichara also. But, when it comes to actual practice, it will do nothing. If there is a serious determination in you to concentrate and, if you put it into actual practice for months steadily and, if the longing for Darshana of God or Self-realisation becomes keen and acute, then alone think that all these kinds of thoughts proceed from your Sattvic Buddhi only.

All Sadhanas aim at the development of Sattva Guna and the attainment of pure, irresistible Will. This will bring about Avidya Nivritti (removal of ignorance) and Paramananda-Prapti (Sat-Chit-Ananda state). Increase of Sattva Guna and pure, strong, determined Will pave a long way in achieving God-realisation.

In the world also, there are persons with a few Sattvic virtues such as patience, generosity, forgiveness, etc. But, a spiritual aspirant tries to develop the mind as a whole, to acquire all Sattvic virtues.

CHAPTER 7

THE PSYCHIC STATES

Sit in silence in a solitary room and watch the various mental phenomena, mental states, moods, impulses, emotions, sentiments, whims, fancies that occur in the mind. It will be of absorbing interest to study the subtle states of the inner psychic world.

INSTINCTS

There are two powerful instincts in the human beings and animals too. They are the instinct of self-preservation and the instinct of reproduction. Hunger is a manifestation of the self-preserving instinct. Lust is a manifestation of reproductive instinct. An instinct is an involuntary prompting to action.

The Jiva or the individual soul with egoism wants power, name and fame. This is for self-aggrandisement. Exploitation is greed. It is the act of using for selfish purposes. Domineering is to command haughtily. The Jiva wants to exercise power over others. This is Jiva-Bhavana. The rootcause for industries, business, commerce, etc., is greed and self-preservation. If you want to have constant Brahma-Bhavana, you will have to give up exploitation and domineering.

There is another third instinct, viz., the herding instinct (the instinct for company). Woman take delight in the company of men. Men take delight in the company of women. The rootcause for this is reproductive instinct. Another reason is that a weak man gains strength in the company of a strong man. But, a man who wants to realise God should shun ruthlessly company—particularly, the company of women and worldly-minded persons. He should live alone. Then he will become very powerful and strong. He will develop a strong individuality. One will find difficulty in the beginning in the practice of living alone. Fear will come in. You will have to overcome all difficulties, one by one, if you want to attain immortality (Amritatva). The reward is very great: *Brahmavit Paramapnoti* (A Knower of Brahman gets the Highest); *Amritamasnute* (He drinks the nectar of immortality).

(55)

IMPULSES

An impulse is a sudden propelling force. There are three kinds of impulses, viz., impulses of thought, impulses of speech and impulses of action. Mouna (silence) checks the impulse of speech. Meditation checks the impulse of wrong thinking and wrong action.

There are two important impulses. They are the sex-impulse and the impulse of speech. There is an intimate relation between impulse and imagination. Imagination induces the impulse. Impulses must be controlled by reason and will and meditation on God.

EMOTIONS

An emotion is a combination of thought and desire. Every idea is charged with emotion. Emotions are desires which are penetrated by the thought element. In other words, emotion is desire mingled with thought. The vibrations of emotions will arouse corresponding excitement in purely mental matter and all the man's thoughts will be disturbed and distorted.

There is emotion-desire. There is emotion-feeling also. If the desire element is predominant, it is emotion-desire. If the pleasure element is predominant, it is emotion-feeling.

Raga and Dvesha (love and hatred) are the two important emotions of the mind and all the different emotions can be classified under these two headings. Wonder is a compound emotion. It is admiration and fear combined. Reverence is a compound emotion. It is awe and respect combined. Amarsha is a compound emotion. It is anger and jealousy combined. As soon as the man is pulled down to a lower level, the anger of the inferior man who was jealous vanishes.

Pleasure is a particular kind of emotion in the mind. The mind expands during pleasure. Coolness prevails in the mind. What takes place of the mind when pleasure feeling arises is not exactly understood by the Western psychologists. It is incapable of being understood also by ordinary persons. Only a Yogi or a Jnani knows this psychic phenomenon. During pain, the mind contracts. Considerable heat is produced in the mind.

Many of the physical desires and emotions in man are akin to those of the lower animals. Anger and sex-impulse in man are the brutal instincts. In the undeveloped man, these desires and emotions which belong to the lower nature (Aparaprakriti) predominate and overpower the higher nature (Paraprakriti).

It is a symptom of weakness to have emotions in the mind. They should be controlled by the intellect and the will.

HOW TO CONTROL EMOTIONS AND IMPULSES

When emotions and impulses trouble you much, be indifferent (Udasina). Say to yourself: "Who am I? I am not the mind. I am Atman (all-pervading Spirit, Suddha Sat-Chit-Ananda. How can emotions affect me? I am Nirlipta (unattached). I am a Sakshi (witness) of these emotions. Nothing can disturb me." When you repeat these suggestions of Vichara, the emotions will die by themselves. This Jnana method of controlling emotions is easier than the Yogic method of driving the emotions and struggling with the mind (*Yogas-chittavritti-nirodhah*).

SENTIMENTS

Religious sentiment, moral sentiment, aesthetic sentiment (or sentiment for the sublime and the beautiful) are the three important sentiments of the mind. Feeling and sentiments are illusory. They are not in Atman. They are deceptions created by the mind.

MOODS

Mood is a mental state. The Sanskrit term is Bhava. This term also does not express the true significance of the word 'mood'. We say, "Mr. Naidu or Mr. Atkinson is a moody gentleman." This means he becomes a slave of the mood quickly. We also say, "That gentleman is in 'good mood' or 'happy mood.'" "I can approach him now for a short interview or talk" or "He is in a very 'angry mood.' I should not see him now."

The English people, during the course of their conversation, use the term 'mood' in a broad sense. They say: "He is in a talking mood"; "He is in a silent mood"; "He is in a mood of hatred"; "He is in a mood of love"; "He is in a mood of selfishness"; "He is in a mood of jealousy"; "He is in a mood of separateness"; "He is in a mood of unity." In the light of Vedanta, these are all Vrittis (thoughts or emotions) only. Dr. Bhagavan Das, the reputed author of "Science of Emotions" classifies these under emotions only.

THE TWO KINDS OF MOODS AND THEIR EFFECTS

In Vedanta, there are only two kinds of moods, viz., Harsha (joy, exultation or exhilaration) and Soka (grief or depression). In the mind, these two kinds of moods prevail. Now there is joy. Five minutes later, there is depression. These currents alternate. They belong to the Shad-Urmis (six waves). They are two waves that affect the mind-ocean.

People of gloomy moods attract to them gloomy things and gloomy thoughts from others and from the Akasic records in the physical ether. Persons with hope, confidence and cheerful spirits attract thoughts of similar nature from others. They are always successful in their attempts.

People with negative moods of depression, anger, hatred do positive injury to others. They infect others and raise these destructive Vrittis in others. They are culpable. They do great damage in the thought-world. People with happy and cheerful moods are a blessing to society. They bring happiness to others.

Just as a young, beautiful lady covers her face and does not like to come out to mix with others in society when she has a nasty festering sore on her cheeks or nose, so also you should not come in public and mix with your friends and other people when you have a mood of depression, a mood of hatred or jealousy. For, you will infect others with these moods. You are a menace to society.

HOW TO CONTROL NEGATIVE MOODS

Sadhakas should try to eradicate depression by prayer, meditation, counter-thoughts of joy, chanting of Om, Vichara and singing divine songs. Never give room for gloomy depression. Repeat Om with Bhava. Repeat "I am Anandamaya," "My Svarupa is Ananda." Depression will vanish. There are various causes for this depression. Cloudy day, association with evil persons, indigestion, influence by astral spirits, revival of old Samskaras of depression—all these induce depression.

When you get a talking mood, practise at once 'Mouna' (silence). This is an antidote to the talking mood. When you are in a mood of hatred, develop the opposite virtue of love. This mood will pass off quickly. When you are in the mood of selfishness, begin to do selfless work. When you are in the mood of separateness, try to mix with others through service, love, kindness and Kshama. When you are in the mood of laziness, do at once some kind of active work, drawing water, gardening, running, brisk walk or biking, etc.

A Jivanmukta is absolutely free from all moods. He has controlled all moods completely. He has become a master of all these moods. In Atman, there are no moods. It is pure consciousness. Identify with Atman. You can destroy all moods very easily.

THE MEDITATIVE MOOD

But, there is one good mood in those who practise meditation. It is termed the "meditative mood." Those who practise concentration and meditation feel this kind of mood. When this mood manifests, you must immediately give up reading, writing, talking, etc. You must immediately sit on the usual Asana (posture) and begin to meditate. Meditation will come by itself without effort. This mood is very favourable for contemplation. Watch for this kind of mood. If light disturbs you, close the windows or put on a curtain along the window. Dark room is favourable for the beginners in meditation.

WHIMS AND FANCIES

A whim corresponds to the term 'Taranga' in Sanskrit. Taranga means a wave. When a sudden change arises in the mind, it is a whim. Whims are Tarangas that arise in the mind. They rise up and break quickly. They drag you hither and thither. They upset you.

Everybody has his own whims. Very often you say, "He is a whimsical man," when anyone is swayed by whims. Whim is also termed caprice. Eccentricity is an exaggerated form of whim. Whim tosses a man hither and thither, if he yields to it. Whimsical actions bring on misery. It is through whim that mind tempts and deceives men. Mind cheats through whims. Whims should be checked by reason.

Do not do actions through whims. Action must be done through Viveka and wisdom. Destroy whims as soon as they arise, through Vichara. Always enquire whether the proposed action will bring you pleasure and spiritual gain or not. Be on the alert.

The word 'whim' always goes with the term fancy. We say, "whims and fancies." A fancy is a phase of the intellectual faculty of a lighter and less impressive cast than the imagination of the active play of this lighter faculty. Fancy is a new and pleasing thought or conception due to this faculty. Fancy is a form of imagination. It helps a poet, but not an aspirant. It is a hindrance in meditation. It builds castles in the air. Check it by Vichara and Viveka.

Just as waves and ripples rise on the surface of the ocean, whims, various caprices, fancies and wrong determinations also arise on the surface of the mind-ocean. The whims represent the ripples. You need not be afraid of these. They come and pass off quickly. You must be careful about the strong waves, wrong determinations. The strong thoughts must be eradicated by strong Vichara and proper reasoning.

IMAGINATION

Prakriti never creates a vacuum in the mind. If one anxiety or worry is over, another anxiety immediately manifests. Mind can never become vacant. It has got infinite preoccupations.

Carefully mark the ways of the mind. It tempts, exaggerates, magnifies, infatuates, unnecessarily alarms through vain imagination, vain fear, vain worries and vain forebodings. It tries its level best to divert you from concentration on your Lakshya.

It took me many years to understand thoroughly the subtle workings of the mind. Mind works havoc through its power of imagination. Imaginary fears of various sorts, exaggeration, concoction, mental dramatisation, building castles in the air, are all due to this power of imagination. Even a perfect, healthy man has some imaginary disease or other due to the power of imagination of the mind. Much energy is wasted on account of imaginary fears.

When his mind is fully occupied with the affairs of the war, the soldier does not feel any serious injury as a gunshot wound in the leg. He is not aware of the loss of a large quantity of blood also. He is filled with enthusiasm. He is not conscious of his body—so to say—for the time being. When the excitement is over, when he sees some blood-spots on his clothing or when some of his friends point out to him the wound in the leg, he gets the consciousness. Then he is alarmed a bit. The power of imagination plays havoc now. He gets a collapse now. The power of imagination always exaggerates.

A man may have a little weakness. When he becomes your enemy, you at once exaggerate and magnify his weakness and Dosha. You even superimpose on this or concoct many more weaknesses and Doshas. This is due to evil imagination on your part.

Whenever the mind of two friends are strained by ill-feelings, these minds begin to exaggerate and concoct things. Fault-finding increases. It is very difficult to get at the truth of the statements of these two broken friends with broken friendship. Their utterances are always coloured by their inner feelings. The power of imagination does havoc now. Maya plays havoc through the mind and its power of imagination.

Mind tempts and deceives. Think of one as a good friend of yours and there the thing is created as a reality. Think of him as your foe and then also the mind perfects the thought into an actuality. He who knows the working of the mind and has controlled it by practice is really happy.

I shall explain to you the nature of "mental dramatisation." Mark the ways of the mind. During conversation with your friends, the mind sometimes imagines in vain that it has hurt the feelings of your friend. It spends much of its energy in unnecessary feeling. You think: "How can I see him tomorrow morning? He may be displeased with me." Next morning when you meet him, nothing happens. Your friend starts a pleasant conversation and smiles. You are surprised. To your great astonishment, the subject of talk takes quite a different turn altogether. A family-man imagines when a severe epidemic of plague ravages: "What shall I do if my wife develops plague and dies now? I have got six children." This is his vain imagination. Nothing happens. Sometimes, when the train moves slowly on the Pamban Bridge over the sea near Ramesvaram, the mind imagines, "If the bridge gives way now, what will become of me? I shall be smashed to pieces." A touch of fear creeps in. There are thousand and one ways of mental dramatisation like these. The power of imagination plays a vital part in mental dramatisation.

When your mind is deeply concentrated, period of two hours passes like five minutes. If the mind is distracted and wandering, half an hour hangs on as two hours. This is everybody's experience. In dream also, many events that represent a period of fifty years take place within ten minutes. Through the play of the mind, a Kalpa is considered by it as a moment and vice versa. Time is but a mode of the mind. It is Kala Sakti. It is also illusory like the objects.

Through the trick of the mind, one furlong at times appears to be a great distance and three miles at other times appear to be a very short distance. You ought to have noted this in your daily life.

Marichi Chaitanya, M.A., Ph.D., a Brahmachari of Rumania and myself sat for dinner in the Kailasa Kutia, Svarga Ashram, on the bank of the Ganga. A dish of potato soup was served. Marichi, who has no idea of Indian preparations, took it for a soup of meat. The colour and appearance of the potato soup was exactly the same as that of meat-soup. This is a case of "mental projection." Marichi projected the idea of meat from his own Samskara within the mind into the potato-soup. Mental projections are all false.

Kalpana in the mind means mental creation or imagination. This is the real Yogamaya. You will have to destroy these various Kalpanas. This is the aim of all the spiritual Sadhanas. Then you will be established in Nirvikalpa state of bliss. Pure Nivritti is needed to attain this after you have got Chitta-Suddhi through Nishkama-Karma Yoga.

TEMPERAMENT AND HOW IT CAN BE MODIFIED

There are secretions from endocrine glands which are ductless viz., Thyroid, Thymus, Parotid, Pineal, Suprarenal, etc. These secretions are directly absorbed into the blood. They play a vital part in constituting the temperament of every individual. The temperament of a man can be greatly modified by environments, education and experience. It can hardly be changed *in toto*. That is the reason why the Gita says: *"Sadrisam Cheshtate Svasyah Prakriter-Jnanavanapi—*Even the man of knowledge behaves in conformity with nature" (Gita, III-33).

CHAPTER 8

THE MENTAL FACULTIES

THE POWER OF THE HUMAN MIND

If you closely study the action of mind upon mind, of mind over matter, of mind over the human body, you will find that each man is a power in himself. You will have to develop the potential faculties by self-restraint and mastery over the passions. When mind is so much powerful, what to speak anything of the glory of Atman, who is the storehouse of everything, who is the infinite, inexhaustible central magazine of power, knowledge and bliss from whom the little mind borrows its light and power!

ILLUSTRATIONS OF THE POWER OF MIND

Whenever any fire-accident or any other kind of accident occurs, how agile and nimble you are! Do you not exhibit wonderful powers? You jump over a huge wall, save many children, run amidst fire boldly and carry things. All psychic faculties, memory, imagination, will, etc., are at play. Chivalry, intrepidity, undaunted spirit, mercy and various other noble virtues are exhibited by you. Wherefrom did you draw these faculties and powers? From this, you can conclude that you are, in reality, all-powerful. There is a big, magnanimous magazine of power inside. Go to the source by meditation and tap it. You will get everything. Rely on the Self within.

If you get a telegram at 12 noon on a hot day in summer, which informs you that your father is seriously ailing in your native village which is twenty miles distant, at once you leave even your food and begin to gallop. Though you yourself are not in good health at that time, you do not mind anything as you are very anxious to see your loving father. You even run the whole distance and reach the place within a couple of hours. Then you begin to wonder, "What! I was myself very sick. The day was very hot. I have covered a distance of twenty miles within two hours. What a marvel it is!" This clearly shows that you are, in reality, all-powerful. The mind possesses various kinds of powers and faculties. They lie dormant. You will have to awaken them.

THE SIX IMPORTANT POWERS OF MIND

There are three Saktis (powers, potencies) in the mind, viz., Ichha Sakti (Will), Kriya Sakti (Action) and Jnana Sakti (Knowledge). A desire arises in the mind. This is Ichha Sakti. The mind exerts to have this desire gratified. This is Kriya Sakti. It plans, schemes and finds out methods, etc., for the achievement of the desired object. This is Jnana Sakti.

Vedana-Sakti (power of perception), Smarana-Sakti or Smriti-Sakti (power of memory), Bhavana-Sakti (Power of imagination), Manisha-Sakti (power of judgment), Ichha-Sakti or Sankalpa-Sakti (will or volition) and Dharana-Sakti (power to hold) are the six important powers of the mind.

Vedana-Sakti

Vedana-Sakti is power of cognition or sensation or power of perception and knowing through Indriyas or senses (Indriya-Jnana or sense-knowledge).

Smriti-Sakti

The Smriti-Sakti does three things. It grasps. It holds. It brings to memory whenever a thing is needed. Though the power of grasping is done by the Vedana-Sakti of the mind (power of perception or cognition), the Smriti-Sakti also participates in the act of grasping.

Suppose you hear the sound of a bell in the temple. The memory Sakti grasps it. Then it retains it through Dharana. When you hear again the sound of the temple bell, it at once reminds you, "This is the temple bell. This is not the hostel bell."

In Dhyana, the mind grasps and takes possession of its perceptions or judgments. It makes the content of the idea its own. It strengthens the Samskaras so that a voluntary recall is rendered easy.

Bhavana-Sakti

You have never seen an elephant riding a cycle. When a man, who has actually seen it, gives you a description, your mind forms a mental picture at once. This is done by the Bhavana-Sakti (power of imagination) of the mind.

Manisha-Sakti

Power of comparing and contrasting, drawing inferences, discussion, conclusion, all belong to Manisha-Sakti of the mind. The Manisha-Sakti (power of judgment) has got two subdivisions, viz., Nirnaya (ascertainment) and Tarka (logical reasoning).

A is mortal. B is mortal. C is mortal. Again, all men are mortal. Mr. Choudhary is a man. Therefore, Choudhary is mortal. These sorts of drawing conclusions through inductive and deductive logic with major and minor premises and middle term or through the five parts of syllogistic reasoning of Gautama Rishi's Indian Logic (Nyaya) are done by Manisha-Sakti of the mind with the help of Nirnaya and Tarka.

Tarka has got two other subdivisions, viz., Anumana (inference) and Paramarsa (discussion). When you see a river in full flood in the morning, you infer that there ought to have been rain during previous night. When you see smoke on the hills, you infer that there ought to be fire also on the hill. This is due to Anumana.

Ichha-Sakti

Will is Atma-Sakti. It is the dynamic aspect of Brahman. Will is Brahman in motion. In Vedanta, will plays a very conspicuous part.

Much has been said about the power of imagination in the West—that it is the most tremendous power in the human mind and that in a conflict between the will and the imagination, the imagination would invariably win the day.

Some people say that the will is greater than imagination. In the East, amongst the Vedantins, will is regarded as a greater faculty than imagination. What would the imagination do without the impelling power of the will to execute with dynamic power the desires, wishes and ideals?

There is correlation, co-ordination and co-operation between the different principles in the mind. Therefore, who can say which is great or small, important or unimportant when each depends upon the other for its power? It cannot be truly said that the one is greater than the other, for their independence and power are derived from one another.

Dharana-Sakti

Dharana-Sakti (power to hold) is really a part of memory or

Smarana-Sakti. In common parlance, we say, "Mr. Rama-krishna is a man of good Dharana in Vedanta." Here it means that Mr. Ramakrishna has got fixed and steady ideas in Vedanta. He cannot be changed by anybody. He is not of a wavering nature. He sticks to Vedanta alone. Nobody can shake him.

Apperception

Apperception is the mind's perception of itself as a conscious agent. The principle of apperception is just like a mail clerk of consciousness receiving, sorting out, correlating, arranging, pigeon-holing, associating and sending out messages.

HOW TO UNFOLD THE LATENT POWERS OF MIND

There are many higher mental faculties latent in man. Mind is a magazine of power. The unfoldment of these latent, psychic powers is possible through proper Sadhana. The Sadhana should be systematic, constant and intense. The student also must have reached the proper stage of development. There must be genuine Sraddha also. Then only sanguine success is possible.

CHAPTER 9

THE THREE DOSHAS

Milk is agreeable to some and disagreeable to others. There is nothing wrong with the milk itself. Surely, there is something wrong with the mind. Doubtless, there is a defect in the mind. The view of a child when it sees its mother is that she is its supporter, nourisher and giver of all comforts. The husband of the woman regards her as an object of enjoyment. A tiger, when it sees the same woman, regards her as its prey. The object, woman, remains the same. The viewpoint differs in these three cases owing to the Dosha of the mind.

Dosha means fault or defect. Mala (impurity), Vikshepa (tossing), Avarana (veil of ignorance) are the threefold defects of the mind.

The mind is tossed about among objects of love and hatred like a light feather in a stormy wind. It ever whirls far and wide in vain among sensual objects away from the association with the wise, like a strolling city dog; but, no results accrue therefrom. This baneful mind whirls at the sight of its much-coveted immense wealth. This ferocious dog of mind, following its mate of desire, ever preys upon poor, ignorant worldlings as on carcasses. It will flit in a moment from Howrah to Paris and from Colombo to Berlin. Not resting on any object firmly, it is characterised by an excessive fluctuating power. It will fluctuate and be confused, will flit away from an object and then return to it, will rejoice in vain and be intoxicated with Ahankara. A mind becomes a prey to fear through its fluctuation.

The mind should be rendered fit for salvation, fit to approach its Adhishthana (substratum), its father, Brahman. Remove the three Doshas.

Mala (such as Kama, Krodha, Lobha, Moha, Mada, Matsarya) is removed by doing Nishkama Karma. Mala means sin also.

Vikshepa is removed by Upasana, Trataka, Pranayama and Raja Yoga.

Avarana is removed by Jnana, study of Vedantic literature, Nididhyasana and Abheda-Chintana after duly understanding the right significance of the Mahavakya, "Tat Tvam Asi."

Without hankering after paltry, terrestrial things and causing your mind to fluctuate thereby, may you be immovable as a rock! Those who have no lower impulses drive away rebirths to a great distance from them.

Study the nature of the mind. Analyse the mind carefully. Get rid of the three Doshas of the mind, viz., Mala, Vikshepa and Avarana. Purify the mind. Steady the mind. Fix the mind on God or Brahman. Get the mind dissolved in God by constant and intense thinking. Practise the Sadhana of Manonasa. Rise above the deceptions and temptations of the mind. This is your duty. You are born for this only; all other duties are self-created and self-imposed owing to Avidya or ignorance.

CHAPTER 10

SUDDHA MANAS AND ASUDDHA MANAS

Through the discriminating mind, the lower mind is powerfully mastered by the wise.

"*Uddharet-atmana-atmanam*—Let him raise the self by the Self."   *(Gita, VI-5)*

THE TWO KINDS OF MIND

Suddha Manas or Sattvic mind (pure mind) and Asuddha (impure) Manas or the instinctive mind or desire-mind as it is called are the two kinds of mind according to Upanishadic teaching. There is the lower mind filled with passion. There is the higher mind filled with Sattva (purity). There are two minds. You will have to make it into one—Sattvic mind only—if you want to meditate. It is through the higher or Sattvic mind that you will have to control the lower or instinctive mind of passions and emotions.

There are two kinds of Buddhi also—Vyavaharic Buddhi and pure Buddhi. There are two kinds of Aham or Ahankara, viz., Suddha Aham which identifies with Brahman (Sat-Chit-Ananda) and Asuddha Aham which identifies with the body. There are two kinds of Sankalpa (resolve, conation), viz., Suddha Sankalpa (thoughts of God) and Asuddha Sankalpa (thoughts of body and the world).

The Asuddha Manas which creates Asuddha Sankalpa, the Vyavaharic Buddhi and Asuddha Ahankara—all these three form a vicious circle. These three work in co-operation. The seed of the mind is Ahankara. Mind is merely a bundle of thoughts. Of all thoughts, the 'I' thought is the root thought. It is the first thought also that emanated from the mind. Therefore, mind is only the thought 'I'. Buddhi is the basis of Ahankara. It is Buddhi that forces you to identify yourself with the physical body. It is Buddhi that creates difference (Bheda) and Nana Bhava (the idea of many in the world).

CHARACTERISTICS OF THE SATTVIC MIND

A Sattvic mind likes solitude, silence, simple living, high thinking, study of spiritual books, philosophical discussions, concentration of mind and company of Sadhus, Mahatmas and Sannyasins. A stainless mind can be judged through speech, face and eyes. Through these expressions, the opinion can be formed whether a person has stainless mind. Higher desires, noble aspirations, lofty ideals, true religious feeling, mercy, sympathy, pure unselfish love, devotion, Vichara (Atmic enquiry), inspiration, genius—all come from the higher, pure Sattvic mind. Suddha Manas (pure mind) is Brahman itself. It is an embodiment of purity itself.

CHARACTERISTICS OF THE RAJASIC MIND

A Rajasic mind likes crowded cities, much talking, luxurious life, low thinking, the company of women, study of romantic novels, eating dainty dishes and selfish works. Instinctive mind is the lower, impure Kama Manas with desires, passions and appetites. The vast majority of persons have this instinctive mind only. Even the so-called civilised and educated persons live on the plane of the instinctive mind. Their senses are very sharp and acute and they run after more refined things for their sense-gratification. They identify themselves with the physical body and the senses. They have no idea of the subtle Atman which is entirely distinct from the body and the Indriyas. Their 'I' is the physical, gross body only though they know that there is a mind.

Sensual enjoyment brings on diseases and destroys the power of discrimination (Viveka). It makes the mind Malina (impure). Therefore, shun Vishayabhoga (sensual enjoyment). Try to realise the Self within wherein lies eternal bliss and immortality.

SATTVIC MIND NEEDED FOR ATMA-VICHARA

A sharp, subtle, one-pointed, Sattvic (pure) mind is needed for Atma-Vichara (enquiry into Atman or the Supreme Spirit) and study of Upanishads. A gross mind or practical (Vyavaharic) Buddhi with selfishness and lust is absolutely unfit for Vichara and philosophical ratiocination. Selfishness clouds understanding. Selfishness is the bane of life. The mind of a worldling is ever ready to absorb sexual thoughts. It cannot imbibe subtle, philosophical ideas. It is callous and cannot vibrate properly to take in philosophical ideas. You can drive a nail in clay, but not in a stone. The mind has to be purified by Nishkama Karma, Japa, Pranayama and other spiritual Sadhanas.

Mind is compared to a mirror. If the mirror is dirty, you cannot see your face clearly. Similarly, if the mind-mirror is dirty (full of Mala, impurities—Kama, Krodha, Lobha, etc.), you cannot see God clearly; you cannot see the Self clearly. The light of Brahman cannot shine efficiently. Clean it up with effort daily, through spiritual Sadhana, meditation, strenuous Nishkama Karma Yoga, devotion, etc. You will realise God.

"*Manasaiva-anudrashtavyam*" is the utterance of the Srutis. Brahman is to be seen by the mind. Here 'mind' means the Suddha Manas (pure mind). Brahman can be seen by a mind which is equipped with the four means of salvation; which is rendered subtle and pure by the practice of Sama, Dama, Yama and Niyama; which is furnished with the sacred instructions of a qualified Guru and which does Sravana (hearing), Manana (reflection) and Nididhyasana (constant musing). Should the pure mind concentrate itself for some time through a study of Jnana Sastras, association with the wise and an uninterrupted practice of meditation, then in such persons developing Jnana, a divine vision will dawn in which there will be a direct cognition of the one Reality.

SLAY THE IMPURE MIND

The enemy of Atman is the impure mind, which is replete with excessive delusion and a host of thoughts. This mischievous and powerful imp of lower mind is the generator of all pains and all fears and the destroyer of all noble, spiritual wealth. Your real enemy is this impure mind only which is full of delusion, Trishnas, Vasanas and host of other impurities. Lest this enemy of mind should spoil you in diverse ways through the "enjoyments" of the many "pleasures" in this world, slay it in the hope of getting eternal bliss and spiritual illumination. Destroy the lower Asuddha (impure) Manas through the higher Suddha Manas. Destroy your instinctive mind through discrimination and help of your higher, Sattvic mind. Then and then alone will you get eternal, infinite peace and bliss of Atman. Then alone will you become a Jivanmukta.

Sattvic minds and Rajasic minds move in diametrically opposite directions. Sattvic mind unifies. Instinctive mind separates and divides. Voice from the instinctive mind will mislead you.

Purify the mind and hear the voice of conscience (Sattvic mind). You will have to develop the Sattvic part of the mind by annihilating the lower, impure, instinctive mind. If the lower mind is done away with through the higher mind alone, then only will you have eternal happiness and peace. Then alone will you attain Moksha, supreme knowledge and perennial bliss. Slay this mind through constant Vichara and meditation on Om and rest in your own Svarupa, Sat-Chit-Ananda state.

HOW TO PURIFY THE MIND

As one iron shapes another iron, the pure. mind of a person which makes efforts in the virtuous path should correct and mould his impure mind. Mind is unfailingly rendered pure through true, virtuous and pure actions and constant Satsanga (association with the wise). Speaking the truth and practice of Daya (pure compassion) are very great purifiers of mind. All lofty aspirations, all-embracing tendencies and pity—all go a long way in increasing the Sattvic material of the mind. The higher Manas is developed.

Sacrifice, gift, compassion, study of the Vedas and speaking the truth: these five are purifying. The sixth is penance well-practised. The last one is highly purifying. Pilgrimage to sacred places is also purifying. You come in contact with holy persons there. You can have good Satsanga.

Charity, Japa, Nishkama Karma, Yajna, Agnihotra, Brahmacharya, Sandhya, Tirtha-Yatra, Dama, Sama, Yama, Niyama, Svadhyaya, Tapas, Vrata, service of saints—all tend to purify the mind. There will be, doubtless, unalloyed bliss in the mind thus purified.

A Mantra purifies the mind. Mere repetition of a Mantra, parrot-like, has very little effect. It has some benefit. It must be repeated with Bhava (feeling). Then it produces wonderful effects. The Mantra, unless inspired with the powerful will-force of one's own mind, cannot produce much effect.

Study of philosophical works, right thinking, exercise of good and noble emotions, prayers and beneficent endeavours and, above all, regular and strenuous meditation are the means to improve the mind. These will bring about the rapid evolution of the mind. When the mind is purified, a hole is formed in the centre through which purity, light and knowledge flow from Brahman.

A goldsmith converts 10 carat gold into 15 carat gold by adding acids and burning it several times in the crucible. Even so, you will have to purify your sensuous mind through concentration and reflection on the words of your spiritual preceptor and the Upanishadic sentences, meditation, Japa or silent repetition of the Name of the Lord, etc.

It takes a long time to purify Harital (yellow oxide of arsenic orpiment). It has to be soaked in cow's urine for seven days, in lime water for ten days and in milk for seven days. Then it has to be burnt out hundred and eight times before a Bhasma or proper oxide (ash) is obtained. Even so, it takes a long time to effect Chitta-Suddhi, purity of mind. Severe Tapascharya (austerity) is needed.

As a result of purification of the mind, it becomes more sensitive, gets easily disturbed by a sound or shock and feels any pressure acutely. An aspirant must be sensitive and yet have the body and nerves completely under his control. The greater the sensitiveness becomes, the more difficult is the task; there are many noises which pass unheeded by an ordinary person, but which are torture to one who is very sensitive. You must do your best to get over this oversensitiveness.

INITIATION OF PURE MIND LEADS TO QUIESCENCE

Purification is the first part of Yoga. When purification is over, the natural tendency of the mind is to go towards liberation, Moksha. If only a disciple whose mind is cleansed of all its impurities, is initiated into the sacred mysteries by a Guru, then his mind will get complete quiescence. He will enter into a Nirvikalpa state. The Nirvikalpa state is termed Asamvedana.

CHAPTER 11

VRITTIS

VRITTI—ITS NATURE AND FUNCTION

Vritti means a whirl-pool. It is a wave of thought that arises in the Antahkarana. Vrittis are modifications of the mind. They are the effect of Avidya. When Avidya is destroyed by Jnana, Vrittis get absorbed in Brahman (Laya), just as water thrown in a heated pan is absorbed in the pan.

Wherefrom does a Vritti arise? From the Chitta or mind. Why does a Vritti arise? It is Svabhava of Antahkarana. What is its function? It causes Avarana-Bhanga (removes the veil of Sthula Avidya that envelops the objects). It helps the evolution of a man till he attains perfection (Jivanmukti). It is Vritti that opens the Kundalini in a Jnani in the Ajna Chakra and joins it in Sahasrara. This is one path.

The Chitta is the mind stuff. It is the mental substance. Vritti or thought-wave is a modification of that mental substance. It is a process. Just as waves and bubbles arise from the surface of the ocean, so also these Vrittis arise from the surface of the mind-ocean. Just as rays emanate from the sun, so also these mental rays (modification of Vrittis) emanate from the mind-sun. Just as the sun merges itself in the horizon at sunset by collecting all its rays, so also you will have to merge in that Sun of suns, Absolute Consciousness, Eternal Peace by collecting all the dissipated mental rays and dissolving the mind itself.

The function of a Vritti in the mind is to cause Avarana-Bhanga (removal of the veil of ignorance covering objects). Sthula Avidya or gross ignorance is enveloping all objects. When the veil is removed, perception of objects becomes possible. The Vritti removes the Avarana or layer of ignorance. When you pass through a big crowd or persons, you are able to notice a few persons. You do not see some persons, though they happen to come in front of you. Why? Because there was not complete Avarana-Bhanga. When this is done, the object shines before you.

According to Raja Yoga of Maharshi Patanjali, Pramana (right notion or right proof), Viparyaya (misconception), Vikalpa (fancy or imagination), Nidra (sleep) and Smriti (memory) are the five mental Vrittis or mental functions. If these five mental functions are suppressed, the suppression of desires and other functions will follow.

VISHAYAKARA VRITTI AND BRAHMAKARA VRITTI

Through its own efforts, the mind assumes the shape of any object, it concentrates itself upon. If it thinks of a woman, it assumes the shape of a woman. This is termed Vritti Tadakara. If it thinks of God or Brahman, Brahmakara Vritti develops. In the former case, Rajas (passion) will be infused into the mind; while in the latter, Sattva (purity) will be infused.

When the mind thinks of objects and dwells on them, it assumes the shape of those objects. It is termed as Vishayakara Vritti. When it thinks of Brahman or Infinity, the Brahmakara Vritti is formed. The Sadhaka should be very vigilant and circumspect in watching the mind and its activities. He must convert Vishayakara Vritti into Brahmakara Vritti. As soon as the mind drops down from Brahmakara Vritti into Vishayakara Vritti, he should again make the mind assume Brahmakara Vritti. There is very hard struggle, indeed.

You cannot have Vishayakara Vritti as Ghatapatadi Vritti (modification of pot, cloth, etc.) and Brahmakara Vritti (thought of Brahman) also at the same time. It is Sruti Virodha (i.e. against the utterances of the Srutis). It is against practical experience also.

It is not the object that binds you. It is Vritti and identification (Tadatmya Sambandha) with the Vritti that causes attachment and bondage. It is through Avidya or ignorance that you identify yourself with Vritti as, for instance, when you say: "I am angry."

KINDS OF VRITTI

Vrittis have been classified into five kinds: (1) Mano-Vritti, (2) Buddhi Vritti, (3) Sakshi Vritti, (4) Akhandakara Vritti and (5) Akhanda Ekarasa Vritti. No. 1 belongs to the instinctive mind. Nos. 2, 3, 4 and 5 belong to the Sattvic mind. Mano-Vritti is the Vishayakara Vritti of worldlings. Buddhi Vritti belongs to

Vivekins. When you identify yourself with the Sakshi Vritti, you can witness the modifications of the mind. When you try to feel that you are the Infinite Self, the Akhandakara Vritti is generated. It is also known as Brahmakara Vritti. There is no Vritti in Brahman.

From Mano-Vritti, you must jump to Viveka Vritti. Mano-Vritti concerns Manomaya Kosha. Viveka Vritti belongs to Vijnanamaya Kosha. By developing the Vijnanamaya Kosha, Mano-Vrittis are conquered. From Viveka Vritti, you must jump to Sakshi Vritti. From Sakshi Vritti, you must jump to Akhandakara Vritti. From Akhandakara Vritti, you must jump to Akhanda Ekarasa which is Brahma Svarupa. This is Kaivalya or final goal of life.

ANTARMUKHA VRITTI AND BAHIRMUKHA VRITTI

When the outgoing tendencies of the mind are arrested, when the mind is retained within the heart, when all its attention is turned on itself alone, that condition is Antarmukha Vritti. The Antarmukha Vritti is the indrawing energy of the mind owing to increase in Sattva. The Sadhaka can do a lot of Sadhana when he has this inward Vritti.

The Bahirmukha Vritti is the outgoing tendency of the mind due to Rajas. When the vision is turned outward, the rush of fleeting events engages the mind. The outgoing energies of the mind begin to play. Further, on account of force of habit, the ears and eyes at once run towards sound and sight. Objects and desire are externalising forces. A Rajasic man full of desires can never dream of an inner spiritual life with Antarmukha Vritti. He is absolutely unfit for the practice of introspection.

You will get Antarmukha Vritti (inward-moving mind) only after you have destroyed all the externalising powers of the mind. Vairagya and introspection help a lot in the attainment of this mental state. You must starve the mind by Vairagya and Tyaga (renunciation of desires, objects and egoism). You must learn the art of making the mind introspective or turned inward upon itself through the Yogic Kriya, Pratyahara (abstraction). Just as you have to take back with care your cloth that is fallen on a thorny plant by removing the thorns one by one slowly, so also you will have to collect back with care and exertion the dissipated rays of the mind that are thrown over the sensual objects for very many years.

You will have to gather them patiently through Vairagya and Abhyasa, through Tyaga (renunciation) and Tapas and then march boldly with indefatigable energy towards God or Brahman. Those who know this practice can really be peaceful. They only can be really happy. When the mental rays are concentrated, illumination begins. Mind cannot do any havoc now. The mind cannot externalise itself. It can be kept inside the Hridaya-Guha (cave of the heart).

DESTRUCTION OF VRITTIS LEADS TO MENTAL STRENGTH

Mind gains great strength when the Vrittis are destroyed. It is not easy to destroy Vrittis (thought-waves) because they are innumerable. They should be taken up one by one and dealt with separately. Some Vrittis are very strong. They demand strong efforts for their destruction. Most of the Vrittis are very weak. Weak Vrittis melt away like rent clouds. Strong thoughts remain and frequently recur daily in the morning as soon as you rise from your bed.

Be silent. Enter silence. Silence is Atman. Silence is Brahman. Silence is centre. Silence is the Hridaya-Guha (heart-cave). When the mind runs from one object to another, that state in the interval wherein you become mindless for a very short time is Svarupasthiti. That is Brahman. When the mind is controlled fully, Vrittis cease. When all the modifications subside, you enter into the silence then and then alone. Realise this, this very moment. Feel the divine glory and Brahmic splendour now by closing the eyes, by drawing the Indriyas, by stilling the mind, by silencing the thoughts, by sharpening the intellect, by purifying the Chitta, by meditating on Om, by chanting Om with Bhava (feeling). Keep up the continuity of Brahmic consciousness throughout the 24 hours. Have an unceasing flow of Atmic consciousness. This is very, very important. This is a *sine qua non*. This is a great desideratum.

When all the Vrittis die, Samskaras and the frame of the mind remain. Samskaras can only be fried up by Nirbija-Samadhi.

CHAPTER 12

THEORY OF PERCEPTION

"When one thinks, then he understands; without having thought, one does not know; it is only after having thought that one understands." *(Chhandogya Upanishad, VII-xxi-1)*
"I was absent-minded; I did not hear. I was absent-minded; I did not see. It is thus evident that a person sees with the mind, hears with the mind. Desire, determination, uncertainty, belief, disbelief, steadiness, unsteadiness, shame, intellect, fear—all these are in the mind alone. Therefore, when touched from behind, a person knows by the mind.
(Brihadaranyaka Upanishad, I-v-3)

There are two compartments in the mind, viz., the thinking portion and the perceiving portion. It is easy to stop the thinking portion, but it is extremely difficult to stop the functioning of the perceiving portion.

It is only the individual mind that sees objects outside. If you see the same objects through a telescope, they appear different. If you can see with the mind directly, you will have a different vision altogether. Hiranyagarbha or Karya Brahman has quite a different vision. He sees everything as a vibration or movement within himself as his own Sankalpa, just as you can imagine within your own mind that a big war is going on and many people are dying on either side. You withdraw your imagination at your will.

THEORIES OF PERCEPTION

There is the elastic theory of the mind. This school of thought says that the mind becomes elastic when several objects come in contact with the various senses and thus puts itself simultaneously into touch with various sense-organs or Indriyas of knowledge (Jnana-Indriyas). When the mind comes in contact with one object and one Indriya, it contracts to a point. This theory is exploded and refuted by the Vedantins as unsound.

There is another school of thought that says that there are different compartments or parts in the mind. One part of the mind connects itself with one sense (Indriya), another part with a second sense and so on. This theory is similarly blown up and discarded by the Vedantins as untenable and unsound.

According to the school of thought known by the name of Drishti-Srishti-Vada, the perceiver and the perceived are one. Just as the spider weaves out the web from its own body, even so the mind throws out this physical universe from its own body during waking state and withdraws the world into its womb during sleep. An object is a mental Vritti externalised or objectified.

The Drishya (what you see outside) is due to mental Avidya. There is only light outside. There is only vibration outside. It is the mind that gives colour and shape. It is all mental deception. This is one view. This is one theory of perception.

The interaction between the mind inside and the Tanmatric vibrations outside is the object or the world that you see outside. This is one theory of perception. Mind is formed out of the Sattvic portion of the five Tanmatras. There is light outside. The sun also emits light. The eye is made up of fire or Agni-Tattva. That portion of the mind which perceives is also made up of Agni-Tattva. So fire sees fire. Only that portion of the mind which is made up of Sabda-Tanmatra can hear. Sound comes from Akasa outside. So Akasa of the mind hears Akasa from outside. But, Atman can see, hear, taste and feel everything. Atman only can be seen by Atman. Therefore, whatever you see outside is Atman only. "*Sarvam Khalvidam Brahma*—Everything is verily Brahman."

THE VIEW OF WESTERN MEDICAL SCIENCE

According to Western medical science, light-vibrations from outside strike the retina and an inverted image is formed there. These vibrations are carried through optic tract and optic thalamus to the centre of vision in the occipital lobe of the brain in the back part of the head. There, a positive image is formed. Then only, you see the object in front of you.

PERCEPTION ACCORDING TO SANKHYA PHILOSOPHY

According to Sankhya philosophy, the real background of perception is the Purusha of whom the Western doctors and psychologists have no idea. Fleshy eyes are only external instruments (Karanas) for perception. Eye is not an organ of vision. The organ of vision is a centre situated in the brain; so is the case with all senses. Mind is connected with the Indriyas, the Indriyas with the corresponding centres in brain and the centres, with the physical organs, to the external object. The mind presents the sensation to Buddhi; Buddhi takes it to the Purusha (which is pure Spirit, which is Immaterial). Now, real perception takes place. Purusha gives order to Buddhi. Then, Buddhi, after proper decision and judgment and after taking into consideration the pros and cons of the subject on hand, gives orders back to the mind, for execution through the motor centres (Karma-Indriyas or organs of action). Buddhi is the Prime Minister and Judge who hears the statements of the Advocate, viz., the mind. Mind plays two parts, viz., (i) that of an Advocate and (ii) that of a Commander-in-Chief. After receiving decisive orders from Buddhi, the mind acts the part of a Commander-in-Chief and executes the orders of Buddhi through the five soldiers, the five Karma-Indriyas. This is the theory of perception according to the Sankhya Philosophy. See how very clear matters are in Hindu Philosophy.

First of all, there is the instrument or Karana—for instance, the fleshy eye. It takes the sense-impressions to the centre or Indriya. The mind is then connected with the centre and the external instruments, namely, the physical eye, ear, etc. The mind carries the impressions still further and presents them to the Buddhi, the determinative faculty, which reacts. Then flashes out the idea of egoism or Ahankara, which self-arrogates and identfies with Abhimana. Then the mixture of action and reaction is presented to the Purusha, the real Soul who perceives an object in the mixture.

Knowledge comes through contact with objects (*Indriyartha-Sannikarsha*). To know a Prapancha Vishaya, Indriya, Antahkarana and Jiva are required. Indriya will see the Vishaya. Mind will make it appear. Buddhi, with the help of Abhasa Chaitanya, will understand it. Mind, senses and the Karanas (external instruments) such as the physical eye, ear, etc., should all be joined together. Then only perception of an object is possible. The object comes in contact with the senses. The senses are linked to the mind. The mind is connected to the Atman. The Atman illumines. This is with reference to the physical plane.

THE VEDANTIC THEORY

According to the Advaitic theory of perception, it is the

Chaitanya within us that makes perception possible. The Chetana within us unites with the Chetana in the object and the result is perception. It does not follow from this that the mind and the senses are useless. The senses are necessary for the adaptation of perception to their approximate things. From the soul's essential nature being intelligence, it does not follow that the senses are useless, for they serve the purpose of determining the special object of each sense.

The Vedantic theory of perception is that the mind comes out through the eye and assumes the shape of the object outside. The Antahkarana-Vritti enters through the opening of the Indriya (eye), removes Vishaya Ajnana, assumes Vishayakara (the shape and form of the object it envelops), presents the objects to your view. The function of Vritti is to cause Avarana-Bhanga (removal of the veil or layer of Sthula Avidya that envelops all objects).

A ray of the mind actually goes out, assumes the shape and form of the object and envelops it. Then only perception takes place. The perception of a book is possible only when the mind has assumed the actual shape of the book. Mental image plus external something is the object. Whatever objects you see outside, have got their own images in the mind.

When you pass through a mango garden, a ray of the mind comes out through the eye and envelops a mango. It assumes the shape of the mango. The ray is termed Vritti. The enveloping process is called Vritti-Vyapti. The function of a Vritti is to remove the Avarana (veil) that envelops the object and the Upahita Chaitanya. The veil that envelops the mango is removed by the Vritti or the mental ray. There is Chaitanya associated with the Vritti (Vritti Sahita Chaitanya). This Chaitanya illuminates the object 'mango'. This is termed Phala-Vyapti. Just as a torchlight illumines an object in a flash, this Vritti-Chaitanya illumines the object. Then only does perception of the mango take place. Mind makes Sankalpa-Vikalpa: Is this a mango or not? Buddhi comes to help the mind and determines (this is a mango) through previous experience. Chitta makes Anusandhana (enquiry): "How can I get the mango? May I ask the gardener or the proprietor?" Ahankara asserts: "I must get the mango anyhow. I want it." Then the command is given by the mind to the Karma-Indriyas for execution.

When you see a mango tree, it is external to you. There is

externality. The mango tree is a mental percept. It is a mental concept also. There is no mango tree apart from the mind. You know the existence of the tree through the mind only. There is a mental image in the mind. The image in the mind plus the external something is the mango tree. Even if you close your eyes, you can get at the image through memory. The green colour of the leaves is due to a certain rate of light vibrations (say, 10 millions of vibrations). These light vibrations strike at the retina and are taken to the vision centre at the back of the brain. The mango-leaves have the power to split the white rays and absorb the green colour only. So says science.

Your body also is as much external to you as that yonder mango tree. It is also a mental percept or mental concept. The mango tree is external to you with reference to your body only. The mango tree itself is a mere appearance that floats in the Absolute or the One Reality. As the mango tree is external to you from the standpoint of your body, and as the body itself is external to you, the idea of externality of the mango tree or this external universe is blown up now. The term internality also has a false existence only. There is internality only with reference to the externality. If the externality goes away, where is the internality? Both the terms internality and externality are mere illusions, creations of the mind. There is only the solid existence, the One Reality or Absolute behind the so-called internality and externality. That is the Real, Infinite 'I'. That is your own Self.

MIND ALONE CREATES DIFFERENCES

The eyes present before the mind some forms or images. It is the mind that creates good and bad forms. It says, "This is good. This is ugly. This is beautiful." Here comes bondage and trouble. Good and bad, ugly and beautiful are pure mental creations. If mind can create, it can destroy also. Similarly, the ears bring some sound vibrations before the mind. It is the mind that says: "This is praise. This is censure." Eyes and ears are not to be blamed at all. They are innocent. Mind causes the mischief.

MENTAL COGNITION TAKES PLACE SERIALLY

Mind can think of only limited things. Mind cannot think of greenness without thinking of a green object.

Mind is Niravayava (without parts, divisions, compartments). It can have only one idea at a time. This is the Siddhanta of Naiyayikas. Even those Vedantins who say that mind is Savayava (with compartments) on the analogy of Chora-Nari (the prostitute whose mind is on the paramour even while she works in her house) admit that the mind can have Visesha Vritti of the lover only and Samanya Vritti of the work on hand at the time.

The human mind has the power of attending to only one object at a time, although it is able to pass from one object to another with a marvellous degree of speed, so rapidly in fact, that some have held that it could grasp several things at a time. Mind is a gate-keeper or guard who can allow only one person, one kind of sense-vibration at a time into the mental factory. You cannot hear and see at the same time. The mind can have only one idea at a time. But it moves with such tremendous lightning speed that an ordinary man thinks that he can have several ideas at a time.

Perception through the finite mind or cognition or experience takes place serially and not simultaneousely. Simultaneous knowledge can only be had in Nirvikalpa Samadhi where past and future merge in the present. Only a Yogin will have simultaneous knowledge. A man of the world with a finite mind can have only a knowledge in succession. Two thoughts, however closely related to each other, cannot exist at the same time. The nature of the internal organism (Antahkarana or Manas) prevents our having more than one aspect of an object at each instant presented to consciousness. Though several objects may come in contact simultaneously with the different sense-organs, yet the mind acts like a gatekeeper who can admit only one person at a time through the gate. The mind can send only one kind of sensation at a time into the mental factory inside for the manufacture of a decent percept and a nice concept.

When the mind gives attention and is attached to the sense of sight, it can only see. It cannot hear. It cannot hear and see at the same time. It is everybody's daily experience. When your mind is wholly absorbed in deep study of some interesting book, you cannot hear even if a man shouts, because the mind was not there (with the sense of hearing). "My mind was elsewhere, I did not see; my mind was elsewhere, I did not hear, for man sees with his mind and hears with his mind."

Brihadaranyaka Upanishad, I-v-3). When you seriously think of a problem, you can neither see nor hear nor feel. All the Indriyas are detached from the mind. There is only the process of Anusandhana (enquiry or investigation) by the Chitta (the mental substance).

The best philosophers and seers, Rishis and sages, the best authorities, Eastern and Western, hold to the "Single Idea" theory as being correct. They are unanimously agreed that the mind cannot actually attend to more than one thing at a time, but when it appears to be doing so, it is only moving with prodigious rapidity backward and forward, from one end to the other. Illiterate people say that they can see and hear at the same time. The mind moves with a tremendous velocity backward and forward and people imagine that mind can do two things at a time. It is a sad mistake. A spark of light presents the appearance of a continuous circle of light if it is made to rotate rapidly. Even so, though the mind can attend to only one thing at a time—either hearing or seeing or smelling—, though it can admit only one kind of sensation at a time, yet we are led to believe that it does several actions simultaneously, because it moves from one object to another with tremendous velocity, so rapidly that its successive attention and perception appear as a simultaneous activity.

COMPENSATORY ADVANTAGE IN SENSE PERCEPTION

In some persons, the sense of hearing is more developed than the sense of sight. Judges have acute hearing. Commanders-in-chief have acute sight. The profession itself forces them to develop the particular sense. Blind people have acute sense of hearing. If one Indriya is defective, nature compensates by developing more another Indriya. One of my friends knows of a blind man who can feel the nature of the colour by mere touch.

Speech is even the sight of the Purusha. Speech means here sound, the object of the sense of hearing. When this sense is enlightened, reflection is produced in the mind. By the mind effort to obtain external thing is made; for by the mind one sees, one hears. When one, at a time at night in the dark, cannot distinguish where sound arises (be it the neighing of horses or the braying of donkeys or the barking of dogs), he resorts there whence speech proceeds.

SUPERSENSORY PERCEPTION

It is the mind that really sees, tastes, smells, hears and feels. When you begin to think of the picture of Lord Krishna with closed eyes, it is through the mind's eye that you see the picture.

An occultist can dispense with his physical, fleshy eyes and can see directly with his mind. A Bhakta (devotee), being one with Isvara (Lord), sees directly with the eye of Isvara (with the eye of Karana-Sarira, seed-body). A Jnanin sees with the eye of Knowledge of Atman (Divya Drishti or Jnana-Chakshus).

HOW BRAHMAN PERCEIVES

In the mind, will and sight are separate. In pure Chit, will and seeing are one; will and sight are combined and no longer, as in the case of mind, separated from each other.

Brahman does not need Antahkarana to sense, think and reason. Brahman does not need eyes to see. He is self-luminous. He gives light to everything. He imparts light to Antahkarana. He gives light and power to the Indriyas. He is Chit-Svarupa. He is Chidghana. He is a mass of knowledge. He knows everything through Self-knowledge. He sees within Himself through Self-knowledge the whole universe as His own Sankalpa, as Vivarta.

HOW TO PERCEIVE BRAHMAN

Brahman is not an object or Vishaya. It is to be felt by Sakshatkara (direct spiritual cognition). Knowledge of Brahman (Existence or Truth Absolute) comes through feeling and meditation (spiritual Anubhava, direct perception or Atma-sakshatkara) wherein the seer, sight and seen merge into the one existence like the bubble in the ocean.

CHAPTER 13

CHITTA AND MEMORY

WHAT IS CHITTA?

Chitta is termed as the mind-stuff or mental substance. It is the groundfloor, as it were. From it proceed the three Vrittis, viz., Manas, Buddhi and Ahankara. This word belongs to the Rajayogic terminology of Maharshi Patanjali. Also in the Gita, Lord Krishna uses the term Chitta in various places.

Chitta is a separate faculty or category in Vedanta. Sometimes it is Antargata, comes under Mind. In Sankhya philosophy, it is included in Buddhi or Mahat-Tattva. The Chitta of Patanjali Rishi's philosophy of Raja Yoga (*Yogas-chitta-vritti-nirodhah*) corresponds to the Antahkarana of Vedanta.

Subconscious mind is termed 'Chitta' in Vedanta. Much of your subconsciousness consists of submerged experiences, memories thrown into the background but recoverable. The Chitta is like a calm lake and thoughts are like waves upon the surface of this lake and name and form are the normal ways in which these waves rise. No wave can rise without name and form.

The functions of the Chitta are Smriti or Smarana, Dharana, attention and Anusandhana (enquiry or investigation). When you repeat the Japa of a Mantra, it is the Chitta that does the Smarana. It does a lot of work. It turns out better work than the mind or Buddhi.

THE FIELD OF SUBCONSCIOUS MENTATION

The mental processes are not limited to the field of consciousness alone. The field of subconscious mentation is of a much greater extent than that of conscious mentation. The mind is not conscious of the greater portion of its own activities. As man can hold in consciousness but one fact at a time, only a fraction of our knowledge can be in the field of consciousness at any one moment. Only ten per cent of mental activities come into the field of consciousness. Ninety per cent of the mental activities takes place in the subconscious mind. Messages, when ready, come out like a flash from the subconscious mind to the surface of the conscious mind through the trapdoor in the subconscious mind.

We sit and try to solve a problem and fail. We walk around, try again and again fail. Suddenly an idea dawns on us that leads to the solution of the problem. The subconscious processes were at work.

You repeatedly fail at night to get the solution for a problem in arithmetic or geometry. In the morning, when you wake up, you get a clear answer. This answer comes like a flash from the subconscious mind. Even in sleep, it works incessantly without any rest. It arranges, classifies, compares, sorts all facts and works out a proper, satisfactory solution.

Sometimes, you go to sleep at 10 p.m. with the thought, "I must get up at 2 a.m. in the morning to catch a train." This message is taken up by the subconscious mind and it is this subconscious mind that wakes you up unfailingly at the exact hour. Subconscious mind is your constant, trustworthy companion and sincere friend.

With the help of the subconscious mind, you can change your vicious nature by cultivating healthy, virtuous qualities that remain dormant in every human heart. If you want to overcome fear, mentally deny that you have fear and concentrate your attention upon the opposite quality, the ideal of courage. When courage is developed, fear vanishes by itself. The positive always overpowers the negative. This is an infallible law of nature. This is Pratipaksha Bhavana of Raja Yogins. You can acquire a liking for distasteful tasks and duties by cultivating a desire and taste for them. You can establish new habits, new ideals, new ideas and new tastes and new character in the subconscious mind by changing the old ones.

MEMORY

Smriti or memory is a function of Chitta (subconscious mind). Memory is used in two senses. We say, "Mr. John has got a good memory." Here it means that Mr. John's capacity of the mind to store up its past experiences is very good. Sometimes we say, "I have no memory of that incident." Here, you cannot bring up to the surface of the conscious mind, in its original form, the incident that took place some years ago. It is an act of remembering. You do not get any new knowledge through memory. It is only a reproduction.

If the experience is fresh, you can have a complete recall of your past experience through memory. In ordinary recollection there is a temporal coefficient. In personal memory there is a specific coefficient. That which acts together with another thing is a coefficient. In Mathematics, the numerical or literal factor prefixed to an unkown quantity in an algebraic term is a coefficient.

HOW DOES MEMORY ARISE

Suppose you have received a nice fan as a present from your amiable friend. When you use the fan, it sometimes reminds you of your friend. You think of him for a Smriti-Hetu (cause of memory).

If your brother is a tall man, the sight of a similar tall man in another place will bring to your mind the memory of your brother. This is memory due to the similarity of objects (Sadrisyata).

Suppose you have seen a dwarf at Madras. When you see a very tall man or Patagonian, this will remind you of the dwarf whom you saw at Madras. The sight of a big palace will remind you of a peasant's hut or a Sannyasin's grass hut on the bank of Ganga. This memory is due to dissimilarity in objects (Viparitata).

When you walk along the road on a stormy day, if you happen to see a fallen tree, you conclude that the tree has fallen owing to the storm. In this case, the memory is due to the relation between cause and effect (Karya-karana-sambandha).

The new Samskaras wash away the old Samskaras. If the Samskaras are fresh and recent, it is easy to recall them back quickly. They come up again from the depths of the subconscious mind to the surface of the conscious mind. Revival of old Samskaras takes place. If you visit once the college wherefrom you received your education, ten years after you became an officer in the Government, all the previous Samskaras of your college days will be revived now. You will remember now your old professors, old friends, old books and various other things.

CHARACTERISTICS OF A GOOD MEMORY

The following are the four good characteristics of a good memory: (1) If you read once a passage and if you can reproduce the same nicely, it is a sign to indicate that you have a very good memory. This is termed Sugamata. (2) If you can reproduce the same thing without increase or decrease, addition or substraction, it is called Avaikalya. (3) If you can preserve a fact or passage or anything for a very considerable period, it is called Dharana (retentive memory). (4) If you can reproduce a passage at once without any difficulty when it is needed, it is called Upaharana.

THE PROCESS OF RECOLLECTION

When you desire to remember a thing, you will have to make a psychic exertion. You will have to go up and down into the depths of the different levels of subconsciousness and then pick up the right thing from a curious mixture of multifarious irrelevant matter. Just as the railway sorter in the Railway Mail Service takes up the right letter by moving the hand up and down along the different pigeon-holes, so also the sorter subconscious mind goes up and down along the pigeon-holes in the subconscious mind and brings the right thing to the level of normal consciousness. The subconscious mind can pick up the right thing from a heap of various matters.

In a big surgical clinic, the assistant surgeon allows only one patient to enter the consultation room of the senior surgeon for examination. Even so, the mind allows one idea only to enter the mental factory at a time through the mind door (Manodvara). The subconscious mind brings to the threshold of the conscious mind, during an act of Smriti (memory), the right thing at the right moment, suppressing all others. It serves the part of a censor and allows only relevant memories to pass by. What a wonderful mechanism it is! Who is the driver for these dual minds? Who created these? What a magnanimous Being He must be! My hairs stand on their ends when I think of Him! My pen quivers when I write. Don't you like to dwell with Him? What a great privilege and joy it is to be in communion with Him!

When you try to remember something, sometimes you cannot remember. After some time, the forgotten something flashes out to the conscious mind. How do you explain this? It is a slip of memory. The Samkaras of the particular thing has sunk deep. The Chitta, which is the storehouse of Samskaras (and whose function is memory), has to exert a bit, to analyse and sort and bring it to the surface of the conscious mind through the trapdoor. After some exertion, revival of the old Samskaras takes place and the forgotten idea, or name of a person, which you wished to recollect sometime back, suddenly flashes to the conscious or objective mind. There ought to have been some congestion in the brain, which might have prevented the revival of a forgotten thing, idea or person. As soon as the congestion is relieved, the forgotten idea floats on the surface of the mind. When the mind is calm, memory becomes keen.

POWER OF MEMORY

Those who overwork mentally, who do not observe the rules of Brahmacharya and who are tormented by many cares, worries and anxieties, lose their power of memory soon. When you show symptoms of losing your memory, as you grow old, the first symptom is that you find it difficult to remember the names of persons. The reason is not far to seek. All the names are arbitrary. They are like labels. There are no associations with the names. The mind generally remembers through associations, as the impressions become deep thereby.

Even in old age, you can remember old events, as there are associations with events. You can remember well in old age some passages that you read in schools and colleges. But, you find it difficult to remember in the evening a new passage you read in the morning. The reason is that the mind has lost its Dharana Sakti (power of grasping ideas). The brain cells have degenerated.

In early boyhood, the power of grasping in the mind is very marked. But, there is no power of understanding. In 16, 18, 20, the power of understanding becomes manifest. The power of retentive memory is also great in this age. The mind becomes settled only after 30. Below 30, there is much Chanchalatva (wandering nature). A man below 30—in the vast majority of cases—is not able to think and decide for himself. He has no power of judgment. After 45, power of grasping begins to decline. Memory also begins to decline. He has power of retention for what he has learnt before. He cannot learn new sciences. Brahmacharya helps a lot to develop the power of retention and various other psychic powers.

CHAPTER 14

SAMSKARAS

WHAT IS SAMSKARA?

Vritti (whirlpool, thought-wave) arises in the mind-ocean. It operates for sometime. Then it sinks below the threshold of normal consciousness. From the surface of the conscious mind wherein it was uppermost for some time, it sinks down deep into the region of the subconscious mind (Chitta). There, it continues to be a subliminal action and becomes a Samskara (impression). A conscious action—whether cognitive, affective or conative—assumes a potential and hidden (Sukshma and Avyakta) form just below the threshold of consciousness. This is termed a Samskara.

MEMORY—A REVIVAL OF SAMSKARA

The Samskaras (impressions) are embedded in the subconscious mind or Chitta. The subconscious mind is otherwise known as the unconscious mind. Subjective mind, subconscious mind, unconscious mind and Chitta are synonymous terms. The seat of this subconscious mind is the cerebellum or hindbrain. You can recall the past experiences from the storehouse of Samskaras in the subconscious mind. The past is preserved even to the minutest detail. Even a bit is never lost. When the fine Samskaras come up to the surface of the conscious mind back again as a big wave, when the past Vritti comes back to the surface of the conscious mind again by recollection, it is called memory or Smriti. No memory is possible without the help of Samskara.

HOW THE SAMSKARA IS FORMED

An experience in the sense-plane sinks down into the depths of the subconscious mind (Chitta) and becomes there a 'Samskara' (impression). A Samskara of an experience is formed or developed in the Chitta at the very moment that the mind is experiencing something. There is no gap between the present experience and the formation of a Samskara in the subconscious mind. A specific experience leaves a specific Samskara. The memory of this specific experience springs from that particular Samskara only, which was formed out of that particular experience. When you perceive an orange and taste for the first time, you get knowledge of an orange. You know its taste. You know the object, orange. A Samskara is formed in the subconscious mind at once. At any time, this Samskara can generate a memory of the object, orange and knowledge of an orange. Though the object and the act of knowledge are distinguishable, yet they are inseparable.

CYCLIC CAUSATION OF THOUGHT AND SAMSKARA

An object awakens or revives Samskaras in the mind through external stimuli. Hence, a Sankalpa or thought arises subjectively from within, without a stimulus from outside. When you think of a cow which you have seen before, you repeat the word 'cow' mentally. Then only, the mental image comes. Then, a thought is formed. Samskara causes Sankalpa, and Sankalpa causes Samskara, just as seed is the cause of the tree, and tree is the cause of the seed, in turn. There is cyclic causation on the analogy of seed and tree (Bija-Vriksha-Nyaya). A Vritti in the mind produces a Samskara, and a Samskara, in turn, causes again a Vritti. Owing to the force of stimuli (Udbodhaka, Vyanjaka) either from within or from without, the seed-like Samskaras again expand and give rise to further activities. This cycle of Vritti and Samskara is Anadi (beginningless), but has an end when one attains Divine Knowledge and liberation. They get Laya (dissolution) into Prakriti. They cease to produce any effect on the Jivanmukta. The Samskaras should be fried up by continuous Samadhi. Then only you will be free from births and deaths.

SAMYAMA OVER SAMSKARAS

Samskara is known as "residual potency" also. When all Vrittis or thoughts die away, the frame of the mind remains with the Samskaras. This is termed the Potential Mind. In Vedantic parlance, it is called Antahkarana Matra.

All Samskaras co-exist in the mind. The Vrittis slowly subside and leave traces in the mind. These traces are the

Samskaras. From these Samskaras springs memory. If you have Yogic vision, you can vividly notice the marvels that take place in the mental factory of an individual, how the Vritti arises in the mind-lake, how it subsides and how a Samskara is formed. You will be struck with wonder. Samyama over these Samskaras brings out the direct knowledge of the residual potencies. A Yogin brings into direct consciousness the previous life-states by getting direct knowledge of their Samskaras. Such knowledge can hardly be acquired in Universities. A Yogin alone can impart this knowledge to deserving aspirants.

VIRTUOUS AND VICIOUS SAMSKARAS

Like forces, Samskaras aid or inhibit one another. When you see a man in serious sickness and when the feeling of mercy arises in your heart, all the Samskaras of your previous merciful actions coalesce together and force you to serve and help that sick man. Similarly, all the Samskaras of charitable actions come forth to the surface of the conscious mind when you see a man in a serious distress and in straitened circumstances and they force you to help this man. You begin to share with him your physical possessions.

When one Samskara or virtuous action comes into play, another Samskara of dissimilar nature may emerge out and come in the way of its fulfilment. This is fight between a virtuous and a vicious Samskara.

When you try to fix your mind on God and think of purity, just at that moment, all evil thoughts and Samskaras burst forth with violence and vengeance to fight against you. This is termed 'crowding of Samskaras'. Good Samskaras also crowd together and help you to drive out evil Samskaras. The father of Sri Swami Advaitanandaji was a great Bhakta of Chandi. At the time of his death, he was semi-conscious. He began to repeat all the Slokas of Chandi-Stotra which he had got by heart while he was young. This is 'crowding of spiritual Samskaras'.

PAST SAMSKARAS CONSTITUTE PRARABDHA

When you are born, the mind is not a mere *Tabula Rasa* (a smooth or blank tablet or a blank sheet of white paper). It is a storehouse of Samskaras, predispositions, predilections, etc. A child is born with his Samskaras. A child is born with his past experiences transmuted into mental and moral tendencies and powers. By experiences, pleasant and painful, man gathers materials and builds them into mental and moral faculties. The earthly experiences are worked up into intellectual faculty. The mind evolves through the impressions received from the universe through the senses. It will take many bodies till it gathers the complete experience of the world. Every man is born with his inborn or inherent Samskaras and these Samskaras are embedded, lodged or imprinted in the Chitta which is the seat for Prarabdha. In earthly life, he gains many more Samskaras or experiences through actions and these are added to the original store and become the future Sanchita Karmas (accumulated actions).

All Samskaras lie dormant in the Chitta as latent activities, not only of this life but of all previous innumerable lives from Anadi Kala (beginningless time). The Samskaras of animal life (those of dog's births, etc.), the Samskaras of a Deva life, the Samskaras of kingly life, the Samskaras of the life of a peasant, are all hidden there in the Chitta. In human life, only those Samskaras which are appropriate to that particular type of birth will operate and come to play. The other kinds of Samskaras will remain concealed and dormant.

"As a merchant closing the year's ledger and opening a new one, does not enter in the new all the items of the old but only its balances, so does the spirit hand over to the new brain his judgments on the experiences of a life that is closed, the conclusions to which he has come, the decisions to which he has arrived. This is the stock handed on to the new life, the mental furniture for the new dwelling—a real memory."

KARMA

The gross body and the mind have, on account of your past Karmas, a tendency to act in a certain way and you act just in accordance with that tendency like a machine. You wrongly impute to yourself the authorship (agency) of these actions and thus make the matters worse. Most of your actions are done more or less automatically.

If you find it difficult to do your actions in a Nishkama spirit, have one desire for liberation in doing all things.

In Svarga or heaven, all earthly experiences of the mind are sorted and analysed. The essence is taken. The Jiva is born again in the physical universe with a new frame and bent of mind according to the nature of the essence extracted in the mental plane.

When you are writing a drama, if sleep comes in, you stop writing and retire to bed. As soon as you get up, you continue to write from where you have left the previous night. Even so, when you take up a new incarnation, you begin to continue the work which you had left unfinished in your previous life in accordance with the current of Vasanas of your past life.

Your next life will depend very largely upon the Karma you perform in this birth. There are probably many things which the man of the world does constantly and may do without much harm resulting in any way; if these things were done by those sincere aspirants who are treading the path of Realisation, they would be decidedly harmful.

Habitual study of abstract problems will result—in another earthly life—in a well-developed power for abstract thinking, while flippant, hasty thinking, flying from one object to another, will bequeath a restless ill-regulated mind to the following birth into this world.

THE ENSLAVING CHAINS OF SAMSKARAS

Mind exercises its suzerainty through Samskaras. From Samskaras emanate Vasanas like swarms of locusts. From Vasana flows the stream of desire and from enjoyment of objects of desires arises Trishna or internal craving (intense longing). Trishna is very powerful. The Samskaras are imbedded in the mind, in the Karana Sarira. There arises a memory of pleasure in the mind. Then the mind thinks of objects. Maya has her powerful seat in the imagination. There comes attachment. The mind plans and schemes. You are swayed by the passions. You exert yourself physically to possess those objects and enjoy them. In your efforts, you favour some and disfavour others through Raga and Dvesha. You will have to enjoy the fruits of your virtuous and vicious actions. Through this six-spoked wheel of Raga and Dvesha, virtue and vice, pleasure and pain, this Samsaric wheel of birth and death moves on without stopping from Anadi Kala (beginningless time).

THOUGHTS AND DESIRES DEPEND UPON SAMSKARAS

The nature of desires and thoughts depends upon the nature of your Samskaras. If you have good Samskaras, you will have good desires and good thoughts and vice versa. Even if you have indulged in vicious actions up to the age of forty, begin practising virtuous actions such as charity, Japa, Dama, Svadhyaya, meditation, service of the poor and the sick, service of saints, etc., from this moment and these Samskaras will prompt you to do more virtuous deeds. They will stimulate good desires and noble thoughts. The Lord says in the Bhagavad-Gita:—

Api chet suduracharo bhajate mam-ananyabhak
Sadhureva sa mantavyah samyag-vyavasito hi sah (IX-30)

"Even if the most sinful worships Me with undivided heart, he too must be deemed righteous, for he has rightly resolved."

EVIL SAMSKARAS—THE REAL ENEMY

Who is your real enemy? It is your own evil Samskaras. Substitute Subha Vasanas in place of Asubha ones. Then you can approach God. The mind will be changed. Old Samskaras will be obliterated. Wrong suggestions of various kinds and crude fantastic superstitions are rooted deeply in your mind. They are harmful. You will have to knock them down by Vichara, sublime suggestions, right thinking. "I am body," "I am Mr. John," "I am a Brahmin," "I am rich"—these are wrong suggestions and wrong Samskaras. Suggest to yourself boldly that you are Brahman. The previous wrong suggestion and Samskara "I am body" will slowly melt away by strenuous efforts.

If you forget your real Brahmic nature even for a minute, the old Samskaras of Ajnana will try to come up and overwhelm you. See how Narada's determination began to fluctuate even though he was absorbed in meditation, when he saw some Deva-girls. He at once experienced the sexual desire in himself. The seed came out, he put it in a pot and Chudala in the form of Kumbha Muni emerged from out of the pot (Yogavasishtha, story of Sikhidhvaja). Therefore, you will have to be very, very careful. Keep yourself away from all kinds of temptations—money, woman, name, fame, etc.

HOW TO ACQUIRE GOOD SAMSKARAS

Try to acquire some good spiritual Samskaras in this birth at least, if you are not able to devote all your time in spiritual pursuit. Do some kind of meditation for a short time at least daily, say for half an hour in the morning and evening. Have a meditation room. Make some kind of Japa of any Mantra. Study the Gita regularly. Have Satsanga. Visit Rishikesh, Nasik, Varanasi, Haridwar, Prayag once a year for a week's stay. Have the Darshana of Mahatmas. By doing so, you will acquire some spiritual Samskaras which will be a valuable spiritual asset for a new, good life. You will have a very good birth. You will be placed in suitable environments in the next birth for unfolding the Divinity that is lurking in your heart, for practice of Yoga. All opportunities and facilities will be given to you by God, through His grace (Isvara-Kripa) for your spiritual Sadhana. Even by a little systematic spiritual practice (Yogabhyasa and Vedantic Sadhana), you can change your mentality, your old vicious Samskaras. You can cut short several future births. By practice for three years, you can free yourself from the clutches of births and deaths. You are bound to become a Sannyasin. Why not now in this very birth? Why don't you cut short the cycle of unnecessary births and consequent miseries? How long do you want to be a slave of the world, a slave of passions and Indriyas? Wake up now. Do Sadhana and get immortality. *Udharet-Atmana-Atmanam*—Rouse the self by the Self.

New, healthy Samskaras can be implanted by new, healthy suggestions. Suppose your brain is a plank in which are driven nails which represent the ideas, habits and instincts which determine your actions. If you find that there exists in you a bad idea, a bad habit, a bad instinct,—a bad nail, as it were, in the plank of your mind—you should take another, viz., a good idea, habit or instinct, place it on the top of the bad one and give a hard tap with a hammer. In other words, you should make a healthy, useful suggestion. The new nail will be driven in perhaps a fraction of an inch while the old one will come out to the same extent. At each fresh blow with the hammer, that is to say, at each fresh suggestion, the one will be driven in a little further and the other will be driven out just that much until, after a certain number of blows, the old habits will be completely replaced by the new habits, new ideas. It demands, doubtless, strenuous efforts. It needs constant repetition of the new, healthy suggestions. Habit is second nature. But, pure, irresistible, determined will is bound to succeed eventually.

When you repeat "OM" or the Mahavakya of the Upanishads "Aham Brahma Asmi" once, one Samskara of the idea that "I am Brahman or the Absolute" is formed in the sub-conscious mind. The object in doing Japa or silent repetition of "OM" 21,600 times daily is to strengthen this Samskara.

DEATH OF SAMSKARAS LEADS TO MOKSHA

The physical body may die. But, the thoughts and Samskaras of actions, enjoyments and thinking follow you after death till you attain Moksha. These are variable Upadhis that accompany you after death. They are variable because you carry different kinds of Samskaras each time when you die. In different incarnations, you create different kinds of Samskaras. The permanent Upadhis that accompany you after death are the five Jnana-Indriyas, five Karma-Indriyas, five Pranas, fourfold mind and the Karana Sarira which is the support or Adhara for the Linga Sarira or astral body. It is the death of the Samskaras, it is the death of the Karana Sarira that leads to the final Moksha. It leads to the attainment of Brahma-Jnana. You will be getting fresh births so long as there are Samskaras. You will have to take birth again and again till all the Samskaras are obliterated or fried up by the acquisition of Brahma Jnana. When the Samskaras are wiped out, Brahmic Knowledge shines by itself in its own glory.

SADHANA CONSISTS IN DESTROYING THE SAMSKARAS

The aim of a Sadhaka is to fry out or burn or obliterate all these Samskaras through Nirbija Samadhi. Sadhana consists in wiping out the Samskaras. Breathing, hearing, seeing, feeling, tasting, smelling—all cause Samskaras or latent Smriti in the mind. The world enters the mind through the eyes, ears, tongue (speech) and old Samskaras. If you remain in seclusion, you can shut out the first three doors. Through Vichara (right enquiry of Supreme Self), you can destroy the fourth route. Then, Jnana (Knowledge of Self) will dawn. A Jnani is without Samskaras. They are fried out by Jnana. No doubt, the force of the Samskaras remains in the Antahkarana. But they are harmless. They will not bind the Jnani.

CHAPTER 15

SANKALPA

THE OPERATION OF THOUGHT

There is the spiritual life in God. This is what relates us to the Infinite. You get everything in Brahman, as He is self-contained and Paripurna (all-full). All your wants and desires are satisfied there. There is then the physical life. This it is that connects us with the universe around us. The thought-life connects the one with the other. It is this that plays between the two.

We have the power within us to open or close ourselves to the divine inflow exactly as we choose. This we have through the power of mind, through the operation of thought. If you are Rajasic, you are far from God. You have shut yourself up from God. If you are Sattvic, you open yourself to the divine inflow.

The sacred Ganga takes its origin in Gangotri (Himalayas) and runs perennially towards Ganga Sagar. Similarly, thought-currents take their origin from the bed of Samskaras (impressions) in the mind, wherein are imbedded the Vasanas (latent subtle desires), and flow incessantly towards the objects both in waking state and dream. Even a railway engine is sent to the engine-shed for rest when the wheels become overhot. But, this mysterious engine of mind goes on thinking without a moment's rest. The expansion of this mind alone is Sankalpa; and, Sankalpa, through its power of differentiation, generates this universe.

Ajnanins have fickle minds with a great deal of fluctuation and myriads of Sankalpas. Their minds ever vacillate through Sankalpas. But, Jnanins will be free from Sankalpas. They will be ever resting in their Atmic Jnana (Jnana-Svarupa) which gives the highest satisfaction (Tripti) and Supreme Peace (Parama Santi).

SANKALPA ONLY IS SAMSARA

When Sankalpa increases prodigiously, it is in no way beneficial. It is for evil only. The cause of bondage is Sankalpa. It is all the Sankalpas and Vasanas which you generate that enmesh you as in a nest. You become subject to bondage through your own Sankalpas and Vasanas like a silk-worm in its cocoon. Sankalpa of the mind itself is pain. Its absence is Brahmic bliss. Sankalpa only is Samsara; its destruction is Moksha.

It is the Sankalpa of the mind that brings about this world with all its moving and fixed creatures. The poisonous tree of the great Maya's illusion flourishes more and more out of the seed of the mind's modifications, full of Sankalpa, in the soil of the variegated enjoyments of the world.

Maya is a big poisonous tree. Trishnas and Vasanas water the tree of Mayaic illusion. Karmas are the fruits. Lust, anger, greed, etc., are the sprouts. Sattva, Rajas and Tamas are the buds. Indriyas are the twigs. Ahankara is the trunk. Raga and Dvesha are the two main branches. Various sensual objects are the leaves.

The individualised mind, which is full of Avidya and is all-pervading, though existing in name, has no form, either external or internal, like the Akasa permeating all space. The mere manifestation in all objects of (seeming) reality is the mind. Wherever there is Sankalpa, there does the mind exist.

The origin and the dissolution of this universe, which is nothing but a mode of consciousness, take place with the complete origination and destruction of the Sankalpas of the mind. Realisation of Brahman can be effected through the mind alone after abandoning its Sankalpas and Vikalpas. You should root out Sankalpa as completely as possible. This destruction of Sankalpa should be intelligently practised.

ANNIHILATION OF SANKALPAS CONSTITUTES MOKSHA

You may perform Tapas for myriads of years; you may be able to travel at once through the three worlds; but, never will you be able to reach the stainless MOKSHA, except through the firm path of annihilation of Sankalpas. Therefore, endeavour to destroy this Sankalpa and, thereby, attain Brahmic bliss which is devoid of pains and heterogeneity.

It is only Sankalpa of the mind destroyed beyond resurrection that constitutes the immaculate Brahmic seat. Why can you not contemplate silently and secretly in your heart upon the destruction of this Sankalpa? Then it will so betide that even the throne of an emperor, who sways his sceptre over the whole earth, will be regarded by you as but a paltry bauble.

Remain without Sankalpa-Vikalpa and Dvaita-Bhavana (idea and feeling of duality). Divest yourself of all Sankalpas and be a Nirvikalpa. This is Brahma-Nishtha or Advaita-Nishtha. Strive hard to get this state. You will be then in perfect peace and joy.

THE SVABHAVA OF MANAS

The mind can very easily think of worldly objects. It is its Svabhava. Thoughts generally flow with ease towards objects. Mental energy will readily flow in that direction. The mental force can easily flow in the old grooves and avenues of mundane thoughts. It finds it extremely difficult to think of God. It is an uphill work for a Samsaric mind of Vyavahara. The difficulty in weaning the mind from objects and fixing it on God is the same as in making the Ganga flow towards Badri Narayan instead of its natural flow towards Ganga Sagar. It is like rowing against the current of the Yamuna. Still, through strenuous efforts and Tyaga it must be trained to flow towards God, much against its will, if you want to free yourself from birth and death. There is no other go if you want to escape from worldly miseries and tribulations.

HOW TO DESTROY SANKALPA

Destroy the stains of Sankalpa or the cloud of Sankalpa through the power of discrimination and constant efforts and be drowned in the ocean of Brahmic bliss with spiritual illumination. When you try to bury your shadow in the earth, it always comes out. Similarly, when you try to destroy the Sankalpas through Viveka-Vritti, they will come out again and again. Withdraw the mind from the objects and act according to your Guru's instructions. Purify the mind and fix it on the Akasa of the heart (Infinite Brahman). The mind will be destroyed in course of time. Be sure of this.

Do not for a moment contemplate upon the things of the universe. You need not exert yourself too much to rid yourself of this Sankalpa. With the checking of all thoughts, one's mind will perish. To crush a full-blown flower in one's hand requires a little effort, but even that little effort is not needed to do away with Sanklpa. Sankalpa is destroyed with the control of thoughts. Having firmly annihilated the external Sankalpa through the internal one and having destroyed the impure mind through the pure one, rest firmly in your Atma-Jnana.

When you are firmly established in the idea that the world is unreal, Vikshepa (through names and forms) and Sphurana of Sankalpa (thoughts) will slowly vanish. Repeat constantly the formula, "*Brahma Satyam Jaganmithya Jivo Brahmaiva Naaparah*" (Brahman alone is real. World is unreal. Jiva is identical with Brahman). You will gain immense strength and peace of mind through the repetition.

Having freed yourself from all desires for the visible objects before you and having made your impure mind firm and steady through your pure mind, eradicate all the Sanklpas that arise in the mind. Now, this mind, which arises through Sankalpas, perishes through it alone like a flame of fire which, though fanned by the wind, is yet extinguishable by the same.

THE STATE OF NISSANKALPA

With the extinction of the base Sankalpas, there is the extinction of Avidya and its effect, mind. Sankalpa is pain. Nissankalpa is all bliss. Sit alone in a solitary room. Close the eyes. Watch the mind and destroy the Vrittis one by one by continuous, energetic efforts. Asamprajnata Samadhi will ensue.

If, with the extinction of the pain-producing Sankalpas, the mind also is destroyed, then will the thick frost of Moha (delusion) affecting you from remote periods dissipate itself. Then, like an unobscured sky in the autumnal season, Brahman alone will shine resplendent, blissful, imperishable, non-dual, formless and without birth and death.

When your thoughts, which are now dispersed, shall be collected together and you will remain in a state of repose, then the eternally happy Atman will shine forth as the reflection of the sun is seen in a clear surface of water. Peace is not in money, woman or eating. When the mind becomes desireless and thoughtless, Atman shines and sheds forth eternal bliss and peace. Why do you search in vain for happiness in objects outside? Search within for bliss in the subjective, Sat-Chit-Ananda Amrita Atman.

CHAPTER 16
THOUGHT CREATES THE WORLD

THOUGHT, THE ORIGIN OF EVERYTHING

Everything in the material universe about us had its origin first in thought. From this, it took its form. Every castle, every statue, every painting, every piece of mechanism—in short, everything—had its birth, its origin, first in the mind of the one who formed it before it received its material expression or embodiment.

Mind has got various preoccupations. When an artist begins to draw a picture on the canvas, he draws the picture out of the material preconceived by the mind.

After all, the world is merely an idea or thought. Just as a seed begins to germinate at its proper time and place, so also the seer (knower) appears as the visible through the Sankalpa of the mind (the visible being no other than the seer itself). When the mind ceases to think, the world vanishes and there is bliss indescribable. When the mind begins to think, immediately the world reappears and there is suffering.

"*Cogito, ergo sum*—I think, therefore I am." This is Descartes's fundamental basis of philosophy. This is in accordance with Sri Sankara's statement that the Atman cannot be illusive; for he who would deny it, even in denying it, witnesses its reality.

The universe is rendered visible by mind. But, it is a pity that nobody has seen the mind save a seer. When you seriously and unceasingly think over the nature of the mind, it is nothing. When you begin to analyse mind, it is nothing. It dwindles to airy nothing. It is a bundle of thoughts and the thought 'I' is the root of all thoughts. This 'I' is a false idea, a non-entity. When the root of all thoughts vanishes into nothing, where is the boasted mind?

The first thought that arose in your mind was 'Aham', 'I'. The last thought or Vritti that will arise in the mind before it is absorbed in Brahman will be Brahmakara Vritti which is produced by your feeling that you are Infinity.

(103)

UNIVERSE, A CREATION OF THE COSMIC MIND

The universe is not mental creation of Jiva. One single, organised thought of the Cosmic Mind (Hiranyagarbha) has materialised as the seeming universe. This phenomenal universe is but an outcome of the Divine Will, seeming to be real through the workings of the mind.

Before you write out a drama, you have a vivid mental picture of the whole drama in your mind. Then you write it out in succession in four acts. When it is staged, it is acted in succession, part by part. Similarly, the universe with its movements is a vivid mental picture in the Cosmic Mind—in the mind of Isvara. There is neither past nor future for Him. Everything is 'Present' for Him. There is neither 'near' nor 'far' for Him. Every place is 'here'. Every time is 'now'. The events come out in succession on the stage of the long world-drama as Time rolls on. Atoms rotate continuously. Old becomes new and new becomes old. In reality there is no such thing as old; there is no such thing as single. The Jivas with individual minds are witnessing the events in succession. But Isvara knows all events at one sweep. He is Sarvajna (all-knowing). He is Sarvavit (all-understanding) also. He knows every detail of His creation. The Cosmic Mind creates the Maya. Individual minds receive things under delusion.

This universe is nothing but a mode of the mind, self-evolved from Brahman, the cause of the universe. All the universes which appear only through Manas are no other than its modes. The mind is subjectively consciousness and objectively it is this universe. Hence, this all-pervading world is nothing but consciousness itself.[3]

ISVARA AND MAYA

All the Samskaras float in Maya. Suppose there is a very big mirror. You can see in the mirror the reflection of all persons who move in the street, all carts, cars, all carriages which pass along the road. You can be simply watching these movements from a distance in the mirror without being affected in the least. Even so, the movements of this whole universe take place in the biggest mirror of Maya. Isvara or the Lord of the universe is simply witnessing everything. He is the silent Sakshi. When the

3 *The Jiva and the universe are Brahman in their innate condition only.*

Adrishta (the hidden power in Karmas) of the Jivas ripens, Isvara simply wills and the universe is projected.

REALITY OF THE UNIVERSE LIES IN SANKALPA OF MANAS

This ever-agitated Manas (mind), having come into existence out of the ineffable Brahman, creates the world according to its own Sankalpa (thoughts). This legerdemain of the universe springs out of the Sankalpa of your Manas. It is through the Sankalpa of your Manas that the universe appears to be and it is this Sankalpa that is asked to be given up by you if you wish to soar to the One Reality beyond the universe. *"Sarvasankalpasannyasi Yogarudhastadochyate*—He is said to be established in Yoga who has renounced all his Sankalpas." (Gita, VI-4)

With the growth of a paltry Sankalpa, there will arise the universe; with the extinction of the former, the latter also will disappear. With the annihilation of Sankalpa, all conception of differences between the seer and the seen will vanish and then the Reality of Brahman will begin to shine uninterrupted. Then the shadow of all the universe—movable and fixed—will be found absorbed in It in a non-dual state.

With the contemplation of 'I', all the train of ideas of the universe will set in; otherwise, all the universe will vanish as instantaneously as darkness before the sun. Mind and 'I' are one. Destroy the 'I', then the mind is destroyed.

"Manah-kalpitam Jagat—(Creation of) world is an imagination of the mind" (Yogavasishtha). This legerdemain of the world is enacted by the mind and the mind alone— *"Manomatram Jagat.* What you call world is the mind only." Mind is world. The mind manifests itself as the external world. This universe is no other than the mind itself. Like a dream generating another dream in it, the mind, having no visible form, will generate non-existent visibles. This perishable universe exists only when the mind exists, but disappears with the absence of the latter. If the mind, which is the insturument of knowledge, perception and activity, vanishes, with it disappears this subjective world also.

There is a corresponding notion and object for every Sabda (sound). There is a notion and an object for the Sabda "Cow." Maya is deceiving you through Sabda-jala. The whole world is a mere notion, mere idea. It is Sankalpamatra. It is Bhrantimatra. It is Kalpanamatra. It is Akasamatra. It exists in name only. "*Vacharambhanam Vikaro Namadheyam Mrittiketyeva Satyam*—all modifications being only names based upon words, the truth being that all is clay." The whole world is a combination of five elements. Analyse, realise the illusory nature of all objects and abandon all false objects. When you begin to analyse, the whole world vanishes and with it the notion, sound, and objects also.

The happiness and misery experienced in this world are caused by the working of the mind. All the hosts of pains and pleasures arise from the mind only. They will perish if the mind perishes through stainless discrimination and spiritual Sadhana. The three worlds are created for the pleasures and pains of the mind. Suspension of the mental activity will cause the three worlds to disappear with their misery. With the destruction of the mind, all the three periods of time vanish into nothing. By controlling the mind, all occult powers are acquired. If the mind is not controlled, all else become useless and painful. Therefore, the mind should be annihilated.

MIND FUNCTIONS WITHIN THE THREE CATEGORIES

Mind always functions within the categories of time, space and causation. These three categories are mental creations only. A coconut tree is not really twenty feet high. The height is only a mental interpretation. There are vibrations only outside. It is the mind that creates length, breadth, height, thickness, dimensions, void, square, etc. A distance of two miles comes out of feeling only. You actually feel that you have walked so much distance. When you transcend the mind, all these categories vanish entirely. Annihilate the mind, therefore, through Brahmavichara. You will enter a realm of Peace and Ananda which is eternal, infinite and causeless (Parama Karana).

THE WHY AND HOW OF THE UNIVERSE
—A TRANSCENDENTAL QUESTION

Mr. Narain, my friend who is standing before me, is my own mental creation. Even this world is my own mental creation.

Abhava or non-existence is said to be an object of perception, since non-existence of a thing means its existence somewhere else.

According to the idealistic theory, there is no world at all in reality. It is all mere mental imagination. This is Vijnanavada of the Buddhists.

According to the realistic theory, the world is a solid reality. Even the dualist shool of Madhva and Visishtadvaita school of Ramanuja and Raja Yogic school of Maharshi Patanjali hold that the world is real (Jagat Satyam).

Kant has demonstrated that space, time and causation are not objective realities, but only subjective forms of our intellect, and the unavoidable conclusion is that the world, so far as it is extended in space, is running on in time and ruled throughout by causality, is merely a representation of our mind and nothing beyond it.

A finite mind that is gross and conditioned by time, space and causation cannot comprehend the why and how of the universe, a question that is transcendental. The question has never been answered by anybody, by any Sastra, by any sage or Acharya. Do not rack your mind on this point. You can never get a solution for this problem. It is Mauja of Brahman to create this universe. It is His Lila-Vilasa. It is His Maya. It is His Svabhava.

NON-EXISTENCE OF THE WORLD—WHAT IT MEANS

The Abhava of Jagat (non-existence of the world) or its Nasa (destruction) does not mean the annihilation of mountains, lakes, trees and rivers. When your Nischaya (determination) that this world is Mithya (unreal, illusory) gets stronger and stronger and when you are well-established on this idea that this world is illusory like Mrigatrishna (mirage), this alone is destruction of the world.

You cannot destroy a mountain, but you can destroy the idea of a mountain.

The universe is like a Svapna in Jagrat. Just as there is the image in the mirror, this world is a big image in the mind-mirror. The mind is like a big *Chaddar* (thick cloth) painted with various pictures. There is neither painter nor canvas nor any material for painting such as brush, dish, oil, powder, etc. The picture of the universe appears depicted on the spotless Jnana-Akasa (knowledge-space).

The play of the mind arising out of Chaitanya (pure consciousness) constitutes this universe. Mind is Maya. Maya is mind. The workings of the mind are nothing but the workings of Maya itself. Attraction or attachment in the mind towards forms is Maya. Identification of one's own self with the mind is Maya.

HOW THE MIND MANIFESTS AS THE WORLD

The motion or vibration of Prana moves the mind. The movement of the mind generates the universe. The mind manifests itself as the external world. Nama-Rupa (names and forms) arise owing to Vikshepa Sakti, one of the powers of Maya. The Vikshepa force operates both in the Jagrat and the Svapna states. The whole world is projected on account of this power only. In sleep, it disappears.

The world enters the mind through the eyes, ears, tongue (speech) and old Samskaras. If you remain in the seclusion, you can shut out these first three doors. Through Vichara (right enquiry of Supreme Self), you can destroy the Samskaras, the fourth route. Then Jnana (Knowledge of Self) will dawn.

All the universes with their heterogeneity, though really Atma-Jnana, shine as worlds only through our illusory mind, like the blueness of the sky which is really non-existent. The Self-light of Para Brahman alone is appearing as the mind or this motley universe. Mind is Prajna-Sakti. Matter is Bhuta-Sakti. Prana is Kriya-Sakti of Brahman. Everything belongs to Brahman. In reality, there is no Jiva. There is Brahman only.

The mind which ever rises and falls with the ebb of desires, fancies this illusory universe to be through its ignorance; but it should be informed of the real nature of this world, then it will cognise it to be Brahman itself.

CHAPTER 17
AVIDYA AND AHANKARA

AVIDYA

The mind itself is a creation of Avidya (ignorance). It is a Karya (effect) of Avidya. It is filled with delusion. That is the reason why it deceives and tempts you. It makes you go astray. If you can destroy the cause of the mind, Ajnana, by getting Jnana (knowledge of the Supreme Self), mind is nowhere. It dwindles into an airy nothing. Manonasa (annihilation of mind) takes place when Jnana dawns.

Avidya works through Upadhis (attributes, limiting adjuncts). All the special apparatus required by Avidya constitute the Upadhis of the soul. Mind is an Upadhi; Buddhi is an Upadhi and Ahankara also is an Upadhi.

The sea of Avidya (ignorance) is in the mind of man. The explanation of the empirical concept must be sought in the nature of our cognitive faculty. Sri Sankara explains Avidya in this way. It is Naisargika; it is innate in our mental faculty. It is Mithyajnananimitta, based on wrong knowledge; and, knowledge is a function of the mind. It is Nityapratyayarupa; it consists in the form of a wrong conception. "All Jivas—human entities—which are really non-existent, are (with all concomitant appearance of birth, death, etc.) mere results of the objectivising tendency of the mind and nothing else."

The whole experience of duality, made up of perceiver and perceived, is pure imagination. There is no Avidya apart from the mind. On destruction of the mind, all is destroyed. The activity of the mind is the cause of all appearance. On account of Avidya or Bhranti (illusion) in the mind, you see the objects, trees, etc., outside and feel as if they are separate from you and real.

So long as there is mind, there are all these distinctions of big and small, high and low, superior and inferior, good and bad, etc. The highest Truth is that in which there is no relativity. If you can transcend the mind by constant and profound meditation on Atman, you will be able to attain the Nirdvandva state (a state beyond the pairs of opposites) wherein lies the supreme peace and highest knowledge.

There is no Avidya outside the mind. The mind itself is Avidya. Imaginations and Sankalpas are products of Avidya. Ignorance is imbedded in the mind. The mind needs thorough cleansing with Japa, Pranayama, Satsanga, Vichara and Nididhyasana, just as a rusty copper plate needs cleansing with earth, ash, tamarind, powder, etc.

AHANKARA—HOW IT DEVELOPS

Atman in conjunction with the Buddhi is Ahankara. The basis of Ahankara is Buddhi. As the Buddhi (Bheda Buddhi) is the cause for this differentiation (this little "I"), Buddhi is the cause or seed for Ahankara. Ahamta and Mamata ('I'-ness and 'mine'-ness) are Jivasrishti. It is Jivasrishti that binds a man to the world. Isvarasrishti (God's creation) helps man in his God-realisation.

The seed of mind is Ahankara. Ahankara is development through the thoughts of the mind. As the first thought is the 'I' thought and as this 'I' thought is at the base of all other thoughts, Ahankara is the seed for the mind. This idea of 'I' will bring in its train, the idea of time, space and other potencies. With these environments, the name Jiva accrues to it. Contemporaneously with it, there arise Buddhi, memory, Manas which is the seed of the tree of Sankalpa.

When you are a boy, the Ahankara is not very potent. It is like a shadow in a glass. It gets developed and firm-rooted during your adolescence after you marry and entangle yourself in the achievement of various worldly desires. You are fearless in your boyhood. The moment this little 'I' becomes stronger in you, side by side, various sorts of fears, various sorts of desires, a host of delusions take firm hold of you. The world appears to you more real, too.

THE CURSE OF EGOISM

Ahankara is, after all, nothing. But, tremendous is its influence! Maya means Ahankara. Mind is another name for Ahankara. World means Ahankara. The sprout of Ahankara ramifies here and there with its long branches of 'mine' and 'thine'. It is inveterate. Ahankara wants to live in flesh (Abhinivesa or clinging to life), to eat flesh and to embrace flesh. This is pure Ajnana (ignorance) only. Look at Maya's deception and wholesale swindling! Beware! Awake! Get Jnana.

Just as the cloud screens the sun, so also this cloud of Ahankara screens the 'Jnana Surya', the Infinite Sun of Knowledge, Brahman. You cannot realise God, if you have the least tinge of egoism, if you have the slightest attachment to name and form, if you have the least tinge of Vasana or if you have the least trace of worldly desire in the mind.

HOW TO ERADICATE AHANKARA

The deep roots of Ahankara should be burnt by the fire of knowledge (Jnanagni). Then you will quite easily get the wealth of Moksha. All tribulations, sorrows, miseries and afflictions will terminate now. Control of the Indriyas and Pranayama help to develop the Buddhi (Vikasa of Buddhi).

You cannot, all at once, eradicate Ahankara altogether. You can easily give up wife, children, money, anger. But it is extremely difficult to give up Ahankara. Try to minimise it little by little. Remove one *anna* ($\frac{1}{16}^{th}$ of a Rupee) of Ahankara within three months. Within four years, you will be able to root it out completely. You will have to remove it either by self-sacrifice through Karma Yoga, or self-surrender through Bhakti, or self-denial through Vedantic Atma-Vichara.

Through the Sankalpas of Manas, Ahankara is generated. If the modification of the mind which leans to sensual pleasures is destroyed, the Atman, divested of its Ahankara, becomes the unnameable Brahmic Reality.

Ahankara is like a thread. It connects or links all the Indriyas on itself. When the thread is broken, all the pearls fall down. Even so, when the thread of Ahankara is broken by 'Aham Brahma Asmi' Bhavana or Sakshi Bhava or self-surrender method by taking the Nimitta Bhava (instrument-in-the-hands-of-the-Lord attitude), all the Indriyas will be broken down or destroyed. The connection with Indriyas will be severed.

Even if you identify yourself with a subtle body inside, it will help you in your Self-realisation. It is only the identification with the fleshy physical body that brings all sorts of troubles through gross Ahankara and 'mineness'. The physical 'I' is a very great menace.

Whenever Ahankara asserts itself, raise a question within thyself, "What is the source of this little 'I'?" Again and again, moot this question and enquire. When you remove layer after layer, the onion dwindles to nothing. When you analyse the little 'I', it becomes a non-entity; it will gradually vanish. It will dwindle into an airy nothing. Body is not 'I'. 'I' remains even after the leg is amputated. Give up Jivasrishti.

Within the time taken to pluck a flower, within the twinkling of an eye, this Ahankara can be easily eradicated by right Sadhana or Brahma-Bhava.

SATTVIC AHANKARA

When you assert 'Aham Brahma Asmi' (I am Brahman), it is Sattvic Ahankara. It is Moksha Ahankara. It will not bind you in any way. It will help you realise Brahman. The fire in a picture will not burn anything. A light in the presence of midday sun will not shine and shed its light. Even so, the Ahankara of a Sattvic person cannot do any harm to any person.

CHAPTER 18

THE POWER OF THOUGHT

THOUGHT IS A LIVING FORCE

Thought is a vital, living force, the most vital, subtle and irresistible force that exists in the universe. The thought-world is more real relatively than this physical universe. Thoughts are living things. Every change in thought is accompanied by vibration of its matter (mental). Thought as force needs a special kind of subtle matter in its working.

Mind assumes the form of anything it contemplates. When you think of an object, your mind shapes itself into the form of that object. When you change your thought, your mind also changes its shape. Many modifications continually arise in the mind. Your thoughts rapidly change. Your mind also changes its shape rapidly. Every moment, mind is continually creating hundreds of these thought-forms and continually dispersing them again. It never holds on steadily to one thought-form for some time.

Every thought has a certain name and a certain form. Form is the grosser and name the finer state of a single manifesting power called thought. But, these three are one. It is the unity in trinity, the three degrees of existence of the same thing. Wherever the one is, the others also are there. Suppose your mind is now perfectly calm, entirely without thought. Nevertheless, as soon as thought begins to rise, it will immediately take name and form. Thus you find that every idea that man has, or can have, must be connected with a certain word as its counterpart.

Language is different, but thought is one. Mental image is the same in all. Sound has got four forms, viz., Para, Pasyanti, Madhyama and Vaikhari. Vaikhari is the ordinary speech. It differs in different countries. But Para, Pasyanti and Madhyama are one and the same. Para is undifferentiated sound that lies dormant in Brahman. The language of the Devatas, the language in the mental plane is one. It is Madhyama. The rotatory vibration of the causal body (Karana-Sarira) is Pasyanti. That is your real name. When you operate through your Karana-Sarira, (lower Prakamya or lower Divya Drishti), you will hear the Pasyanti sound, your real name.

THOUGHT IS SUBTLE MATTER

Thought is subtle matter. A thought is as much solid as a piece of stone. You may die, but your thoughts can never die. They have form, size, shape, colour, quality, substance, power and weight. A spiritual thought has yellow colour; a thought charged with anger and hatred is of a dark red colour; a selfish thought has a brown colour; and so on. A Yogin can see directly with his inner Yogic eye all these thoughts.

The stronger the thoughts, the earlier the fructification. Thought is focussed and given a particular direction and, in the degree that thought is thus focussed and given direction, it is effective in the work it is sent out to accomplish.

THOUGHT IS A CREATIVE FORCE

Thought is a great force. Thought is a dynamic force. Thought moves. Thought is infectious. Thought creates. You can work wonders with the power of thought. Through the instrumentality of thought, you acquire creative power. There are nowadays numerous books on thought-power, thought-dynamics and thought-culture. Study them. You will then have a comprehensive understanding of thought, its power, workings and usefulness.

The power of thought is very great. Every thought of yours has a literal value to you in every possible way. The strength of your body, the strength of your mind, your success in life and the pleasures you give to others by your company—all depend on the nature and quality of your thoughts. You must know thought-culture.

THOUGHT GIVES HEALTH

If you entertain healthy thoughts, you can keep good health. If you hold on to sickly thoughts in the mind, thoughts of diseased tissues, thoughts of weak-nerves, thoughts of improper functioning of organs or viscera, you can never expect good health, beauty and harmony. The body is the product of the mind. If you hold on vigorous thoughts in the mind, then the physical body also will be vigorous.

Evil thoughts of all kinds befoul and infure the mind and, if persisted in, will become veritable diseases and maimings of the mind, incurable during the period of life.

THOUGHT BUILDS CHARACTER

"As a man thinketh, so he is." "Man is created by thought; what a man thinks upon, that he becomes." Think you are strong; strong you become. Think you are weak; weak you become. Think you are a fool; fool you become. Think you are God; God you become. A man forms his own character, becoming that which he thinks. If you meditate on courage, you shall work courage into your character. So with purity, patience, unselfishness and self-control. If you think nobly, you shall gradually make for yourself a noble character, but if you think basely, a base character will be formed. Steady persevering thought sets up a definite habit of the mind and that habit manifests itself as a quality in the character. The thread of thought is woven into mental and moral qualities and these qualities in their totality form what we call character. You can build your character as surely as a mason can build a wall, working with and through the law.

The first step towards a deliberate creation of character lies then in the deliberate choosing of what we will think and then of thinking persistently on the quality chosen. Ere long, there will be a tendency to evince that quality; a little longer, its exercise will become habitual. Thought makes character. You spin the thread of thought into your destiny.

THOUGHT WEAVES DESTINY

That which man thinks upon in one life, he becomes in another. If the mind dwells continually upon one train of thought, a groove is formed into which the thought-force runs automatically and such a habit of thought survives death and since it belongs to the ego, is carried over to the subsequent earth life as a thought tendency and capacity.

Every thought has got its own mental image. Every man has a mental world of his own, his own views, his own sentiments, his own feelings, his own habitual thoughts, his own experience and his own mode of thinking. The essence of the various mental images formed in one particular physical life is being worked out in the mental plane. It constitutes the basis for the next physical life. Just as a new physical body is formed in every birth, so also a new mind and a new Buddhi are formed in every birth.

It is difficult to explain the detailed workings of thought and Karma. Every Karma produces twofold effects, one on the individual mind and the other on the world. Man makes the circumstances of his future life by the effect of his actions upon others.

Every action has a past which leads up to it; every action has a future which proceeds from it. An action implies a desire which prompted it and a thought which shaped it. Each act is a link in an endless chain of causes and effects, each effect becoming a cause and each cause having been an effect; and each link in the endless chain is welded out of three components—desire, thought and activity. A desire stimulates a thought; a thought embodies itself in an act.

Selfish coveting of the possessions of others, though never carried out into active cheating in the present, makes one a thief in a later earth-life, while hatred and revenge secretly cherished are the seeds from which the murderer springs. So again, unselfish loving yields as harvest the philanthropist and the saint; and every thought of compassion helps to build the tender and pitiful nature which belongs to one who is a friend to all creatures.

LIKE ATTRACTS LIKE

The great law, "Like attracts like," is ever operating. This is a great cosmic law. This is a law in nature. This law operates in the thought world also. People of similar thoughts are attracted towards each other. That is the reason why the maxims run as follows: "Birds of the same feather flock together... A man is known by the company he keeps." A doctor is drawn towards a doctor. A poet has attraction for another poet. A songster loves another songster. A philosopher likes another philosopher. A vagabond likes a vagabond. The mind has got a 'drawing power'. You are continually attracting towards you, from both the seen and the unseen sides of life-forces, thoughts, influences and conditions most akin to those of your own thoughts and lives.

In the realm of thought, people of similar thoughts are attracted to one another. This universal law is continually operating whether we are conscious of it or not. We are all living, so to speak, in a vast ocean of thought; and the very atmosphere around us is continually filled with the thought-forces that are being continually sent or that are continually going out in the form of thought-waves. We are all affected more or less by these thought-forces either consciously or unconsciously and in the degree that we are more or less sensitively organised or in the degree we are negative and so are open to outside influences, rather than positive, which thus determine what influences shall enter into the domain of our thoughts and hence into our lives.

Carry any kind of thought you please about with you and so long as you retain it, no matter how you roam over land or sea, you will unceasingly attract to yourself, knowingly or inadvertently, exactly and only what corresponds to your own dominant quality of thought. Thoughts are your private property and you can regulate them to suit your taste entirely by steadily recognising your ability to do so. You have entirely in your own hands to determine the order of thought you entertain and consequently the order of influences you attract and are not mere willowy creatures of circumstances, unless indeed you choose to be.

GOOD THOUGHTS AND EVIL THOUGHTS

A good thought is thrice blessed. First, it benefits the thinker by improving his mental body (Manomaya Kosha). Secondly, it benefits the person about whom it is entertained. Lastly, it benefits all mankind by improving the general mental atmosphere.

An evil thought, on the contrary, is thrice cursed. First, it harms the thinker by doing injury to his mental body. Secondly, it harms the person who is its object. Lastly, it harms all mankind by vitiating the whole mental atmosphere.

Every evil thought is as a sword drawn on the person to whom it is directed. If you entertain thoughts of hatred, you are really a murderer of that man against whom you foster thoughts of hatred. You are your own suicide, because these thoughts rebound upon you only.

A mind tenanted by evil thoughts acts as a magnet to attract like thoughts from others and thus intensifies the original evil.

Evil thoughts thrown into the mental atmosphere poison receptive minds. To dwell on an evil thought gradually deprives it of its repulsiveness and impels the thinker to perform an action which embodies it.

THE PROGENY OF THOUGHTS

It is not sufficient that your thoughts are not bad. You must transmute bad thoughts into good thoughts. This is the first part of your Sadhana. You must make them helpful thoughts. When they are sent out, they must be capable of doing immense good and benefit to the suffering humanity and your neighbours.

Thoughts are your own real children. Be careful of your progeny of thoughts. A good son brings happiness, name and fame to the father. An evil son brings infamy, discredit to his father. Even so, a noble thought will bring happiness and joy to you. An evil thought will bring misery and trouble to you. Just as you rear up your children with great care, so also you will have to rear up good, sublime thoughts with great care.

THOUGHT IS CONTAGIOUS

Thought is very contagious, nay, more contagious than the Spanish Flu. Thought moves. It actually leaves the brain and hovers about. It enters the brains of others also. A sympathetic thought in you raises a sympathetic thought in others with whom you come in contact. A thought of anger produces a similar vibration in those who surround an angry man. It leaves the brain of one man and enters the brains of others who live at a long distance and excites them. A cheerful thought produces cheerful thought in others. A thought of joy creates sympathetically a thought of joy in others. You are filled with joy and intense delight when you see a batch of hilarious children playing mirthfully and dancing in joy.

In broadcasting, a singer sings beautiful songs at Calcutta. You can hear them nicely through the radio-set in your own house at Delhi. All messages are received through the wireless. Even so, your mind is like a wireless machine. A saint with peace, poise, harmony and spiritual waves sends out into the world thoughts of harmony and peace. They travel with tremendous lightning speed in all directions and enter the minds of thousands and produce in them also similar thoughts of harmony and peace. Whereas a worldly man whose mind is filled with jealousy, revenge and hatred sends out discordant thoughts which enter the minds of thousands and stir in them similar thoughts of hatred and discord.

Thought is very contagious. Keep a good and honest man in the company of a thief. He will begin to steal. Keep a sober man in the company of a drunkard. He will begin to drink.

THOUGHT-TRANFERENCE OR TELEPATHY

What is the possible medium through which thoughts can travel from one mind to another? The best possible explanation is that Manas or mind-substance fills all space like ether and it serves as the vehicle for thoughts as Prana is the vehicle for feelings, ether is the vehicle for heat, light and electricity, and air is the vehicle for sound. Mind is Vibhu (all-pervading) like Akasa. Hence, thought-transference is possible. Thought-transference is telepathy.

If we throw a piece of stone in a tank or a pool of water, it will produce a succession of concentric waves travelling all around from the affected place. The light of a candle will similarly give rise to waves of ethereal vibrations travelling in all directions from the candle. In the same manner, when a thought, whether good or evil, crosses the mind of a person, it gives rise to vibrations in the Manas or mental atmosphere, which travel far and wide in all directions.

While electricity travels at the rate of 1,86,000 miles per second, thoughts virtually travel in no time, their speed being as much faster than electricity as their vehicle Manas is finer than ether, the medium of electricity.

Thoughts are like things. Just as you hand over an orange to your friend and take it back, so also you can give a useful, powerful thought to your friend and take it back also. You must know the right technique to handle and manipulate a thought. The science is very interesting and subtle. You can aid a friend in trouble by sending him thoughts of comfort, a friend in search of Truth by thoughts clear and definite of the truths you know. You can send into the mental atmosphere thoughts which will raise, purify and inspire all who are sensible to them.

If you send out a loving, helpful thought to another man, it leaves your brain, goes directly to that man, raises a similar thought of love in his mind and returns back to you with redoubled force. If you send out a thought of hatred to another man, it hurts that man and hurts you also by returning back to you with redoubled force. Therefore, understand the laws of thought, raise only thoughts of mercy, love and kindness from your mind and be happy always.

When you send out a useful thought to help others, it must have a definite, positive purpose and aim. Then only it will bring out the desired effect. Then only that thought will accomplish a definite work.

THE DUTY OF AN ASPIRANT

You should learn the method of sending out helping, loving thoughts to others and the whole world at large. You should know how to remove distraction and collect all thoughts and send them out as a battalion of helpful forces to do good to the suffering humanity. Thought-transference is a beautiful science. It is an exact science.

Just as the flowing Ganga brings joy and coolness to those who live on its banks, so also your strong thoughts of love and peace must flow out as a healing stream to bring solace, peace and glee to those persons whose minds are filled with care, worry, anxiety, tribulation, affliction, etc.

Even some good natured householders entertain some occasional good thoughts and send out into the world some helpful thoughts. This is not sufficient for an aspirant in the path of Truth. A continuous stream of helpful thoughts must gush out from his mind. It must be a perennial, healing stream of loving, helpful thoughts. He must be able to charge groups of twenty persons, masses of hundreds and thousands with love, joy and cheerfulness. He must stir them with a mere glance and a few sweet, powerful words into enthusiasm, high spirits and exalted moods and exhilaration. That is spiritual strength, will-force (Atma-Bala).

HOW SANNYASINS SERVE THE WORLD THROUGH THEIR THOUGHT-VIBRATIONS

Indians have now imbibed the missionary spirit of the West and cry out that Sannyasins should come out and take part in social and political activities. It is a sad mistake. A Sannyasin or a Yogin need not become the President of an Association or the leader of a social or political movement. It is a foolish and puerile idea. A true Sannyasin can do everything through his thought-vibrations.

It is not necessary that a Sannyasin, a saint should appear on the platform to help the world, to preach and elevate the minds of people. Some saints preach by example. Their very lives are an embodiment of teaching. Their very sight elevates the minds of thousands. A saint is a living assurance for others for God-realisation. Many draw inspiration from the sight of holy saints. No one can check the thought-vibrations from the saints. Their pure, strong thought-vibrations travel a very long distance, purify the world and enter the minds of many thousands of persons. There is no doubt in this.

A sage living in a Himalayan cave can transmit a powerful thought to a corner of America. He who practises Nishkama Karma Yoga in the world purifies himself through disinterested works and he who meditates in a cave in the Himalayas and tries to purify himself really purifies the world, helps the world at large through his spiritual vibrations. Nobody can prevent his pure thoughts coming out and passing to others who really want them. Worldly-minded social workers cannot understand this point.

CLEAR THINKING—HOW IT IS ACCOMPLISHED

The common man does not know what deep thinking is. His thoughts run riot. There is a great deal of confusion in the mind sometimes. His mental images are very distorted. It is only thinkers, philosophers and Yogins who have well-defined, clear-cut mental images. They can be seen through clairvoyance very vividly. Those who practise concentration and meditation develop strong, well-formed mental images.

Most of your thoughts are not well-grounded. They come and slip away. They are, therefore, vague and indefinite. The images are not clear, strong and well-defined. You will have to reinforce them by clear, continuous and deep thinking. Through Vichara (ratiocination), Manana (deep reflection) and meditation, you will have to make the thoughts settle down and crystalise into a definite shape. Then the philosophical idea will become firm. Through right-thinking, reasoning, introspection and meditation, you will have to clarify your ideas. Then confusion will vanish. The thoughts will get settled and well-grounded.

Think clearly. Clarify your ideas again and again. Introspect in solitude. Purify your thoughts to a considerable degree. Silence the thoughts. Do not allow the mind to bubble. Let one thought-wave rise and settle down calmly. Then allow another thought to enter. Drive off all extraneous thoughts that have no connection with the subject-matter you are handling at the present moment.

INDEPENDENT AND ORIGINAL THINKING

Thinkers are very few in this world. Most of us do not know what right thinking is. Thinking is shallow in the vast majority of persons. Deep thinking needs intense Sadhana (practice). It takes innumerable births for the proper evolution of the mind. Then only it can think deeply and properly. A man who speaks the truth and has moral purity has always powerful thoughts. One who has controlled anger by long practice has tremendous thought power. If a Yogin whose thought is very powerful speaks one word, it will produce tremendous impression on the minds of others.

Independent and original thinking is resorted to by the Vedantins. Vedantic Sadhana (Manana, reflection) demands a sharp intellect. Hard thinking, persistent thinking, clear thinking, thinking to the roots of all problems, to the very fundamentals of the situations, to the very presuppositions of all thoughts and being is the very essence of Vedantic Sadhana. You will have to abandon an old idea, however strong and ingrained it may be, when you get a new, elevating idea in its stead. If you have no courage to face the results of your thinking, to swallow the conclusions of your thinking, whatever they may mean to you personally, you should never take the trouble to philosophise. Take up to devotion.

APPLIED THINKING AND SUSTAINED THINKING

Applied thinking applies the mind to the object and sustained thinking keeps it continually engaged; rapture brings about the expanding and bliss of the developing mind whose motives for non-distraction have been accomplished by those two kinds of thinking. Meditation can arise when applied and sustained thinking, rapture, bliss and collectedness of mind arise.

Thought is a great force. It has got tremendous power. It becomes a matter of great moment to know how to use this power in the highest possible way and to the greatest possible effect. This can best be done by the practice of meditation.

CHAPTER 19

THOUGHT-CULTURE

If a pebble in our boot torments us we expel it. We take off the boot and shake it out. Once the matter is fairly understood, it is just as easy to expel an intruding and obnoxious thought from the mind. About this there ought to be no doubt, no two opinions. The thing is obvious, clear and unmistakable. It should be as easy to expel an obnoxious thought from your mind as it is to take a stone out of your shoe; and till a man can do that, it is just nonsense to talk about his ascendency and conquest over nature. He is a mere slave and prey to the bat-winged phantoms that flit through the corridor of his brain. Pitiable, indeed, is the lot of these creatures!

BENEFITS OF THOUGHT-CONTROL

Thoughts lead to action. Thoughts are the sources of all actions. Thought is the real Karma. Thinking is the real action. If you can root out all evil thoughts in the beginning, you will not do any evil action. If you can nip them in the bud, you will be free from the miseries and tribulations of this world. Watch your thoughts with vigilance and introspection.

Thought is the real action. Activities of the mind are the real Karmas. Once the Vikshepa of the mind vanishes, you will get good Nishtha (meditation). The mind will be very, very calm. Get rid of the impurities of the mind. Have mastery over the mind. Then all the miseries of the Samsara with births and deaths will come to an end. If you free yourself from the clutches of the mind, Moksha (liberation) will come by itself. There is no doubt about this.

A wise man watches his thoughts and eradicates all evil thoughts as they arise from the surface of the mind. So he is happy. He has always pure thoughts. By meditation on God, pure thoughts emanate from the mind, because God is purity (Nitya Suddha).

If you have control over your thoughts, you can turn out immense work with intense concentration. Mental torments of all sorts, cares, worries and anxieties will disappear. The peace that you will enjoy cannot be adequately described.

Those who have even a little control over their thoughts and speech will have a calm, serene, beautiful, charming face, sweet voice and brilliant, lustrous white eyes. Just as sweet perfume continuously emanates from an incense stick, so also divine perfume and divine effulgence (magnetic, Brahmic aura) radiate from a Yogin who has controlled his thoughts and who is constantly dwelling on Brahman or the infinite. The effulgence and perfume of his face is Brahma-Varchas. When you hold in your hand a bouquet made of jasmine, rose and Champaka flowers, the sweet perfume pervades the whole hall and tickles all alike. Even so, the perfume of fame and reputation (Yasas and Kirti) of a Yogin who has controlled his thoughts spreads far and wide. He becomes a cosmic force.

Radium is a rare commodity. There are only 16 grains in the world. Yogins who have controlled their thoughts are also very rare in the world, like radium.

CONSERVATION AND PROPER UTILISATION OF THOUGHT-ENERGY

Just as energy is wasted in idle talk and gossiping, so also energy is wasted in entertaining useless thought. Therefore, you should not waste even a single thought. Do not waste even an iota of energy in useless thinking. Conserve all mental energy. Utilise it for higher spiritual purposes in divine contemplation, Brahma-Chintana and Brahma-Vichara. Conserve all thought-energy and utilise it for meditation and helpful service to humanity.

Do not store in your brain useless information. Learn to unmind the mind. Unlearn whatever you have learnt. They are now useless for you. Then only you can fill your mind with divine thoughts. You will gain new mental strength as all the dissipated mental rays are collected now.

In physics you have the term 'power of orientation'. Though the mass of energy is there, the current will not flow. It must be connected to the magnet and then the electric current will flow through the power of orientation. Even so, the mental energy which is dissipated and misdirected in various worthless worldly concerns should be well-directed in proper spiritual channels.

NEGATIVE THOUGHTS

Drive away from your mind all unnecessary, useless and obnoxious thoughts. Useless thoughts impede your spiritual growth; obnoxious thoughts are stumbling blocks to spiritual advancement. You are away from God when you entertain useless thoughts. Substitute thoughts of God. Entertain only thoughts that are helpful and useful. Useful thoughts are the stepping-stones to spiritual growth and progress. Do not allow the mind to run into the old grooves and to have its own ways and habits. Be on the careful watch.

You must eradicate through introspection all sorts of mean thoughts, useless thoughts, unworthy thoughts, impure thoughts, all sexual thoughts, thoughts of jealousy, hatred and selfishness. You must annihilate all destructive thoughts of disharmony and discord. You must develop thought-culture of good, loving, sublime thoughts, divine thoughts. Every thought must be of a constructive nature. It must be strong, positive and definite. The mental image must be of a clear-cut and well-defined nature. You must develop right thinking. Every thought must bring peace and solace to others. It should not bring even the least pain and unhappiness to anyone. Then you are a blessed soul on the earth. You are a mighty power on the earth. You can help many, heal thousands, spiritualise and elevate a large number of persons as did Jesus and Buddha.

Just as you grow jasmine, rose, lily, honolulu flowers in a garden, so also you should cultivate the flowers of peaceful thoughts of love, mercy, kindness, purity in the vast garden of Antahkarana. Through introspection, you have to water this garden of mind with meditation and sublime thinking and remove the weeds of vain, useless discordant thoughts.

INCONSISTENT THOUGHTS

Generally, in untrained persons, four or five kinds of thoughts occupy the mind at a time. Household thoughts, business thoughts, thoughts of office, thoughts of body, thoughts of food and drink, hope and anticipation, some kind of planning to get money, some kinds of thoughts of revenge, some habitual thoughts of answering calls of nature, bathing, etc., occupy the mind at a time. When you are studying a book with interest at 3.30 p.m., the idea of pleasure of witnessing a cricket match at

4 p.m. disturbs your study every now and then. It is only a Yogin with Ekagra mind, who can have only one thought at a time and can keep it as long as he likes.

If you watch the mind carefully, you will find that many thoughts are inconsistent. The mind wanders at random aimlessly. There will be some thoughts of the body and its wants, some thoughts of friends, some thoughts of acquiring money, some thoughts of eating and drinking, some thoughts of your boyhood, etc. If you can study the mind and if you have consistent thoughts of one subject or one kind only to the exclusion of all other thoughts, this itself is a very great achievement, is a great step in advancement in thought-control. Do not be discouraged.

HAUNTING THOUGHTS OF SIN

Thoughts of sin haunt the minds of some persons. One man always thinks, "I have committed a very heinous sin. I do not know what to do." Again and again, this one idea haunts his mind. This is a bad habit. These people do not know how to divert their minds. They become prey to these 'haunting thoughts'. Virtue and sin are relative terms. They are creations of the mind. Sin is nothing but a mistake. Japa of God's Name, charity and fasting will destroy at once any amount of sin. Why are you afraid? Even the worst sinner can attain salvation, can become holy of holies. What was the state of Valmiki, Jagai and Madhai and Ajamila in the beginning? Were they not rogues of the first water? Repeat OM, Rama and assert boldly, 'I am pure now' 'I am holy now'. Where is the room for despair? *Nil desperandum*. Do virtuous actions. Remember Him always. Be true to the Antaryamin (Indweller of your heart).

TECHNIQUES OF THOUGHT-CONTROL

The following are some of the auto-suggestions for controlling your thoughts: (1) I shall not think of anything. (2) I shall get peace, if I do not think of anything. (3) My will is growing strong. I can control my thoughts. (4) I will get perfect peace when I am thoughtless. I eagerly long for that thoughtless state.

Each thought, by itself, is extremely weak, because the mind is distracted into countless and ever-varying thoughts. The more the thoughts are restrained, the more is the mind concentrated and, consequently, the more does it gain in strength and power. Destroy the evil thoughts one by one. It doubtless needs patient work.

As soon as you slowly wake up in the morning, the first thought that comes is 'I'. Then comes the memory of the events of the previous evening. The strong thoughts that float in the mind this evening slowly emerge out the moment you rise from your bed in the following morning and materialise. Then come the thoughts that are to fructify in the course of the day. Watch this carefully.

When a thought hovers in the mind, fulfil it. Do not allow it to linger on for a long time. It will frequently recur again and again. It will be a source of great trouble. Whenever a thought flashes out to write a letter to your friend, then and there finish that piece of work. Do not procrastinate it.

There are four ways of destroying evil thoughts. A Jnana Yogin (student of the path of Knowledge) does it by living in OM or Truth. He destroys the evil thoughts by Vichara and attitude of indifference. He says, "This has nothing to do with me. I am Satchidananda-Svarupa, Sivoham, Sivoham. These impulses belong to the mind. I am distinct from the mind." A Bhakta destroys the same by prayer and self-surrender. He says, "O God! I have surrendered myself, the fruits of all actions and the actions themselves to Thee. Give me strength to drive away and destroy these evil thoughts." He gets help from God through self-surrender. God sublimates the sex-impulse into Sattva or Ojas (spiritual energy). The Raja Yogin destroys evil thoughts either by destroying the Vrittis as they arise or by substituting opposite, positive thoughts of Sattvic nature, by supplanting sublime thoughts in their stead (Pratipaksha-Bhavana).

Brahma Vichara

The first and foremost of all thoughts—the primeval thought—is 'I'. It is only after the birth of this thought that any other thought can rise at all. It is only after the first personal pronoun 'I' has arisen in the mind that the second personal pronoun 'You' and the third personal pronoun 'He', etc., can make their appearance. If 'I' vanishes, 'You' and 'He' will disappear by themselves. Eradicate this false little 'I' of an illusory nature through proper Brahma Vichara. There is no other way.

Thinker is different from thought. Remember this. This gives the clue to the fact that you are the silent witness of the modifications that arise in the mind. You are Kutastha Brahman. You are Pratyagatman.

Destruction of Sankalpas

Raja Yoga teaches *Yogas-chittavrittinirodhah*:—"Yoga is the restraint of the mental modifications." It gives you the power of expelling the thoughts or, if need be, of killing them dead on the spot. Naturally, the art requires practice, but like other arts, when once acquired, there is no mystery or difficulty about it. It is worth practising.

Mark how one Sankalpa expands into many Sankalpas (imaginations) in a short time. Suppose you get a Sankalpa to have a tea-party for your friends. One thought of tea invites instantaneously the thoughts of sugar, milk, tea-cups, tables, chairs, table-cloth, napkins, spoons, sweetmeats, salted things, etc. So this world is nothing but the expansion of Sankalpas. There is no such thing as the world, independent of and apart from, thoughts. The expansion of thoughts of the mind towards objects is bondage (Bandha). Renunciation of Sankalpas is liberation (Moksha). In the string of Sankalpa, countless thoughts are strung like so many beads. If the string be cut into pieces, then you may infer what will become of the illusory thoughts which are strung on it. You must be very watchful and nip the Sankalpas in the bud. Then only will you be really happy. Mind plays tricks. You must understand its nature, ways and habits. Then only you can control it very easily.

Pranayama

Prana (energy) is the outer overcoat for the mind. The vibration of the subtle, psychic Prana gives rise to the formation of thought. By Pranayama (control of Prana or restraint of breath), you can also increase the mental energy and develop thought-control and thought-culture. This will help concentration and meditation. This will make the mind steady. This will remove Rajas and Tamas (passion and inertia). This will burn the dross in the mind.

Pratipaksha Bhavana

If you think again and again of impure things, an evil thought gains new strength by repetition. It gets the force of momentum. You must drive them immediately. If you find it difficult to do so, entertain counter-thoughts of God. Cultivate sublime and elevating thoughts. Evil thoughts will die by themselves. A noble thought is a potent antidote to counteract an evil thought. This is easier than the former method. By repetition of God's Name thousands of times daily, good thoughts gain new strength by each repetition. By repeating 'Aham Brahma Asmi' thousand times daily, the idea that you are the spirit (Atman) becomes stronger. The idea that you are the body becomes weaker and weaker.

Control of Body and Speech

If you are not able to control any evil thought, control the body and speech first. Slowly you will gain mental strength and will-force and will be able to control the thoughts gradually. If, for a moment you think you will not succeed in vanquishing an evil thought, at once get up and set about some work involving physical labour. One effort after another will make gradually the task easy and, in a few weeks, you will obtain a complete control over your thoughts.

Control the physical body and the speech first. Then slowly proceed to control thoughts. Do not speak ill of others. Control the Indriya of speech first. Gradually the mind will not think ill of others. The mind will say unto itself: "Why should I think ill of others when the organ of speech is not prepared to express what I think?" You can control your actions only when you have become moral. When you speak ill of a man, you poison the mind of several people. It is extremely ignoble to speak ill of others. But just comment without hatred or malice is permissible occasionally.

Do not allow useless or evil thoughts to develop themselves into words. Curb the speech. Divert the mind at once to some good thoughts. Try to remember some Slokas from the Gita or repeat some prayers. Keep some 'word-image' as "Om Hari," "Om Siva," "Om Narayana." Observance of Mouna (vow of silence) for a couple of hours daily will check the impulses of speech and thinking, will conserve energy and help meditation and thought-control and thought-culture.

Vigilance

Fully realise for yourself the grave and ruinous consequences of evil thoughts. This will set you on your guard when the evil thoughts would come. The moment they come, exert yourself or divert the mind to some other object of divine thoughts, prayer or Japa. A real earnestness to drive away the evil thoughts will keep you on the alert so much so that even if they appear in dream, you will at once wake up. Should the enemy appear when you are awake, it will not be very difficult for you to cope with him, if only you are sufficiently watchful.

Keep the Mind Fully Occupied

When the mind is vacant, evil thoughts try to enter. Evil thinking is the beginning or starting point of adultery. Through a lustful look only, you have already committed adultery in the heart. Mental actions are the real actions. Remember this. God judges a man by his motives; worldly people judge a man by his external physical actions. You will have to look to the motive of the man. Then you will not be mistaken. Keep the mind fully occupied. Then evil thoughts will not enter. An idle brain is the devil's workshop. Watch the mind every minute. Always engage yourself in some work—stitching, cleaning vessels, sweeping, drawing water, reading, meditating, counting the beads, singing divine songs, praying, serving the elders or nursing the sick. Avoid loose talk and gossip. Fill the mind with sublime thoughts, such as those contained in the Gita, the Upanishads, the Yogavasishtha, etc.

Sattvic Background of Thought

The vast majority of people will always want something concrete to hold on to, something around which, as it were, to place their ideas, something which will be the centre of all thought-forms in their minds. That is mind's very nature. A background of thought is needed for fixing the mind.

Have a Sattvic background of thought or mental image. The mind assumes the shape of any object it intently thinks upon. If it thinks of an orange, it assumes the shape of an orange. If it thinks of Lord Krishna with flute in hand, it assumes the shape of Lord Krishna. You must train the mind properly and give it proper, Sattvic food for assimilation.

You must have Sattvic background of thought to take you to the goal (salvation). If you are a devotee of Lord Krishna, have a background of thought of His picture and the repetition of His famous Mantra "Om Namo Bhagavate Vaasudevaya" and His qualities (Form-formula-qualities). A Nirguna Upasaka (Vedantin) should have a background of thought of 'OM' and its meaning (Infinite Ocean of Light, Satchidananda, Vyapaka, Paripurna Atman). Work in the world, and the moment the mind is free, begin to think of the background of thought—either Saguna or Nirguna background according to taste, temperament and capacity for Sadhana. By constant thinking, a habit in the mind will be formed and, without effort, the mind will run towards the background of thought.

It is a pity that the vast majority of persons have no ideal, no programme of life at all and no Sattvic background of thought. They are doomed to destruction. The background of thought of a young married lady is usually lustful. The background of thought of an old mother is the affection towards her sons and grandsons. The background of thought of the vast majority of persons is hatred and jealousy. Even the so-called educated persons with many university qualifications, which is only husk when compared with spiritual knowledge, have no ideal, no programme of life and no background of thought. A deputy collector, after getting pension, marries a third wife and goes on as a minister of a State.

A worldly-minded person is a prey to sexual thoughts and thoughts of hatred, anger and revenge. These two types of thoughts actually take possession of his mind. He is a slave to these two sets of thoughts. He does not know how to divert his mind and fix it on some other good, noble thought. He does not know the laws of thought. He is quite unaware of the nature and subtle workings of the mind. His position is extremely deplorable despite his earthly possessions and bookish knowledge obtained in universities. Viveka has not awakened in him. He has no Sraddha in saints, Sastras and God. He is unable to resist an evil desire, craving or temptation on account of his weak will. The only potent remedy to remove his world-intoxication, world-charm, world-delusion is constant Satsanga or association with Sadhus, Sannyasins and Mahatmas.

After retirement, everybody should have a background of thought and should spend his time in philosophical studies and divine contemplation. Old habits of loose thinking must be replaced by cultivating fresh habits of good thoughts. At first, a tendency to think of good thoughts will be formed. By continued practice, a positive definite habit of thinking of virtuous, helping thoughts will be developed. You will have to struggle very hard. The old habits will try to recur again and again. Till you are firmly established in the habit of thinking of good thoughts only, you will have to fill the mind again and again with Sattvic thoughts, divine thoughts, thoughts of the Gita, Lord Krishna, Lord Rama, the Upanishads, etc. New grooves and avenues will be formed now. Just as a gramophone-needle cuts a small groove in the plate, Sattvic thinking will cut new, healthy grooves in the mind and brain. New Samskaras will be formed.

GLORY OF THE WAVELESS JNANIN

Through constant and intense practice, you can become waveless (thought-free). The waveless Yogin helps the world more than the man on the platform. Ordinary people can hardly grasp this point. When you are waveless, you actually permeate and pervade every atom of the universe, purify and elevate the whole world. The names of waveless Jnanins such as Jada Bharata and Vamadeva are even now remembered. They never built Ashrams. They never lectured. They never published books. They never made disciples. Yet, what a tremendous influence these waveless Jnanins had produced on the minds of the people. Glory to such waveless Jnanins!

CHAPTER 20

VASANAS

VASANAS—HOW THEY MANIFEST

Vasana (desire in subtle form) is a wave in the mind-lake. Its seat is the Karana Sarira. It exists there in the form of a seed and manifests in the mind-lake. Just as flowers are latent in seeds, Vasanas are latent in the Antahkarana and the Karana Sarira (seed-body). Daily new flowers blossom out. They fade out in a day or two. Similarly, Vasanas blossom out like flowers one by one, come out to the surface of the mind, generate Sankalpas in the mind of Jivas and goad them to strive to possess and enjoy the particular objects of enjoyment. Vasanas cause actions, and actions strengthen the Vasanas. This is a Chakra, vicious circle. On the advent of knowledge of Brahman, all Vasanas are fried out. The real enemies are the Vasanas within. Annihilate them. Eradicate them. They are inveterate.

The whole mango tree with branches, leaves and fruits is contained in a subtle form in the seed. It takes time for manifestation. Even so, the Vasana of lust lurks in the mind when you are a boy, manifests at 18, fills the whole body at 25, works havoc from 25 to 45 and then it gradually declines. Various forms of wrong-doing and mischief are done by human beings between 25 and 45. This is the most critical period of life. There is no particular difference between a boy and a girl in their characteristics when they are young. After attaining puberty they exhibit their characteristic qualities.

CHAPALATA

Chapalata is Vasana of a mild type. It lasts for a short time only. There are two kinds of important Chapalatas. There is the Jihva-Chapalata of the tongue where the tongue wants to eat the various things every now and then. It is a form of morbid appetite. Rich people who lead a luxurious life have this form of Chapalata. The other variety is the Upastha-Chapalata wherein the sex Indriyas wants to taste again and again the sexual enjoyment (Sparsa).

VASANA CAUSES RESTLESSNESS AND BONDAGE

Vasana is the cause of restlessness of mind. As soon as a Vasana manifests, there is an intimate connection between the mind and the object through overflowing Vishaya-Vritti-Pravaha. The mind will not retrace its steps till it gets the object and enjoys it. The restlessness will continue till the object is enjoyed. The Vritti will flow towards the object till it is obtained and enjoyed. The common run of men cannot resist or suppress any Vasana owing to weak will.

It is the Vasana in the mind that causes attraction towards objects and brings about bondage; with the disappearance of Vasanas, bondage naturally vanishes. There will not be any attraction, admiration or excitement for any object outside, if there is no Vasana inside your mind. It is the Vasana that is at the bottom of all your miseries and troubles. There is no pain from Isvara-Srishti (objects created by the Lord). Water quenches your thirst. Breeze gives you comfort. Sunshine enlivens you. Fire gives warmth. It is Jiva-Srishti that brings about bondage. Ahankara, anger, Abhimana, attachment are all Jiva-Srishtis. Have Suddha Sankalpa, but no Vasanas.

By mere ethical training, jealousy, Raga, Dvesha, Krodha, Kama, etc., can be suppressed though not eradicated completely. These impure, Asubha Vasanas can be considerably attenuated (Tanu-Avastha) by moral culture. They attain a subtle condition. They cannot harm the individual. They remain under perfect control.

ERADICATION, NOT SUPPRESSION, THE PROPER REMEDY

A Vasana may be suppressed for the time being by an aspirant. But it again manifests with redoubled force when a suitable opportunity arises. Like a minister obeying the king, the five organs of the body act in accordance with the dictates of the mind. Therefore, you should through your own pure mind and proper efforts eradicate the Vasanas for objects. You should rend asunder, the long rope of Vasanas tied to the vessels of man, whirled on the ocean of Samsara, through enormous efforts on your part. Vasanas should be thoroughly eradicated. If these Vasanas are destroyed by Vichara (enquiry of Atman) and discrimination, the mind which is ever restless will get quiescence like a gheeless lamp.

HOW TO DESTROY VASANAS

Sama

Vijnanamaya Kosa serves as a great fortress for the aspirant. From there he can attack the Vasanas when they try to emerge from the seed-body (Karana Sarira) into the mind. Through the practice of Sama, the aspirant should destroy the Vasanas one by one with the help of Vijnanamaya Kosa (Buddhi). He should crush them as soon as they try to raise their heads on the surface of the mind-lake. He must not allow them to sprout forth. This is Vasana-Tyaga. This attack or fight is from inside.

When a Vasana or Sankalpa arises in the mind, the mind gives a push to the Antar-Indriya. From the Antar-Indriyas, this push is communicated to the Bahyakaranas (external instruments) such as hands, legs, eyes, ears, etc. The practice of Sama stops this very push which is the root cause of motion of all the Indriyas and Karanas.

Sama is peace of mind produced by the eradication of the Vasanas (Vasana-Tyaga). The Antahkarana of a man who possesses this virtue is cooler than ice. Even the coolness of the moon cannot compete with coolness of the Antahkarana of a man of Sama. Generally, the Antahkarana of a worldling is a blazing furnace. A man of Sama is neither exalted when he gets a desired object (Ishta) nor depressed when he gets an undesired thing (Anishta). He keeps a balanced mind always. He has no enemies. The happiness of an emperor is nothing, nothing when compared with the supreme spiritual bliss of a man of Sama. Sama is one of the four sentinels of Moksha. If you have Sama, you will get the company of the other three friends, viz., Santosha (contentment), Vichara (enquiry into Atman) and Satsanga (association with the wise and saintly).

Dama

The attack should commence from outside also. Bahyavritti-Nigraha should be done through Dama (restraint of the Indriyas). You must not allow sense-vibrations to enter from outside into the mind through the avenues of Indriyas. This is also necessary. Sama alone is not sufficient. The senses must be rendered blunt by Dama. The Vasana for sweets, for instance, should be destroyed by Sama through Vasana-Tyaga, by crushing the Vasanas within as soon as a desire arises; and the Bahyavritti, which arises by the sight of sweetmeat should be destroyed by withdrawing the eyes from the same when you move about the bazaar and by giving up taking sugar. Dama supplements Sama in the control of mind. Dama is an auxiliary for the complete eradication of Vasanas.

If you give up an old habit of taking tea, you have controlled to a certain extent the sense of taste. You have destroyed one Vasana. This will give you some peace, because the craving for tea has gone and you are freed from your efforts and thinking in getting tea, sugar, milk, etc. Thinking is pain, seeing is pain, hearing is pain for a philosopher and a Sadhaka. It is all pleasure for a worldling. The energy that was agitating you to run after tea is now transmuted into will. You gain peace and will-power by giving up one thing. If you give up fifteen things, your peace of mind will be still greater and the will still more powerful. This is the fruit of Tyaga. So, you are not a loser in Tyaga. You gain more knowledge, more bliss and more power. You give up something in favour of something higher. Is there anyone who will not give up black sugar in favour of white sugar? If you once control one Vasana, it will be easy for you to control other Vasanas too, because you gain strength and power.

Svadhyaya and Meditation

Increase your Sastra-Vasana in the beginning. Occupy your mind with the study of standard philosophical books. Thereby you can decrease your Deha-Vasana (thought of the body) and Loka-Vasana (desire for name and fame, Kirti, Pratishtha, etc). Later on, you will have to give up Sastra-Vasana also. You must entirely devote all your time and energy in meditation and meditation alone. Vasana-Kshaya (destruction of Vasanas) is caused through well-conducted deliberation (Vichara), Brahma-Dhyana, Vairagya and Tyaga.

Vichara and Brahma-Bhavana

The wise know that the mind associated with Vasana tends to bondage while the mind absolutely free from Vasana is said to be an emancipated one. Just as a lion that is shut up in a cage emerges out by breaking the bars of the cage, so also a Jnani comes out of this cage of physical body victoriously by breaking or by destroying the Vasanas of the mind through constant Vichara (Atmic enquiry), constant Nididhyasana (profound and constant meditation on 'OM' and its meaning) and Brahma-Bhavana. The more you attenuate your Vasanas by Svarupa-Bhavana or the Brahma-Bhavana, the happier you will become. In proportion to the thinning of the Vasanas, the mind also is proportionately thinned out. Mind is nothing but a bundle of Vasanas. Mind is no other than the Vasanas which generate an endless series of rebirths. The true nature of the mind is the Vasanas. The two are synonymous.

Conquest of Ahankara

If you destroy egoism (Ahankara, this false little 'I') and control the Indriyas (the senses), the Vasanas will die by themselves. The root cause for all troubles is Ahankara. Just as the dependants of a family hang upon the chief of the house—the father—similarly, all Vasanas, Trishnas, Kamanas, etc., hang upon Ahankara, the chief of this house-body.

Constantly generate from the Sattvic mind-battery the Akhanda electric current 'Aham Brahmasmi'-Vritti (Brahmakara Vritti). That is the potent antidote. Keep it safe in the pocket; smell it when an apoplectic attack of the Ahankaric false 'I' idea overcomes you. It is only when you eradicate the painful Ahankara of the mind and conquer the foes of organs (Indriyas) that the ever-waking Vasanas will subside.

THE MEANING OF MOKSHA

The illusory Samsaric Vasanas that have arisen through the practice of many hundreds of lives never perish except through the practice of Yoga for a long time. Therefore, O Aspirants! After having put away at a distance the desire of enjoyment by discriminative efforts, practise the state of mind absolutely devoid of Vasana.

Moksha does not mean physical separation from all worldly affairs, but only a state of mind bereft of all impure Vasanas or clinging to worldly things, but yet working as usual amidst them. You must realise God in and through the world. This is the central teaching of the Gita. "But the disciplined (lower) self, moving among sense-objects with senses free from attraction and repulsion and mastered by the higher Self, goeth to Peace" (Gita. II-64). This is the central teaching of Yoga Vasishtha also.

There is no Vasana in Brahman. Complete annihilation of the Vasanas takes place only in Nirvikalpa Samadhi. Only Nirvikalpa Samadhi can completely fry up the seeds of impure Vasanas. Through the knowledge of Brahman, there will be an extinction of all Vasanas, which form the medium of enjoyments. With the extinction of all Vasanas, the undaunted mind will get quiescence like a gheeless lamp.

CHAPTER 21

DESIRES

"Sweep out the sphere of your mind:
Make a place for Loved One to sit.
Dust out all thoughts of this world
So that His throne may be fit.
A million desires engulf you,
A million ambitions and aims:
How can you make room for His Presence
Unless they vacate His domain?"

WHAT IS DESIRE?

Desire is a mode of the emotive mind. It has got a power of externalising the mind. Desire is the fuel; thought is the fire. The thought-fire is kept up by the desire-fuel. If you withdraw the supply of fuel, the fire will be withdrawn into its womb. If you stop thinking by cutting off desires, the mind will be withdrawn into Brahman.

It is only when the mind, being divested of all its desires, is indifferent to pleasures and pains and is not attracted by any object that it will be rendered pure, free from the grip of the great delusion like a bird freed from its cage and roaming freely in the Akasa.

Desire, thought and Ahankara form one vicious circle. If you can destroy any one of them, the other two will die by themselves. These are the three pillars or corner-stones of the edifice of mind. They are the three links of the mind-chain. Destroy any one of the links; the whole chain will be broken.

WHY DO DESIRES ARISE?

Why do desires arise in the mind? On account of Ananda-Abhava (absence of Ananda or spiritual bliss). The cause for desire is the existence of objects outside. Curiosity becomes a desire in the mind. Interest and feeling precede a desire. Hope and expectation fatten the desire.

VIKSHEPA—THE VERY NATURE OF MIND

Just as heat is inseparable from fire, Vikshepa or the tossing of the mind is inseparable from the mind. It troubles the Sadhakas a lot. It destroys all of a sudden the determinations of strong-willed persons also. The mind ceases to exist if it is destitute of this oscillation. This fluctuating mind alone creates the universe. Even Mala (impurity) can be removed easily. It demands strenuous efforts for a protracted time on the part of the Sadhaka to remove this Vikshepa. The undaunted Uddalaka suffered a lot from this distracting Vikshepa when he tried to enter into Nirvikalpa state. Raja Bhartrihari underwent the same difficulty when he tried to overcome this troublesome fluctuating Sakti of the mind. Vikshepa is Maya. Vikshepa is impure Vasana (Asuddha Vasana). You will have to destroy this Vikshepasakti by constant Upasana or Yoga or ceaseless Atmic enquiry (Brahmavichara). Then, peace (Santi) will come by itself.

TYPES OF DESIRE

Desire in the mind is the real impurity. Sexual desire, vulgar attraction for the opposite sex, is the greatest impurity. This causes the real bondage. You can even give up wife, children and wealth. But, it is extremely difficult to give up ambition, name and fame. Ambition is a serious obstacle in the path of Yoga. This is the most powerful weapon of Maya with which she slaughters worldly-minded persons. Even if there is a tinge of desire for name and fame, Truth will not manifest. Truth will shine by Itself. It does not need any pompous advertisement. It is the very Self of all beings and objects.

ANIRBUDDHA OR SUBTLE, HIDDEN DESIRES

Even after you have renounced all the desires, there may remain in the mind some subtle, hidden desires (Sukshma, Anirbuddha) that cannot be comprehended. These are very dangerous ones. Therefore, you will have to be very, very careful. The lurking under-currents of desires will throw you down at any moment if you are not very vigilant and cautious, will destroy your Vairagya (dispassion) and will bring about your downfall eventually. I have witnessed many Yogabhrashtas who had fallen from Yoga owing to the overpowering influence of these subtle, hidden desires. So long as you have these subtle, hidden, Anirbuddha (unnoticeable) desires in your mind, you can never dream of entering into the Nirvikalpa state without any modification of the mind. You can never develop real Paravairagya (supreme non-attachment and dispassion) also.

CRAVING OR TRISHNA

You may become old, your hairs may turn grey, but your mind is ever young. The capacity may vanish, but the craving remains even when you have reached advanced senility. Cravings (Trishna) are the real seeds of birth. These craving-seeds give rise to Sankalpa and action. The wheel of Samsara is kept revolving by these cravings. Nip them in the bud. Then only will you be safe. You will get Moksha. Brahma-Bhavana, Brahma-Chintana, meditation on OM and devotion will root out these craving-seeds which are laid deep. You will have to dig them out properly in various corners and burn them beyond resurrection. Then only will your efforts bear the fruit of Nirvikalpa Samadhi.

"Love and kill," "Marry and observe Brahmacharya," "Enjoyment without desire," "Action without fruits" are paradoxical terms. A man with gross Vyavaharic Buddhi can hardly understand these terms. A subtle, pure intellect is needed. Suppose you were a terrible smoker for the last fifteen years. Then you gave up smoking for five years. The craving for smoking also died. Suppose one of your friends offers you a cigar in the sixth year. You have no craving for smoking now. If you take it now and enjoy it just to please your friend, it will be called a Suddha Bhoga only. You have enjoyed it without a craving or a desire. Isvara enjoys Suddha Bhoga.

SATISFACTION OF DESIRE YIELDS ILLUSORY HAPPINESS ONLY

Desire excites the mind and senses. When desire is gratified by enjoyment of the objects of desire, satisfaction (Tripti) comes in temporarily. Rapture is delight in the attainment of the desired object. Bliss is the enjoyment of the taste of what is attained. Where rapture is there is bliss; but where bliss is there is not, quite of necessity, rapture. Rapture is like a weary traveller who hears or sees water or a shady wood. Bliss is the enjoying of the water or entering the forest shade.

When there is desire, then alone is there pleasure. The cause for pleasure is desire. When there is no desire, there cannot be any pleasure. When there is no hunger, delicious

food can give you no pleasure. When there is no thirst, any refreshing beverage will have no effect. So, hunger is the best
sauce. The first cup of hot milk gives pleasure. The second cup
induces disgust. After the enjoyment is over, Tripti comes.
Hence, disgust arises when the second cup is taken. There is
no real pleasure in milk. The happiness is in Atman only. It is reflected in the object (milk) owing to ignorance, owing to Bhranti
(illusion). It is Bhranti-Sukha. If there were real happiness in
milk, it should induce pleasure always and in every person. It is
not the case.

A desire arises in the mind. There is a Vritti now. This Vritti
agitates your mind till you get satisfaction through enjoyment of
the desired object. There is Santi or peace or happiness after
the enjoyment is over. Another desire arises in the mind. Now,
in the interval between the gratification of one desire and the
manifestation of another, there is pure bliss, because there is
no mind then. It is at rest. You are in union with Brahman. That
state of pure bliss between two desires is Brahman. If you can
prolong that period of bliss through Sadhana by keeping up the
idea of Brahman and by not allowing another Vritti or desire to
crop up, you will be in Samadhi. The period between one Vritti
and another Vritti is the real Sandhi (juncture).

DESIRES ARE INSATIABLE

Mind plays havoc through desires. As soon as a desire arises,
you think you will get all happiness by its realisation. You exert
yourself to achieve the desired object. As soon as you get it, a
little satisfaction (false Tushti or gratification) is experienced for
a short time. Again, mind becomes restless. It wants new sensations. Disgust and dissatisfaction come in. Again, it wants
some new objects for its enjoyment. That is the reason why this
world is termed as mere Kalpana (imagination) by Vedantins.

Desires are innumerable, insatiable and unconquerable.
Enjoyment cannot bring in satisfaction. It is a mistake to think
so. Enjoyment fans the desire. It is like pouring ghee in fire. Enjoyment strengthens, increases and aggravates a desire. See
the case of Raja Yayati of yore. He borrowed the youthful state
from his son to have sexual enjoyment for thousands of years.
At last, he cries out in his old age with bitterness, "Alas! What a
fool I am! Still my sexual desires are waxing. There is no end of
desires. I have wasted my life. O God! Have mercy on me. Lift

me up from this mire of Samsara." This comes in Mahabharata. In the Gita, Chapter III-39, you will find *"Kamarupena Kaunteya Dushpurena-analena cha*—desire which is insatiable as a flame."

FREEDOM FROM DESIRES NECESSARY FOR JNANA

You can attain Jnana only if you are free from sensuous desires and immoral mental states. Aloofness of body from sensuous objects and aloofness of mind from immoral states of mind are needed for the attainment of Jnana. Then only will Divine Light descend. Just as a bungalow is cleaned of cobwebs and all kinds of dirts and the garden of all its weeds for the reception of the Viceroy, the mental palace should be cleansed of all vices, desires and immoral states for the reception of the Holy Brahman, the Viceroy of viceroys.

When a desire arises in the mind, a worldling welcomes it and tries to fulfil it; but, an aspirant renounces it immediately through Viveka. Wise people consider even a spark of desire as a very great evil. Therefore, they will not entertain any kind of desire. They will be ever delightful in Atman only.

HOW TO CONTROL DESIRES

In this ocean of Samsara, desires are the crocodiles. Kill them as soon as they arise on the surface of the mind. Do not yield to them. Do not become despondent under your trials. Make friendship with the pure, Sattvic mind and destroy the impure mind with the help of the pure mind. Make your mind rest in the blissful Atman. Desires should be crushed the very moment they arise in the mind, by discrimination and dauntless, indefatigable efforts.

Whenever a desire arises in the mind, consult always your Viveka (power of discrimination). Viveka will at once tell you that the desire is attended with pain, that it is only a vain temptation set up by the mind and that Vairagya and Tyaga alone can bring about satisfaction and peace of mind. It will advise you to renounce the desire immediately and take to the study of Upanishads, repetition of OM and to have Samadhi-Nishtha in a solitary place on the bank of the sacred Ganga. Think deeply again and again whether the new desire will give you more happiness or more spiritual gain. Viveka will guide you to take up the help of will and drive the desire immediately. Viveka and will are two potent weapons for an aspirant on the Jnana Yogic path to destroy evil Mara (temptation) and remove all major and minor impediments.

Never accept gifts from anybody, even from your closest friends. It will produce slavish mentality, weak will and attachment. Asking is begging. Recommending is begging. A beggar is absolutely unfit for freedom and spiritual pursuits.

Just as you starve a plant by depriving it of water, so you may starve out obnoxious desires by allowing the mind not to dwell upon such desires. You have no desire for a thing till you know what it is like. It is only after you have seen it or heard of it or touched it that you get a longing for it. Therefore, the best principle for a man is not to take, touch or see anything that is likely to taint the imagination. You will have to turn aside the attention resolutely and particularly the imagination from the subject. In course of time, all objectionable desires will die out.

It is desire in the mind that has created this body. The nature of the desire depends upon the quality of Samskaras. If these are good, virtuous Samskaras, good desires will crop up and, if they are bad, they will give rise to evil desires. Buddhi also is Karmanusarini (according to the nature of Karmas). It has to be specially trained by repeated efforts to think and act according to the holy injunctions of sacred scriptures. Desire becomes the thought and thought becomes the action. An evil desire sets up an evil thought which leads to evil action. Do always virtuous action—charity, Tapas, Japa, Dama, Dhyana and study of scriptures. Give up Nishiddha Karma (actions prohibited by Sastras). Have constant Satsanga. This is very important. It is the only means of changing the evil Samskaras of the mind.

The mind with half-developed Jnana feels severe pain when it relinquishes all desires. It demands aid, through prayer, from higher souls.

A counter-desire, a desire for God, one strong desire to attain Brahman will destroy all other worldly desires. Put down vicious desires through virtuous desires. Then give up virtuous desires through one strong desire—Mumukshutva (desire for liberation). Abandon this desire for God also in the long run. Give up Asubha Vasana through Subha Vasana. Give up Subha Vasana through Svarupa Vasana. Give up Svarupa Vasana by Nididhyasana. Desires will become extinct with the rise of discrimination. When desires cease, Jivahood becomes extinct.

Brahma-Chintana will destroy all desires. There are no desires in Brahman. Brahman is All-Purity. Repeat OM. Repeat the Mantra, "All purity I am." All the desires will vanish.

Kill the thoughts. Practise thoughtlessness. You can destroy desires. Mind associated with thoughts of gratifying the passionate desires, blindly goads a man to seek for sensual pleasures. Uncontrolled thoughts are the roots of all evils. Sublime thoughts will easily destroy lower, base thoughts. Do not entertain any base thought.

DESTRUCTION OF DESIRES LEADS TO ATMIC BLISS

Vasanasahita mind (mind associated with desires) is Bandha (bondage). Mind free from desires is Mukta (free). Desires are themselves pain. Non-desire is itself pure Atmic Bliss. Mere annihilation of Maya is Moksha. With the extinction of the base Sankalpas, there is also the extinction of Avidya. Should all longings for the visibles cease, then such an abnegation of mind is itself the destruction of Ajnana or the mind. Such a bliss is generated through one's efforts only. There is nothing like Purushartha (right exertion). Purushartha changed the destiny of Markandeya. He became a Chiranjivi.

Desire is the enemy of peace. You have become the beggar of beggars through desires. A desireless man is the richest man in the world. It is the mind that makes a man rich.

Free yourself from the firm grip of crocodiles of desires. Do not get disheartened under trials. Cheer yourself up. Stand up like a lion. Destroy the impure mind with the help of the pure mind. Make friendship with the Sattvic mind and rest yourself peacefully in Atman.

CHAPTER 22
RAGA-DVESHA

Raga-dvesha-viyuktaistu vishayanindriyais-charan
Atmavasyair-vidheyatma prasadam-adhigacchati

"But the disciplined (lower) Self, moving among sense-objects with senses free from attraction and repulsion and mastered by the Higher Self, goeth to Peace." (Gita, II-64)

RAGA-DVESHA, THE CAUSE OF BONDAGE

Raga (attraction), Dvesha (repulsion) and Tatastha Vritti (indifference) are the three important Vrittis of the mind. Raga and Dvesha (like and dislike or love and hatred or attraction and repulsion) are the two currents in the mind which bind a man to the Samsaric wheel of birth and death. Raga and Dvesha are the two Doshas or faults in the mind that have brought you to this world. The Svarupa of Bandha (bondage) is Raga and Dvesha. The Svarupa of Ajnana is Raga and Dvesha. All the emotions come under the category of Raga-Dvesha. These two currents are the Dharma (characteristics) of the mind and not of the spirit. Pleasure and pain, Harsha and Soka, exhilaration and depression are due to Raga-Dvesha. If Raga and Dvesha vanish from the mind, Harsha-Soka also will disappear.

SELFISH LOVE AND DIVINE LOVE

When two forces of equal quality or power meet, a third force is formed. When two people of equal force and quality are attracted towards each other, a third force is formed between them. That is termed love. This is the scientific way of explaining what love is. Attraction is Akarshana-Sakti. Repulsion is Vikarshana-Sakti. When I see myself in another man, when I see him as my own self, I begin to love him as my own self. When I find something in you that I myself possess, I am naturally drawn towards you and begin to love you. This is Vedantic way of explaining love. Love is pouring forth one's affection (Prema) on another. Love is God. Love is of two kinds, viz., selfish or physical love and real Love or divine Love which is unselfish and lasting. The first kind is love with attachment. The second one is love without attachment. He who is a real aspirant of Vedantic path, who feels his own self everywhere and a real Bhakta who sees Narayana everywhere in everything can really love' others. When an inferior person hangs on another person for his happiness or existence, physical attachment crops up. Attachment causes slave mentality and weak will. Attachment is death. Physical love is death. *"Asangasastrena dridhena chhitva*—Cut all sorts of attachment by the sword of non-attachment." (Gita, XV-3)

RAGA AS PAINFUL AS DVESHA

Raga (attraction) in the mind is as much dangerous as Dvesha (hatred or repulsion). Whenever there is Raga, there is Dvesha also. Not only the Dvesha-Vritti (the modification of dislike), but also the Vritti of Raga gives pain to man. If an object gives pleasure, you get Raga for the object. But when there is Viyoga (separation) from the object, as in the case of death of your dear wife or son, you get immense pain which is indescribable. Suppose you are in the habit of taking fruits after food. Fruits give you pleasure. You get Raga (liking) for fruits. But if you cannot get fruits in a place, you get pain.

Whenever there is pleasure and Raga, there exist side by side fear and anger. Anger is only a modification of desire. Fear and anger are two old associates of pleasure and Raga. Fear and anger are hidden in Raga. They constantly torment the mind.

Fear is hidden in Raga. When you have got Raga for body, fear of death comes in. When you have Raga for money, there is fear of losing money, as money is the means of getting objects of enjoyment. When you have Raga for a woman, you always take care in protecting her. Fear is a very old, intimate friend of Raga.

THE DIFFERENT STATES OF RAGA-DVESHA

Raga-Dvesha has four Avasthas, viz., Dagdha (burnt up), Tanu (attenuated or thinned out), Vicchinna (concealed) and Udara (fully expanded). The first two states pertain to a Yogin; the last two to worldlings. In a fully developed Yogin, the Vrittis of Raga-Dvesha are burnt up by Nirvikalpa Samadhi. They are Dagdha (like burnt-up seeds). In a Yogin who is practising, the impressions of Raga-Dvesha are tenuous. They are in a fine state. He has control over these two Vrittis. In those who are given to enjoyments (ordinary mortals), they are concealed and fully expanded. In the Vichhinna state, they are concealed. When the wife shows affection to her husband, when the Raga-Vritti is in operation, her anger and hatred remain concealed for the time being. The moment she gets displeased with him for some reason or other, the Dvesha-Vritti manifests itself. In the last (expanded) state, the Samskaras of Raga-Dvesha, having favourable surroundings, attain to great activity. A worldly-minded man is a mere slave of Raga-Dvesha currents. He is tossed about hither and thither by these two currents of attraction and repulsion.

In sleep, these two emotions exist in a man in a Bija state (seed form). They are not destroyed. As soon as the man gets up from sleep, they begin to operate again.

In children, these twin currents manifest for a short time and disappear soon. They fight in this second and join together with joy the very next second. They do not keep up any ill feelings in their minds. They do not brood also over the wrongs done by others. They do not exhibit any grudge. The wave comes and passes away. As the child grows, these currents assume a grave phase by constant repetition and become inveterate.

Dvaita slowly develops when the child reaches the second year. Place a baby within one year of age in any place. It will remain there like a block of stone. It will laugh and see alike all people without any Raga-Dvesha. Ask a child of two years of age to sit. It will stand. Ask the child to come near. It will recede back to a distance. Tell the child, "Do not go to the street"; it will immediately march to the street. It will do contrary actions, because Dvaita is developing now in the child.

THE CAUSES OF RAGA-DVESHA

Raga-Dvesha is due to the Anukula-Pratikula Jnana. You have Raga for things favourable (Anukula) and Dvesha for things unfavourable (Pratikula). When this Anukula-Pratikula Jnana which depends upon Bheda Jnana disappears, Raga-Dvesha will vanish.

Raga-Dvesha is also due to Abhimana-Ahankara. As soon as Abhimana manifests, there comes Raga-Dvesha.

When you conceive yourself as husband, there comes the attachment (Raga) for your wife. As soon as you conceive yourself to be a Brahmin, there comes the love of the Brahmins. Give up Abhimana, if you want to eradicate Raga-Dvesha. If this Abhimana, the result of Avidya (ignorance) vanishes, Raga-Dvesha will vanish.

Some minds hang on you through Raga, while some others hang on you through Dvesha. Ravana's mind was hanging on Sri Rama through hatred and fear. He was seeing Rama everywhere and in everything through constant, intense thinking of Rama. Similarly, Kamsa's mind was hanging on Sri Krishna. This is also a form of Bhakti (Vaira-Bhakti). Anyhow their minds were on God.

RAGA-DVESHA CONSTITUTES REAL KARMA

Raga-Dvesha in the mind is the real Karma. It is the original action. When the mind is set in motion or vibration through the currents of Raga-Dvesha, real Karmas begin. Real Karma originates from Sankalpas of the mind. It is the actions of the mind that are truly termed Karmas. External actions manifest later on. It is desire that sets the mind in motion. When there is a desire, Raga and Dvesha exist side by side in the mind. Desire is a motive force. Emotions and impulses co-exist with desire.

From Avidya emanates Aviveka (non-discrimination). From Aviveka originates Ahankara and Abhimana. From Abhimana emanates Raga-Dvesha. From Raga-Dvesha comes Karma. From Karma comes the body. From body comes misery. This is the chain of bondage with seven links. This is the chain of misery.

If you do not want misery, do not take up the body. If you do not want body, do not do Karma. If you do not want to do Karma, give up Raga-Dvesha. If you want to give up Raga-Dvesha, give up Abhimana. If you want to give up Abhimana, give up Aviveka. If you want to give up Aviveka, give up ignorance. O Rama! If you do not want ignorance, get Brahma-Jnana.

This Samsara or world process is kept up by the six-spoked wheel, viz., Raga, Dvesha, merit, demerit, pleasure and pain. If the root cause, the original Avidya, is destroyed by attainment of Brahma-Jnana, the whole chain of Abhimana, Raga, Dvesha, Karma, body, merit and demerit, pleasure and

pain will vanish. One link hangs upon another. All the links will
be broken totally on the advent of Jnana. Sruti says: *"Rite
Jnananna muktih*—Liberation comes from knowledge of Brahman."

ABSENCE OF RAGA-DVESHA MAKES FOR FREEDOM

That Yogin or Jnanin who has destroyed these two Vrittis of
Raga and Dvesha is the highest man in the three worlds. He is
the real King of kings, Emperor of emperors. The chief Linga or
distinguishing mark of a Jivanmukta or a liberated soul is freedom from Raga-Dvesha. Even if a Jnanin or Yogin sometimes
exhibits traces of anger, it is Abhasamatra (mere appearance).
Just as the impression made in water with a stick passes away
soon, as also the anger will disappear in the twinkling of an eye,
even though it manifests in a Jnanin. This can hardly be understood by worldly people.

He who has no Raga but possesses Titiksha (power of endurance) can do anything. He can move about wherever he
likes. He is as free as the atmospheric air. His happiness, freedom and peace are unbounded. Their extent can hardly be
imagined. The freedom and joy of such Sannyasins cannot be
imagined by the poor, petty-minded worldlings. It is Raga and
luxury that have enfeebled the householders.

DESTRUCTION OF RAGA-DVESHA CONSTITUTES
THE ESSENCE OF SPIRITUAL SADHANA

I shall tell you the gist or essence of spiritual Sadhana. Destroy
the true modifications of the mind, Raga-Dvesha, by Vichara
and Brahma-Chintana (right thinking and meditation). Go beyond the Dvandvas (pairs of opposites). You will get eternal, infinite bliss and peace. You will shine in Brahmic glory. You will
become Brahman. YOU ARE BRAHMAN.

Just as heat in fire can be removed by Mantra and
Oushadha (recitation of God's Name and medicine), so also
the Raga-Dvesha currents, the characteristics of the mind, can
be removed by Yogic Kriya (practices of Yoga). These can be
completely fried up by Nirvikalpa Samadhi or Asamprajnata
Samadhi.

Amongst the several Vrittis in the mind, Raga-Dvesha and
Moha are very deep-rooted. They demand strenuous and per-

sistent efforts for their eradication. In your mental lives, you can either keep hold of the rudder and so determine exactly what course you take, what points you touch or you can fail to do this and, failing, you drift and are blown hither and thither by every passing breeze, by every emotion, by petty Raga-Dvesha currents.

CHAPTER 23

PLEASURE AND PAIN

PLEASURE AND PAIN PERTAIN TO MIND

Pleasure and pain are the effects of virtue and vice. They are two kinds of emotions that pertain to the mind alone. It is the mind alone which brings pleasures and pains on itself and enjoys them through its excessive inclination towards objects. Mind contracts during pain and expands during pleasure.

Ahankara creates the body. Prana does all sorts of Cheshtas (efforts). Mind experiences pleasure and pain. If you perform actions through a stainless mind (with Akartri Bhava and Nishkama Bhava), your body will not share their fruits.

There are only facts, vibrations or phenomena outside. Prakriti is blind. Prakriti is quite indifferent. There is neither pleasure nor pain in objects. It is all mental creation, mental perception, mental jugglery. It is only the mental attitude or certain kind of mental behaviour towards objects that brings joy or grief, pleasure and pain. Maya has her powerful seat in the imagination of the mind.

All pains are not equally felt. There is no pain when you are asleep. It is only when the mind is connected with the body that pains arise. It is the identification with the mind and body, Abhimana owing to Avidya, that causes pain.

When the mind is intensely fond of anything, there will be no perception of pain even if destruction awaits the body. When the mind is completely drowned in any object, who else is there to observe and flee from the actions of the body?

When you put one drop of oil on the surface of water, it spreads throughout the surface of water and makes it oily. Even so, a little pain for a luxurious man spoils all his pleasures and makes all objects appear very painful. When you are in acute agony, a cup of coffee, milk or tea does not give you any pleasure. When you are in acute agony, the whole world which appeared to you to be full of bliss while in good health, appears quite dreary. The world loses all its charms while you are seriously ailing.

If the pessimist changes his mental attitude, the world will appear to him to be full of Ananda.

Mind always runs after pleasure, because it is born of Ananda Brahman. You love a mango, because it affords you pleasure. Of all things, you love your own self most. This love of the self gives the clue to the fact that Ananda or bliss must be the nature of the Self.

ATMAN HAS NO PLEASURE AND PAIN

Freedom from the body and mind is the real nature of the Self or Atman and, consequently, there being no possibility of virtue and vice, very much less is the chance for any effects of these on the Atman, hence, pleasure and pain do not touch Atman. Atman is Asanga, Anaasakta, Nirlipta (unattached). It is Sakshi of the two modifications, pleasure and pain that arise in the mind. Mind enjoys. Mind suffers. Atman is a silent witness. It has nothing to do with pleasure and pain.

SENSE-PLEASURE IS ONLY A MENTAL DECEPTION

Pleasure and pain, beauty and ugliness are all false imaginations of the mind. Mind is a false illusory product. Conceptions of the mind also must, therefore, be false. They are all Mrigatrishna (like a mirage in the desert). What is beautiful for you is ugly for another. Beauty and ugliness are relative terms. Beauty is only a mental concept. It is only a mental projection. it is only a civilised man that takes much of symmetry of form, good features, graceful gaits, elegance of manners, graceful form, etc. An African negro has no idea of all these things. Real beauty is in the Self only. Pleasure and beauty reside in the mind and not in the objects. Mango is not sweet; the idea of mango is sweet. It is all Vritti. It is all mental deception, mental conception, mental creation, mental Srishti. Destroy the Vritti; beauty vanishes. The husband stretches his own idea of beauty in his ugly wife and finds his wife very beautiful through passion. Shakespeare has rightly expressed this in his "Mid-summer Night's Dream": "Cupid is painted blind. It finds Helen's beauty in the brow of Egypt."

Pleasure arising from external objects is evanescent, transitory and fleeting. It is mere nerve-titillation and mental deception. Jiva joins with mind and Vritti and enjoys the Vishayas (sense-objects). The thing that gives you pleasure gives you pain also. *"Ye hi samsparsaja bhoga duhkhayonaya eva te*—The delights that are contact-born, are verily wombs of pain." The body is an abode of misery and disease. Wealth brings a lot of trouble in acquiring and keeping safe. Sorrow springs from every connection. Women are a perpetual source of vexation. Alas! People prefer this path of misery to that of spiritual enjoyment.

No true, lasting satisfaction comes from the enjoyment of worldly objects. Yet, people rush headlong towards objects even when they know that the objects are unreal and the world is full of miseries. That is Maya. When the mind rests on Atman, then only Nitya-Tripti (eternal satisfaction) will come; because, Atman is Paripurna (all-full), you get everything there. It is self-contained. All desires are gratified by realisation of Atman.

Some say that children are very happy. It is wrong. They only become exuberant. They get serious reaction also. They have no balanced mind. They weep for hours together for nothing at all. It is only a man of balanced mind that can really be happy.

PLEASURE ARISES FROM VRITTI-LAYA: NOT FROM SENSE-OBJECTS

Really, there is no pleasure in objects. Atman gives a push to the mind and sets it in motion. A Vritti or thought-wave arises in the mind on account of the force of a Vasana. The mind is agitated and runs towards the particular object. The agitation will not subside till the mind gets the desired object. It will constantly think of the object. It will scheme and plan various methods to achieve the desired object. It will be ever restless. It will be ever assuming the shape of the object. As soon as the object is obtained and enjoyed, the particular Vritti that was causing agitation in the mind gets dissolved. Vritti-Laya takes place. When Vritti-Laya takes place, you get peace and Ananda from the Svarupa or Atman within only and not from the object outside. Ignorant persons attribute their pleasures to external objects. That is a serious blunder, indeed.

There is no happiness at all in any of the objects of the world. It is sheer ignorance to think that we derive any pleasure from the sense-objects or from the mind. Whenever we feel our desires are satisfied, we observe that the mind moves towards the heart, towards Atman. In pleasure also, there is exercise of the mind. It expands. It turns inward and moves to its original home, the place of its origin, Atman and enjoys Atma-Sukha (Bliss of the Self).

REAL HAPPINESS LIES WITHIN

Why do you search, in vain, for your happiness, O worldly fools, outside, in objects, money, women, titles, honours, name and fame, which are false, worthless and like cow-dung? You cannot get your happiness there. You are entirely deluded. Search within the heart, subjectively in the Atman, the source and fountain of all happiness.

Real happiness is within you. It is in the Atman. It is subjective. It is in the Sattva Guna and beyond Sattva. It manifests when the mind is concentrated. When the Indriyas are withdrawn from the objects outside, when the mind is one-pointed (Ekagra), when there is Vasana-Kshaya (annihilation of the Vasanas) and Manonasa (annihilation of the mind), when you become desireless and thoughtless, Atmic bliss begins to dawn; spiritual Ananda begins to thrill.

ATTACHMENT AND PLEASURE

The mind is the cause of attachment to delusive objects. It is the mind which is the germ of all Karmas. It daily agitates this body of ours to work and secure for its enjoyment various pleasurable objects.

The mind always wants to be doing something and, when it attaches itself with the objects it cherishes, feels amused and happy. A play at cards has nothing in it; but, the attachment and attention produce pleasure.

There can be attraction without attachment. You can be attracted by a beautiful cabbage rose or a young lady. But it is not necessary that you must be attached either to the rose or to the lady. Attachment comes after possession and enjoyment.

Attachment, love and Ananda (bliss)—all go together. You are attached to your wife and children; you love them also, because they give you Ananda. As this world is illusory and as through Bhranti (illusion) pain appears as pleasure, you must cut asunder all worldly attachments ruthlessly and direct your love and attachment towards the Reality, Brahman, the Adhishthana (substratum or basis) that lies at the back of mind and all objects and is the Sakshi (witness) for all the activities that take place in Buddhi.

It is difficult to divert the mind which, from infancy, has fallen into the pernicious habit of seeking external pleasure and it shall evei persist in doing so, unless you give it something superior to be amused with, a greater form of pleasure to delight in.

KINDS AND DEGREES OF PLEASURES

Intellectual pleasure is far superior to sensual pleasure. Ananda from meditation is far superior to intellectual pleasure. Spiritual bliss or Atmic bliss from Self-realisation is infinite, immeasurable and unbounded. It is Anandaghana (solid mass of bliss).

THE GOLDEN MEAN

Keep the mind in a state of moderation or happy, golden mean. Never let it run to excesses. People die of shock from extreme depression as well as from extreme joy. Do not allow Uddharsha to crop up in the mind. It is excessive merriment. Mind always runs to extremes—either to extreme depression or extreme joy. Extremes meet. Extremes bring about reaction. Mind can never be calm in excessive joy. Let the mind be cheerful but calm.

Be always cheerful. Laugh and smile. How can a mind that is gloomy and dull think of God? Try to be happy always. Happiness is your very nature. This is termed Anavasada (cheerfulness). This spirit of cheerfulness must be cultivated by all aspirants.

Study spiritual books. Have constant Satsanga. Repeat OM 21,600 times daily with Bhava. It will take you three hours. Meditate on Atman or Krishna. Realise Brahman. Only this will free you from all mundane miseries and afford you eternal peace, knowledge and bliss.

With the growth of mind, pains increase; with its extinction, there will be great bliss. Having lorded over your mind, free yourself from the world of perceptions, in order that you may be of the nature of Jnana. Though surrounded by pleasurable or painful objects to disturb your equilibrium of mind, remain immovable as a rock, receiving all things with equanimity. The final cool joy and laugh consequent upon it is the bliss arising from the mind merging into the stainless Brahman.

CHAPTER 24
VIVEKA

WHAT IS VIVEKA?

When you are fully aware of the magnitude of human sufferings in this miserable, relative world, you will naturally begin to discriminate between what is real and what is unreal. Brahman is real and Jagat is unreal. This is Viveka. Then sincerity or Sraddha will develop. Then aspiration or keen longing to realise God will be felt. Then you will have to remember the Truth constantly. Then you will have to assert constantly: "*Aham Brahmasmi*—I am Brahman." By incessant practice, Nama, Rupa and Sankalpa will vanish and you will realise Brahman. This is Vedantic Sadhana. Discrimination, sincerity, aspiration, remembering Truth always, assertion and then Realisation are the various stages or means for realisation of Brahman.

AIDS TO VIVEKA

Viveka or power of discrimination is only awakened by constant Satsanga and Sravana (hearing of Srutis). Those who have done countless virtuous Karmas in their previous births will have the fortune through the grace of God to have Satsanga of Mahatmas, Sadhus, Bhaktas, Yogins, Jnanins and Sannyasins.

BENEFITS OF VIVEKA

Mind wants repetition of a pleasure once enjoyed. Memory of pleasure arises in the mind. Memory induces imagination and thinking. In this way, attachment arises. Through repetition, a habit is formed. Habit causes strong Trishna. Mind then exercises its rule over poor, helpless, weak-willed worldlings. As soon as discrimination arises, the power of the mind becomes weakened. The mind tries to recede, to retrace its steps to its original home—the heart. Its poisonous fangs are extracted by discrimination. It cannot do anything in the presence of discrim-

(159)

ination. It gets dethroned. The will becomes stronger and stronger when discrimination is awakened. Thanks to Viveka which enables us to get out of this miserable Samsara.

CHAPTER 25
VAIRAGYA AND TYAGA

WHAT IS VAIRAGYA?

If the mind is constantly thinking of tea and if it gets pain when you do not get it, it is said that you have got 'Aasakti' (attachment) for tea. This 'Aasakti' leads to bondage. The practice of 'Vairagya' (dispassion) demands you to renounce this 'Aasakti' for tea. Mere giving up of taking tea does not constitute the essence of 'Vairagya'.

Study Vairagya-Prakarana in Yoga Vasishtha. You will have a comprehensive understanding of the real Svarupa of Vairagya. A clean description of the actual dispassionate mental state of Sri Rama is given. Palatable dishes, refreshing beverages, affectionate father and mother, brother, dear friends, diamonds, pearls, flowers, sandal, ornaments, soft beds, gardens had no attraction for him. On the contrary, their very sight gave him intense pain.

In Vairagya, Brahmacharya is Antargata (hidden). Vairagya includes celibacy in thought, word and deed.

TWO KINDS OF VAIRAGYA

Vairagya (dispassion, indifference, non-attachment) is of two kinds, viz., (i) Karana Vairagya (Vairagya on account of some miseries) and (ii) Viveka-Purvaka Vairagya (Vairagya on account of discrimination between real and unreal). The mind of a man who has got the former type of Vairagya is simply waiting for a chance to get back the things that were given up. As soon as the first opportunity offers itself, the man gets the downfall and goes back to his former state. Vishaya does havoc in him with a vengeance and redoubled force from reaction. But the other man who has given up the objects on account of Viveka, on account of illusory nature of objects, will have spiritual advancement. He will not have a downfall.

HOW VAIRAGYA DAWNS

Note how Vairagya arises in the mind. The transitory and perishable nature of all things creates a sort of disgust in all minds and, in proportion to the depth and subtlety of nature, this reaction from the world works more or less powerfully in the mind of every individual. An irresistible feeling arises in our mind, viz., that the finite can never satisfy the Infinite within us, that the changing and perishable cannot satisfy the changeless and deathless nature of ours.

When you are not impressed with the idea of rich living, rich style of living cannot attract you. When you are impressed with the idea that meat and wine are not at all pleasurable, they cannot tempt you. In that case, if you do not get meat and wine or rich living, you will not be agonised at all in your mind. Why are you attracted towards a young, beautiful lady? Because, owing to your ignorance, you vainly think you will get pleasure through her. If you have got Viveka, it will at once tell you that you will get immense pain through her. Then the mind will recede or withdraw from the object, woman.

SADHANA WITHOUT VAIRAGYA GOES TO WASTE

When Vairagya appears in the mind, it opens the gate to Divine Wisdom. From dissatisfaction (with the sense-objects and worldly sense-enjoyments) comes aspiration. From aspiration comes abstraction. From abstraction comes the concentration of the mind. From the concentration of the mind comes meditation or contemplation. From contemplation comes Samadhi or Self-realisation. Without dissatisfaction or Vairagya, nothing is possible.

Just as cultivation in a stony land or saltish earth becomes absolutely fruitless, so also Yogic practices and Atma-Vichara (enquiry of the Soul) done without Vairagya (dispassion and indifference to the sensual enjoyments) becomes fruitless. Just as water, when it leaks into the rat-holes, instead of running into the proper channels in agricultural fields, becomes wasted and does not help the growth of plants, grains, etc., so also, the efforts of an aspirant become a wastage if he has not got the virtue Vairagya. He gets no spiritual advancement.

INTENSE VAIRAGYA NECESSARY FOR MOKSHA

There must be intense (Tivra) Vairagya in the minds of the aspirants, throughout the period of their Sadhana. Mere mental adhesion will not do for success in Yoga. There must be intense longing for liberation, a high degree of Vairagya plus capacity for Sadhana (spiritual practice). Then only they will get Nirvikalpa Samadhi and Moksha. It was only Raja Janaka and Prahlada who had Tivra Vairagya (intense dispassion). This kind of Vairagya is necessary for quick realisation. It is very difficult to cross the ocean of Samsara with a dull type of Vairagya. The crocodile of sense-hankering (Trishna) for sense-enjoyments and sense-objects will catch the aspirants by the throat and, violently snatching away, will drown them half-way.

ENEMIES OF VAIRAGYA

The Curse of Affection

Delusion proceeds from affection. It is a common observation that a person is distressed if the cat eats his domestic fowl; but when his affections are not touched, for instance, if the cat eats a sparrow or a mouse, he expresses no sorrow. You must, therefore, root out affection, which is the cause of vain attachment. The body generates numerous germs which people are anxious to remove; but to one variety they give the name "children," for which their lives are wasted away. Such is the delusion of the world.

At the back of affection and love, there is grief and sorrow. Affection is mixed with sorrow. At the back of pleasure, there is pain. Pain is mixed with pleasure. Man sows the poisonous seed of sorrow under the name of love, from which quickly spring up shoots of affection which contain a fire dangerous as lightning; and from these shoots, grow trees of sorrow with innumerable branches which, burning like a heap of covered straw, slowly consume the body.

The knot of affection is strengthened by long indulgence. Affection has entwined its threads around the hearts of men. The principal means to get rid of affection is to consider that this is a fleeting existence. In this wide world, how many millions of parents, wives, children, uncles and grandfathers have passed away! You should consider the society of friends as a momentary flash of lightning and, revolving this often in your mind, enjoy felicity.

Hope and Anticipation

Hope and anticipation are the opposite of Vairagya and Tyaga.

They fatten the mind. To be perfectly hopeless is a very high state for a philosopher. It is a very bad state for worldlings. They always say with contempt: "He is a hopeless man." Worldlings and philosophers move towards diametrically opposite poles.

HOW TO DEVELOP VAIRAGYA

Those who do not develop the painless Vairagya inherent in one's self and that with great felicity and happiness are, at best, but vermins in human shapes. When a bee finds that its feet are stuck in the honey, it slowly licks its feet several times and then flies away with joy. Even so, extricate yourself from the mind's sticking and clinging to this body and children-honey owing to Raga and Moha through Vairagya and meditation and fly away from this cage of flesh and bone to the Source, Brahman or Absolute.

It is very difficult to wean some children. They suck the breast even when they are three or four years old. The mother applies some nim-paste to the nipples. The child is weaned quickly. Even so, you will have to get a medicine of nim-paste for the mind to get it weaned from sensual objects. Sit in a solitary room. Think of the miseries of this earthly life, its cares, worries, anxieties, hunger, thirst, sins, temptations, passion, fighting, fears, vanity, disease, death, old age, sorrow, grief, tribulation, loss, failures, disappointments, hostility, scorpion stings, mosquito bites, etc. This will serve as an efficient nim-paste to wean the mind from Samsara. You must think in the above-manner daily.

Remember constantly the pains of various kinds pertaining to this mundane existence. Moha will vanish if you repeat the following line of Chapter XIII of Gita several times daily: "*Janma-mrityu-jara-vyadhi-duhkha-dosha-anudarsanam*—Insight into the pain and evil of birth, old age and sickness." Always make the mind understand clearly that there is only pain in this world. Reflect often on the instability of this world. This is the first Sadhana for aspirants. They can thus develop Vairagya. The mind will be weaned from objects. Attraction for sense-objects will gradually vanish.

RENUNCIATION BRINGS ABOUT MOKSHA

Shun the earthly objects as fire or poison or offal. Renounce all desires and cravings. This itself is Moksha (freedom). Renunci-

ation of desires brings about the annihilation of the mind. Annihilation of the mind brings on the destruction of Maya, because
the mind alone is Maya. Maya is enthroned in the imagination
of the mind. How cunning she is! A Viveki knows her tricks well.
She is awfully afraid of the man of renunciation and
Atmavichara. She bows to him with folded hands.

WHAT IS TRUE RENUNCIATION?

The mind is the all-in-all and its mastery leads to the renunciation of all. Chitta-Tyaga alone constitutes the renunciation of
all. True renunciation lies in the abnegation of the mind. It consists in renouncing all desires and egoism and not world-exis-
tence. Through such a mental abnegation, you will be able to
free yourself from all pain. Then will come immortality in life or
enjoyment of the infinite delight of existence free from ego,
founded on oneness of all in Brahman.

SANNYASA—A MENTAL STATE

Sannyasa is a mental state only. It is Gerua or colouring of the
heart and not of cloth alone. He is a veritable Sannyasin who is
free from passions and egoism and who possesses all the
Sattvic qualities, even though he lives with the family in the
world. Chudala was a queen-Yogini-Sannyasini, though she
was ruling a kingdom. That Sannyasin who lives in the forest,
but who is full of passions is worse than a householder and a
worldly-minded fool. Sikhidhvaja was a worldly man, though he
lived in the forest naked for very many years.

   True renunciation is the renunciation of all passions, desires, egoism and Vasana. If you have a stainless mind, a mind
free from attachment, egoism and passion, you are a
Sannyasin—no matter whether you live in a forest or in the bustle of a city, whether you wear white cloth or an orange-col-
oured robe, whether you shave the head or keep a long tuft of
hair.

   Shave the mind. Someone asked Guru Nanak, "O saint,
why have you not shaved your head? You are a Sannyasin."
Guru Nanak replied, "My dear friend, I have shaved my mind."
In fact, the mind should be cleanly shaved. Shaving the mind
consists in getting rid of all sorts of attachments, passions, egoism, Moha (infatuation), lust, greed, anger, etc. This is the real

shaving. External shaving of the head has no meaning so long as there is internal craving, Trishna.

Many have not understood what true renunciation is. Renunciation of physical objects is no renunciation at all. The real Tyaga (renunciation) consists in the renunciation of egoism (Ahankara). If you can renounce this Ahankara, you have renounced everything else in the world. If the subtle Ahankara is given up, Dehadhyasa (identification with the body) automatically goes away.

Vedanta does not want you to renounce the world. It wants you to change your mental attitude and give up this false, illusory 'I'-ness (Ahamta) and mineness (Mamata). The snake-charmer removes only the two poisonous fangs of the cobra. The snake remains the same. It hisses, raises its hood and shows the teeth. In fact, it does everything as before. The snake-charmer has changed his mental attitude towards the snake. He has a feeling now that it has got no poisonous fangs. Even so, you must remove the two poisonous fangs of the mind, viz., Ahamta and Mamata only. Then you can allow the mind to go wherever it likes. Then you will have always Samadhi only.

You must renounce the Tyagabhimana also. The Tyagabhimana is very deep-rooted. You must renounce the idea, "I have renounced everything." "I am a great Tyagi"—this Abhimana of the Sadhus is a greater evil than the Abhimana of householders, "I am a landlord; I am a Brahmin, etc."

CHAPTER 26

CONTROL OF INDRIYAS

INDRIYAS, A PROLONGATION OF THE MIND

Indriyas are objectified desires. Will to see is the eye. Will to hear is the ear. The Indriyas (senses) have two states, static and dynamic. When the desire begins to operate, the Indriyas are put in motion. This is the dynamic state. This is the dynamic state. As soon as the desire is gratified, the Indriyas shrink through Tripti (satisfaction). This is the static or passive state.

Mind and Indriyas are one. Indriya is a prolongation of the mind. The sea is fed by the rivers; the sea cannot exist without the rivers. Even so, mind is fed by Indriyas and cannot exist without Indriyas. If you have controlled the Indriyas, you have already controlled the mind. Indriya is another name for mind.

Mind is a mass of Indriyas. Mind is a higher power than the Indriyas. Mind is a consolidated Indriya. Indriya is mind in manifestation. Just as a minister obeys the king, so also, the five Jnana-Indriyas act in accordance with the dictates of the mind. Indriyas represent backwaters. The desire in the mind to eat has manifested as tongue, teeth and stomach. The desire in the mind to walk has manifested itself as legs and feet. If you can control mind, you can control the Indriyas.

Eyes can only see. Ears can only hear. Tongue can only taste. Skin can only touch. Nose can only smell. But, the mind can see, hear, taste, touch and smell. Mind is the common sensory. The five senses are blended there. It can directly see, hear, smell, taste and feel independent of the senses. It is an aggregate of the five senses. All the sense-faculties are blended in the mind. You can see and hear directly through the mind by Yogic practice (clairvoyance and clairaudience). This blows out the Western psychological theory of perception.

Mind is termed the sixth sense: "*Manah shashthanindriyani*—the senses of which mind is the sixth" (Gita, XV-7). The five senses are the five Jnana-Indriyas (organs of knowledge, sensation or perception).

Ayatana means mind (Chhandogya Upanishad, IV-vii)

which is the substratum of the experiences of all other organs. Senses cannot do anything, if the mind is not connected with them. When you are wholly absorbed in the study of an interesting newspaper, you do not hear when your friend loudly calls you. You are not aware that the clock has struck five. It is everybody's daily experience. The mind was away at that time. It was not then connected with the sense of hearing. The eyes may be wide open during sleep. They do not see anything, because the mind is not there.

SISTER INDRIYAS

Nose and anus are sister Indriyas. They are born of the same Prithvi-Tanmatra, nose from the Sattvic portion, anus from the Rajasic portion. These two Indriyas are the least mischievous. The olfactory sense and the olfactory nerve do not trouble you much. They can be controlled very easily.

Tongue and genitals are born of Jala-Tanmatra, the former from the Sattvic portion and the latter from the Rajasic portion. They are sister Indriyas. Eating strengthens the reproductive Indriyas.

Eye and feet are of Agni-Tanmatra, eye from the Sattvic Amsa (portion), feet from the Rajasic Amsa. They are sister Indriyas. Eye likes to see 'sights'. Her sisters, feet, say, "We are ready to take you to the Kumbha Fair at Allahabad. Be ready."

Skin and hands are born of Vayu-Tanmatra, skin from the Sattvic Amsa and hands from the Rajasic Amsa. They are sister organs. Skin says, "I want silk and other smooth articles for my enjoyment." Her sister, hand, says, "I can feel through my tactile corpuscles. I shall get for you fine soft silk. Do not be afraid, my dear sister."

Speech and ear are born of the same Akasa-Tanmatra, ear from the Sattvic Amsa and speech from the Rajasic Amsa. They are sister Indriyas. They help each other in the economy of Nature.

In a bungalow you will find two gates, one for entrance, another for exit. Our body is also a nice bungalow for the Lord. Eyes and ears are entrance gates for the reception of forms and sounds. These are avenues of sense-knowledge (sight and hearing). Upastha Indriya (organ of reproduction) and Guda (anus, organ of excretion) are exit gates. They throw out urine and faeces.

TONGUE, THE MOST DIFFICULT TO CONTROL

The most mischievous and troublesome Indriya is the genera-
tive organ. Then comes tongue. Then comes speech. Then comes ear. Then comes eye. Control of the organ of taste is far
more difficult than control of the genitals, because you have
been enjoying delicious articles of food even from your very
birth. Lust manifests itself just before eighteen. You indulge in
sexual pleasure only for a short period in every birth. But, you
have to take food even in advanced senility. Control of tongue
means control of all Indriyas.

Music, cinema, sight-seeing are enjoyed in human births
only. Ants and rats do not enjoy cinema-show. The Indriya of
sight is not so powerful as the tongue.

The organ of sight serves as a loving comrade to the organ of taste. The mind is at once tickled at the sight of a yellow
colour of the mango. The eyes see a beautiful mango and the
different dishes that are served on the table. At once, the
glosso-pharyngeal nerves are stimulated. You get good appetite and relish. The food is rendered more palatable. A blind
man may not have as good a relish as a man with sharp sight
has.

OBJECT OF SADHANA—TO PREVENT
EXTERNALISATION BY THE INDRIYAS

The three organs of eye, ear and tongue externalise the mind
and make a man altogether worldly. Eyes and ears are the avenues of sense-knowledge or Vritti-Jnana. Close the eyes. Shut
the ears either with balls of cotton or balls of cotton beaten with
yellow bee's wax or with the two thumbs making Yoni-Mudra.
Now you have destroyed two-fifths of the world. Do not allow
anything to enter the mind through these two doors of
sense-knowledge.

The object of Sadhana is to internalise the mind by introspection or Antarmukha Vritti and to realise the Truth within
yourself. Control the three organs of eye, ear and tongue. Then
you can bring the mind under discipline and prevent the mental
energy from flowing externally. These organs are the main
causes of making the mind restive. Control over them helps the
purpose of concentrating the energy internally.

He is a real Kshatriya who wages internal war with the

mind, who fights with the Indriyas, the Svabhava, through Viveka and will-force and obtains absolute mastery over the mind. He is a real Kshatriya who fights with the host of evil Samskaras and evil thoughts, the Rajasic and Tamasic, by awakening and increasing the Sattva Guna. He is a real Kshatriya whose Sastra is Will, and Astra is Viveka, whose battle-field is within, whose band is chanting of Pranava and Udgitha of the Chhandogya Upanishad and whose coat-of-arms is the three qualifications, viz., Viveka, Vairagya and Mumukshutva.

HOW TO CONTROL THE INDRIYAS

There are six ways of controlling the Indriyas: (i) through Vichara, (ii) by will-force, (iii) by Kumbhaka (retention of breath in Pranayama), (iv) by Dama (restraint), (v) by Pratyahara (abstention) and (vi) by Vairagya and Tyaga. Perfect control can be made only through Vichara.

Dama

Dama is restraint of the Indriyas. Dama blunts the Indriyas. Perfect control of the senses is not possible through Dama alone. If the senses are very sharp and acute, they carry away the minds of even good Sadhakas impetuously, just as the gale carries away the ship in stormy weather (Gita, II-67). They can be controlled perfectly through the help of the mind, through Vichara.

When you walk along Mount Road, Madras, each Indriya tries its level best to get hold of its objects of enjoyment and revelry. The Indriyas revolt vehemently if you do not procure them these objects. Tongue drags you to the coffee hotel or Hotel de Angelis. Tvak (skin) says, "Let me go to the Bombay Sait's shop and have a piece of fine China silk." Ear says, "Let me have a gramophone or harmonium." Nose says, "Let me have a bottle of *Otto de Rose*." The mind is at the bottom of these Indriyas to instigate. A tumultuous internal fight goes on between the five organs of knowledge, each trying to have a lion's share of enjoyment. Use Viveka, power of discrimination, always. Indriyas tempt and deceive you. Indriyas are the jugglers. Maya spreads her Moha-Jala through mind and Indriyas. Be on the alert. Practise Dama through Vairagya and Vasana-Tyaga. Happiness comes through calmness of

Indriyas, through calmness of mind (Uparati). Go to the sweets' bazaar with plenty of money in hand. Walk hither and thither for fifteen minutes. Look with a greedy eye at the various sweets. Do not purchase anything. Return home. Even if dainties are served that day at home, reject them. Have a plain diet. By so doing, you will control the tongue which is at the root of all troubles. You will eventually control the mind also. You will develop will-power.

Give up all luxurious food and all articles of sensuous enjoyment. Practise rigid penance. Tapas thins out the Indriyas and eventually leads to control of mind. If you give up tea, you have really controlled a small portion of the mind; control of tongue really means control of mind.

Pratyahara

When the Indriyas give up the objects, they take up the form of the mind-stuff. They are drawn into the mind. This is termed Pratyahara or abstraction. When the Indriyas are withdrawn from their respective objects, it is Indriya-Pratyahara. Mental abstraction takes place when the mind is disconnected with the Indriyas. Pratyahara is a general, broad term which includes Dama also. The effect of Dama (restraint of Indriyas) is Pratyahara.

If you can do consciously Pratyahara at will, consciously attaching and detaching the mind to and from the senses, you have gained really a great control over the mind. You can check at any time the outgoing tendencies or outgoing forces of the mind. Pratyahara is the stepping-stone to inner spiritual life. He who has succeeded in Pratyahara can concentrate his mind quite readily for a very long time. Dharana and Dhyana come automatically if Pratyahara is perfect. An aspirant has to struggle hard to have mastery over Pratyahara. Perfect Vairagya is indispensable for success in Pratyahara. You can succeed after strenuous and incessant struggle for some years. *"Tatah parama vasyatendriyanam—Thence arises the supreme control of the organs"* (Patanjali Yoga Sutras, II-55). If Pratyahara is perfect, all the organs are under perfect control.

During the period of Sadhana, do not mix much; do not talk much; do not walk much; do not eat much; do not sleep much. Observe carefully the five 'do-nots'. Mixing will cause disturbances in the mind. Talking much will cause distraction of the mind. Walking much causes exhaustion and weakness.

Eating much induces Alasya and Tandri (laziness and sleepiness).

Control of Thought—A Great Desideratum

If you have the reins of the horses under your control, you can have a safe journey. The Indriyas are the horses. If you have the senses under your efficient control, you can have a safe journey in the path of Moksha. Indriyas cannot do anything without the help of the mind, their master and commander. Control of the Indriyas means control of the mind only. Control of thoughts leads to the control of mind and Indriyas also. It leads to the attainment of infinite bliss and eternal life. Control of thought is indispensable—a great desideratum for all.

REMEMBER YOUR ORIGINAL HOME

O Mind! Do not ruin yourself by keeping company with the senses and their objects. Enough. Enough. Now get yourself concentrated on Brahma-Svarupa. That is your original home. That is your real, happy home. Remember this constantly when you chant OM. Brahmakara or Akhandakara Vritti will arise thereby. Svarupa is your original home. I have to repeat this again and again, as you always forget your real nature. You have taken your birth from Svarupa. Now, go back to your original home or birth-place through the help of Brahmakara Vritti generated by constant Nididhyasana (profound and constant meditation), through Mahavakya-Anusandhana or Chintana (enquiry into or thinking on the deep and real significance of the great sentence "*Tat Tvam Asi*" or "*Aham Brahmasmi*".) Then the Avidya (nescience) will be destroyed and you will be free from all kinds of miseries and pain and will attain the Paramananda state (highest knowledge coupled with infinite bliss). When the Svarupakara Vritti arises, all your vain Sankalpas will vanish. You will reach the Turiya state with Sahajananda (bliss which is your very nature). Then, O mind, you will be free from birth and death. You will no longer have to enter again this filthy house of physical body. You will not be clothed again by flesh and bone. You will be merged in Sat-Chit-Ananda Brahman, your Adhishthana or repository.

CHAPTER 27

MOUNA AND INTROSPECTION

MOUNA—ITS PRACTICE AND BENEFITS

Miscellaneous talking is a very bad habit. It distracts the mind. It keeps the mind always Bahirmukha (outgoing) and makes a man unspiritual. A vow of silence must be practised once a week. Much energy is wasted in talking.

The Vag-Indriya (organ of speech) seriously distracts the mind. "Speech is the fourth 'foot' of Mind-Brahman, because it is by means of the 'foot' of speech that the mind approaches the denotable objects such as cow, goat, etc. Therefore speech is like a foot of mind. In the same manner, nose is a 'foot', because it is through nose that the mind approaches objects of smell. Similarly, the eye is a 'foot'; the ear is another 'foot'. This constitutes the four-footed character of the Mind-Brahman" (Chhandogya Upanishad).

Do not allow anything to come out from the mind through the Vag-Indriyas (organ of speech). Observe Mouna (a vow of silence). This will help you. Considerable peace follows Mouna. The speech energy becomes transmuted into spiritual energy (Ojas). Sankalpas become much decreased. Will becomes stronger. Now you have shut out a big source of disturbance. You will rest now in peace. Meditate on God or Brahman now in right earnest.

Spiritual aspirants must observe Mouna for some hours daily.

Be careful in the selection of your words before you speak. Think thrice before you speak. Consider what effect the words will produce on the feeling of others. Observe Mouna for a couple of years. It is Tapas of speech.

Do not argue unnecessarily. Argument brings about hostility, heated feelings and wastage of energy. Every man has got his own views, his own opinion, ideas, sentiments, beliefs and convictions. It is very difficult to change the views of others. Do not try to convince others. When you are an aspirant, when you are gathering facts and knowledge from the study of sacred lore, do not argue with others till your thoughts have become mature and steady.

Imagination in the mind always exaggerates. Exaggeration is a modification of lie. Aspirants should not exaggerate. They should utter words with mathematical and scientific precision.

An aspirant is asked to give up company and observe Mouna, because on account of Raga, he will multiply acquaintance; on account of Dvesha, he will incur the displeasure of others by uttering some unpleasant words. There is a sword in the tongue. Words are like arrows. They injure the feelings of others. By observing Mouna and giving up company, one can control the Vag-Indriya and remove Raga. Then the mind will become calm.

There are fifteen Doshas that arise from company. An aspirant should, therefore, preferably remain alone during the period of Sadhana. The Doshas of company are: (1) Misunderstanding, (2) Ill-feeling, (3) Displeasure, (4) Raga-Dvesha, (5) Jealousy, (6) Vampirism, (7) Attachment, (8) Mental sharing of pain of another man, (9) Criticisms of others, (10) Anatma topics, (11) Habit of talking, (12) Bahirmukha Vritti, (13) Idea and Samskara of duality, (14) Slavish mentality and weak will, (15) Contempt. Love little, but love long.

When you take a vow of silence, never assert from within very often, 'I won't talk'. This will produce a little heat in the brain, because the mind wants to revenge on you. Simply once make a determination and then remain quiet. Attend to other affairs. Do not be thinking always, 'I won't talk, I won't talk.'

In the beginning, when you observe Mouna, you will find some difficulty. There will be a severe attack of Vrittis. Various kinds of thoughts will arise and force you to break the silence. There are all vain imaginations and deceptions of the mind. Be bold. Concentrate all energies on God. Make the mind fully occupied. The desire for talk and company will die. You will get peace. The Vag-Indriya (organ of speech) considerably distracts the mind.

MOUNA OF THE MIND

Mouna of the mind is far superior to Mouna of Vak (speech). Mouna should come of itself. It must be natural. Forced Mouna is only wrestling with the mind. It is an effort. If you live in Truth,

Mouna will come of itself. Then only will there be absolute peace.

What is wanted is natural Mouna and mental nudity. Physical nudity has no meaning. It is Tamasic Tapas of fools, that is not countenanced by Sastras and reason. In a Jivanmukta or a liberated soul, nudity comes of itself as he is absorbed in Brahman, when he is in the Saptama Jnana-Bhumika (the seventh stage of knowledge).

INTROSPECTION—WHAT IT IS AND WHAT IT DOES

The self-existent Brahman created the mind and senses with outgoing tendencies. The mind has a pernicious habit of externalisation from time immemorial. So you behold the external universe and not the internal Self. It is the Vikshepa-Sakti or Maya that draws you out. From your childhood, you are taught to look to the external world and not to the internal, psychic world. You have entirely lost the faculty of introspection. To have a comprehensive understanding of what is going on in the inner 'mental factory', a Suddha Buddhi (pure reason) and subtle intellect with power of introspection is needed. You will have to turn the mind inside, then concentrate all its powers and throw them upon the mind itself, in order that it may know its own nature and analyse itself. This is Raja Yoga.

Make a vigorous and earnest search within. Do not trust the mind and the Indriyas. They are your enemies. Woman and wealth are your bitter foes. These are two great evils.

In introspection, the mind itself is the subject of study. A portion of the mind studies the remaining portion of the mind. The higher mind studies the lower mind. Introspection is apperception. Just as you watch the work done by a coolie, a portion of the mind watches the movements of the rest of the mind. If you are one with the mind, if you identify yourself with the mind, you cannot know your defects. If you are a Sakshi or silent witness of the mind and if you practise introspection, you can know your various defects.

By a careful watch, many defects are detected and removed by suitable Sadhana. Enter a quiet room. Enter into silence daily for about fifteen minutes, morning and evening. Introspect. Watch the mind carefully. The mind will be doing either thinking, planning, feeling, knowing or willing. You will have to find out through subjective introspection what the mind is exactly doing at a particular time. To go through this practice, you must have Antarmukha Vritti, a subjective mind and a subtle Buddhi. Buddhi can be rendered subtle by study of philosophical books, Satsanga, control of Indriyas (Dama) and Sattvic food. The constant utterance of holy Names of God as Hari, OM, Narayana, Rama, Siva purifies the mind-stuff and helps make the mind introspective (Antarmukha).

HOW TO PRACTISE INTROSPECTION

You are the best judge of your mind. Introspect by living alone in solitude or retiring into a calm room for an hour. You must sit quiet in a solitary room alone, with closed eyes and watch the activities of the mind. You will then know your defects and weaknesses very clearly.

You should afterwards feel the necessity of removing them. Then your Svabhava should agree to change. You must know the right method to remove the defect. You must apply the method constantly. Then only improvement will set in. Constant application of the Sadhana is an indispensable requisite. You must watch the improvement every now and then, say, once a week, a fortnight or a month. You will have to keep a record of your progress (spiritual daily diary). You must watch carefully whether you are progressing in the spiritual path, whether you remain stationary or retrograding, whether the mind is distracted or concentrated. If it is distracted, you must remove the distracting causes one by one with patience and vigilance by suitable methods. If one method fails to bring about the desired results, you will have to combine two methods (the Yogic methods and Vichara).

Remember the triplet, viz., self-analysis, self-reliance, self-determination. It will be of immense use in your spiritual Sadhana. Analyse your self through introspection. Find out the nature of your Vrittis. Find out what Guna (quality) is predominating at a particular moment, whether it is Sattva, Rajas or Tamas. How long can the mind be absolutely fixed on your Lakshya (point of meditation)—either God, Brahman, idea or object, whether internal or external? How long can the mind be fixed on the object, rose and rose alone to the exclusion of all other objects—whether two seconds or two minutes or five minutes or half an hour? This is self-analysis. Rely on your self alone. You are your own redeemer and saviour. Nobody can give you Moksha. You will have to tread the spiritual path step by step. Books and Gurus can show the path and guide you. This is self-reliance. Make a strong self-determination, "I will realise God. I will have Atma-Sakshatkara or Brahmanubhava this very moment and not in the uncertain future." This is self-determination.

Wordlings have no time to think over even for a few minutes the life-problems, the mystery of life, etc. They get up in the morning. Their minds usually run to the special objects of enjoyment on account of Raga. Their mental energies are poured forth in the usual grooves and avenues—in thoughts of body, thoughts of eating and dressing, thoughts of wife, children, friends and also thoughts of office-work and business; and thus, the day is over. The same routine follows day after day, week after week. Years roll on and life is wasted. It is highly lamentable, indeed!

Only he who does Manana (reflection) and introspection through Antarmukha Vritti can change his worldly nature. In him only the idea of Brahman can get permanently lodged.

CHAPTER 28

EVIL VRITTIS AND THEIR ERADICATION

Kama, Krodha, Lobha, Moha, Mada, Matsarya, Darpa (arrogance), Dambha (hypocrisy), Asuya (a form of jealousy), Irshya (intolerance), Ahankara, Raga (attachment), Dvesha (repulsion) are some of the evil Vrittis. They bind a man to Samsara (transmigration). Pride, illusion and desires are so many binding cords of the mind.

LUST, A POWERFUL FORCE

Kama (lust), Krodha (anger), Lobha (covetousness), Moha (delusion), Mada (pride), Matsarya (jealousy) are the six passions of the mind. If lust is conquered, anger, Lobha, etc., which are auxiliary weapons, will become ineffective. If this inveterate enemy, lust is destroyed, its followers or retinue can be quite easily conquered. If the commander is killed, it is easy to kill the soldiers. If lust, which is the source of all enjoyments, ceases, then all worldly bondage, which has its substratum in the mind, will cease. How, without its renunciation, can you expect to attain the rare Nirvikalpa Samadhi or Brahma Nishtha?

Lust arises in him who develops attachment specially towards a person of the opposite sex. Love's principal weapon is woman or lust. Therefore, attachment should not be developed, specially towards the opposite sex.

The love between a husband and wife is mainly physical. It is of a selfish, ephemeral and changing nature. He who has realised Atman can really love all with sincerity of heart. The love between two aspirants based on psychological affinity and intellectual parity is real and lasting. Get rid of selfishness. Selfishness is a major dirt. It clouds the understanding. Remove it by selfless service, charity, study of Vedantic literature and Satsanga.

In a Jnanin, the sexual craving is entirely eradicated. In a Sadhaka, it remains well-controlled. In a householder, when not controlled, it does havoc. It exists in him in its fully expanded state. He cannot resist it. He yields to it helplessly on account of his weak will and lack of firm resolution.

If you keep lemon juice or tamarind juice in a golden cup, it is not spoiled or tainted. If you keep it in a brass or copper vessel, it is at once spoiled and rendered poisonous. Even so, even if there are some Vishaya-Vrittis (sensual thoughts) in the pure mind of a person, they will not pollute him and induce Vikara (sensual excitement). If there are sensual thoughts in persons with impure minds, they cause excitement in them when they come across sensual objects.

Remembrance of image of a woman unsettles the mind. When a tiger has once tasted human blood, it always runs after killing human beings. It becomes a man-eater. Even so, when the mind has once tasted sexual pleasures, it always runs after women. Lust is powerful. It carries a flowery bow equipped with five arrows, viz., Mohana (fascination), Stambhana (stupefaction), Unmadana (maddening), Soshana (emaciation) and Tapana (inflaming).

In the Bhagavad-Gita, you will find it mentioned that senses, mind and Buddhi are the seats of passions. Pranamaya Kosha is another seat. Desire is all-pervading in the body. Every cell, every atom, every molecule, every electron is surcharged with passion. There are under-currents, cross-currents, inter-currents and submarine currents in the ocean of passion. You must completely annihilate each one of them.

Be careful in destroying passions. It is easy to control the conscious mind. But, it is very difficult to control the subconscious mind. You may be a Sannyasin. You may be a moral man. Mark how the mind behaves or conducts itself in dreams. You begin to steal in dreams. You commit adultery in dreams. The sex-impulses, ambitions, low desires are all ingrained in you and deep-rooted in the subconscious mind. Destroy the subconscious mind and its Samskaras through Vichara, Brahma-Bhavana, meditation on 'OM' and its meaning. A man who is established in mental Brahmacharya can never have even a single thought of evil in dreams. He can never have a bad dream. There is lack of Vichara or Viveka in dream. That is the reason why you get bad dreams, even though you are pure in the Jagrat state through the power of Viveka and Vichara.

That state of mind wherein no single sexual thought enters the mind is termed mental Brahmacharya. Bhishma had this state. If you are not established in mental Brahmacharya, at least try to control the body when the sex-impulse is troubling you.

A SOURCE OF PERPETUAL DANGER TO SADHAKAS

The presence or recollection of a woman usually excites unholy ideas in the minds of recluses who have abandoned this world and devoted themselves to spiritual exercises and thus deprives them of the fruit of their austerity. It is very difficult to understand the presence of subtle lust in the minds of others, particularly in spiritual Sadhakas, though eye (look), tone, gestures, gait, behaviour, etc., may give a clue.

THE EXAMPLE OF JAIMINI

Once upon a time, Sri Vedavyasa was holding his Vedanta class amongst his students. In the course of his lecture, he mentioned that the young Brahmacharins should be very careful and should not mix with young ladies and that, with all their vigilance and circumspection, they may fall a victim as lust is very powerful. One of his students, Jaimini, the author of Purva-Mimamsa, was a little impertinent. He said, "Guruji Maharaj! Your statement is wrong. No lady can attract me. I am well-established in Brahmacharya." Vyasa said, "Jaimini, you will know that soon. I am going to Benares. I will return within three months. Be careful. Do not be puffed with pride." Sri Vyasa, through his Yogic powers, assumed the form of a beautiful young girl, with piercing eyes and very charming face, well-dressed in a thin silken garment. The lady was standing underneath a tree at sunset. Clouds gathered together. It began to rain. Accidentally, Jaimini was passing along the side of the tree. He saw the girl, felt pity and addressed her: "O lady, you can come and stay in my Ashrama. I shall give you shelter." The lady asked, "Are you living alone? Is any woman living there?" Jaimini replied, "I am alone. But, I am a perfect Brahmacharin. No lust can affect me. I am free from any sort of Vikara. You can stay there." The lady objected: "It is not right for a young virgin girl to stay with a Brahmacharin alone at night." Jaimini said, "O damsel, do not be afraid. I promise you of my perfect Brahmacharya." Then she agreed and stayed in his Ashrama at night. Jaimini slept outside and the lady was sleeping inside the room. At the dead of night, Jaimini began to feel the influence of lust in his mind. A little sexual craving arose in his mind. In the beginning, he was absolutely pure. He knocked at the door and said, "O lady, the wind is blowing outside. I cannot bear the cold blasts. I want to sleep inside." She opened the door. Jaimini was sleeping inside. Again, the sexual craving became a little more intense and keen, as he was very close to a lady and as he heard the sound of her bangles. Then he rose up and began to embrace her. At once, Sri Vyasa assumed his original form with his long beard and said, "O, my dear Jaimini, what about the strength of your Brahmacharya now? Are you established in your perfect celibacy now? What did you say when I was lecturing on this subject?" Jaimini dropped his head down in utter shame and said, "Guruji, I am wrong. Kindly pardon me."

Even Jesus was tempted by Satan. Buddha had to fight severely with Mara (lust) just before he attained his Nirvana or Buddhahood.

BEWARE OF MAYA—A WARNING TO ASPIRANTS

Therefore, oh, dear aspirants, you will have to be very, very careful. During the period of Sadhana, avoid the company of women. You must never mix with young ladies, however strong you may be. Maya works through under-currents so stealthily that you may not be aware of your actual downfall.

Keep the mind fully occupied with spiritual pursuits. Keep yourself at the farthest distance from everything that would stir up your passions. Then only you will be safe.

Do not live with householders. Do not test your spiritual strength and purity when you are a beginner on the spiritual path. Do not rush into evil associations when you are a spiritual neophyte to show that you have the courage to face sin and impurity. It will be a serious mistake. You will be running into a grave danger. You will have a quick downfall. A small fire will be very easily extinguished by a heap of dust.

Mind has a great power of imitation. That is the reason why a spiritual aspirant is prohibited from mixing with householders. His mind will try to imitate the minds of worldlings. Downfall will ensue.

If an aspirant moves with rich people, Zamindars and Rajas, his mind begins to imitate the luxurious habits of these people and, ere long, he gets an unconscious downfall. Certain bad habits creep in him unconsciously. And he finds it difficult to tear out or remove these bad habits. After forty, it is difficult to tear out old habits and establish new healthy habits.

An aspirant can live only for a short time in his native place if there is an urgent call. Yogic rules and laws cannot permit him to stay there for a sufficiently long period, however suitable the place may be and whatever may be the degree of Vairagya (dispassion) of the aspirant. The force of Samskaras (impressions) is tremendous. Unless all the Samskaras are thoroughly burnt through pure Asamprajnata Samadhi or Nirvikalpa Avastha (seedless state), it is not safe for one to stay for a long time in one's own native place. He is still within the danger zone.

After seclusion for five years, the aspirant should test his mental state by coming into the world and mixing with the worldly people. If there is no attraction for objects, he can be quite sure that he has reached the third Jnana-Bhumika—Tanumanasi—a stage wherein the mind is thinned out like a slender thread.

HOW LUST DEVELOPS AND RUINS

From the bed of Samskaras and Vasanas emanates imagination, through memory. Then comes attachment. Along with imagination, emotion and impulse manifest. Emotion and impulse exist side by side. Then comes sexual irritation, sexual craving, excitement and burning in the mind and throughout the body. The irritation and burning in the mind penetrate into the physical body just as water in the pot penetrates into the surface of the pot. If you are very vigilant, you can drive off the imagination itself in the very beginning and avert the danger. Even if you allow the thief imagination to enter the first gate, keep a careful watch at the second gate when the irritation manifests. You can stop the burning now. You can stop also easily the strong sexual impulse from being transmitted to the Indriya itself. Draw the sex energy up towards the brain through Uddiyana and Kumbhaka. Repeat OM mentally with force. Divert the mind. Pray. Meditate.

METHODS TO CONTROL LUST

Just as you control the itching sensation in an eczematous part of the leg or scabies of the hand, you must control the itching from lust by Viveka, Vichara, Brahma-Bhavana, light Sattvic diet, fasting, Pranayama, Uddiyana Bandha, Satsanga, study of the Gita, Japa, prayer, etc. Then only can you enjoy spiritual bliss.

Vichara and Brahma-Bhavana

It is through constant Vichara and Brahma-Bhavana that the mind has to be weaned from lustful thoughts and tendencies. You must remove not only the sexual craving and the sexual impulses, but also sex-attraction. Think of the miseries that you get from a married life with its various entanglements and bondage. Make the mind understand by repeated auto-suggestions and hammering that sexual pleasure is false, worthless, illusory and full of pain. Place before the mind the advantages, bliss, power and knowledge of a spiritual life. Make it understand that the exalted, eternal life is in the immortal Atman. When it hears constantly these useful suggestions, it will slowly leave off its old habits. The attraction for the sex will slowly die. Then only real sex-sublimation will take place. You will become then only an Urdhvaretas.

Atman is sexless. There is no sex in the five elements. It is the mind that creates the sex idea. Sukadeva had no sex idea. Consider that a woman is a combination of five elements, a mass of electrons or atoms. The sex idea will slowly vanish.

Pure Reason

There are two kinds of force in the mind, viz., hostile or antagonistic force and friendly or favourable force. Passion is hostile force that drags you down. Pure reason is a favourable force that elevates you and transmutes you into Divinity. Develop, therefore, my child, pure reason to get unalloyed bliss and supreme Brahmic knowledge. The passion will die itself.

Sattvic Food

Take light Sattvic food, such as milk, fruits, etc. You can control passions in this way. The wise say that purity of food leads to purity of mind.

Fasting

Fasting weakens the sex Indriya. It destroys sexual excitement. Passionate young men and ladies should take recourse to occasional fasting. It will prove highly beneficial.

Pranayama

By Pranayama, the mind gradually proceeds from the gross to

the subtle. It, therefore, exercises a wholesome check upon the sexual irritation. When some evil thought disturbs your mind, at once take to Padmasana or Siddhasana and practise Pranayama. The thought will leave you immediately.

Satsanga and Svadhyaya

Do not study romantic novels. Do not talk on sexual subjects. Do not keep company with men who indulge in sex. Strive your best to divert your mind and eyes from external objects that prompt sexual desires. Keep company with Sadhus and Sannyasins. Read sublime books such as the Gita, the Upanishads and the Yogavasishtha. Practise Mantra-Japa and Pranayama.

Keep the Mind Ever Engaged

Keep the mind fully occupied. You can be established in mental and physical Brahmacharya. I shall give here the routine of work: six hours for sleep (10 p.m. to 4 a.m.); six hours for meditation (4 a.m. and 7 a.m. and 7 p.m. to 10 p.m.); six hours for study; four hours for Nishkama work, service of the poor, service of the sick, etc., two hours for walking or indoor exercise. This will keep the mind ever engaged.

BENEFITS OF BRAHMACHARYA

Mind, Prana, Virya (seminal energy) are three links of one chain. They are three pillars of the edifice of Jivatman. Destroy one pillar—either mind, Prana or Virya and the whole building will fall to pieces. If you can observe Akhanda Brahmacharya for a period of 12 years, you will enter into Nirvikalpa Samadhi spontaneously without any effort. The mind will be controlled by itself. Seminal energy is a potent Sakti. Semen is Brahman itself. A Brahmacharin who has practised unbroken celibacy for full twelve years will reach to Nirvikalpa state the moment he hears the Mahavakya "Tat Tvam Asi" (That thou art). His mind is extremely pure, strong and one-pointed. He need not have repeatedly undergone the lengthy process of Sravana (hearing) and Manana (intellection).

A drop of semen is made out of 40 drops of blood. The energy that is spent in one act of copulation is tantamount to expenditure of mental energy through mental exertion for 24 hours or expenditure of physical energy through physical exertion for three days. Mark how valuable and precious is semen!

Do not waste this energy. Preserve it with great care. You will have wonderful vitality and energy. When it is not used, it is all transmuted into Ojas-Sakti (spiritual energy) and stored up in the brain. Western doctors know little of this salient point. Most of your ailments are due to excessive seminal wastage.

A true Brahmacharin in thought, word and deed has wonderful thought-power. He can move the world. If you develop strict celibacy, Vichara-Sakti (power of enquiry) and Dharana-Sakti (power of grasping and holding the Truth) will develop. If a man persistently refuses to yield to his lower nature and remains as a strict celibate, the seminal energy is deflected upwards to the brain and is stored up as Ojas-Sakti (spiritual power). Thereby, the power of the intellect is intensified to a remarkable degree. The strict celibate has keen and acute memory even in old age. The celibate who has achieved the transmutation of the seminal energy will find that sexual desires no longer trouble him. Such celibate is known as Urdhvaretas. Hanuman, Bhishma, Lakshmana, Swami Dayananda and Swami Vivekananda were Urdhvareto-Yogins.

ANGER—HOW IT ARISES

Anger arises in him who thinks of his enemy. Even if you have forgotten the feeling of annoyance, it lurks in the mind in a dormant form. The effect is there for some time. If you renew a number of times the same kind of thought of jealousy, envy or hatred about the same person, the effect lasts longer. Repetition of angry feeling intensifies hatred. Mere ill-feeling develops into intense malice by repetition of anger.

On days when you have many troubles, vexations, worries from the morning to evening, a trifling causes much irritation in the mind. The balance of mind is upset by a paltry affair. A single harsh word throws you out of the balance, whereas when you are peaceful throughout the day, even a strong abuse and severe censure do not produce any effect whatsoever.

Anger resides in the Linga Sarira or astral body. But, it percolates into the physical body just as water percolates through the pores into the outer surface of an earthen pot.

ILL-EFFECTS OF ANGER

Just as heat melts lead, just as heat and borax melt gold, even so, Kama and Krodha, the heating factors of the mind, melt it. When you are angry, the mind becomes disturbed. Similarly, when the mind is disturbed, the body also becomes disturbed. The whole nervous system is agitated. You become enervated.

Anger spoils the brain, nervous system and blood. When a wave of anger arises in the mind, Prana begins to vibrate rapidly. You are agitated and excited. Blood becomes hot. Many poisonous ingredients are formed in the blood. When the blood is agitated, the semen also is affected.

Once a child sucked the breast of his mother when she was in a fit of violent fury or rage and died immediately on account of poisoning by virulent chemical products that were thrown into the blood of the mother when she was in great excitement. Many such cases have been recorded. Such are the disastrous effects of anger. Even three minutes of violent hot temper may produce such deleterious effects in the nervous system that it will take weeks or months for the repair of injury.

Anger clouds understanding. When the mind is violently agitated, you cannot understand a passage of a book clearly. You cannot think properly and clearly. You cannot write a letter with a cool mind. When the lamp is flickering through wind, you do not see the objects clearly. Even so, when the Buddhi (mind) is flickering or agitated by anger, chaos arises in the Buddhi and you are not able to see and understand things properly. Buddhi is all light.

A man who is a slave to anger, may have washed himself well, anointed himself well, dressed his hair and put on white garments; yet he is ugly, being overcome by anger. There are symptoms on the face to indicate the presence of anger in the mind. If you get anger, you will lose the battle of life. If you have an easily irritable mind, you will not be able to do your daily duties and business in an efficient manner.

HOW TO CONTROL ANGER

There are three ways of destroying the anger and lust Vrittis: (1) You can drive them through will-force. This is, no doubt, difficult and taxing. It exhausts your energy much. (2) Pratipaksha-Bhavana method: Entertain counter-thoughts— thoughts of purity and love. This is easy. (3) Live in Truth or Brahman. There are no Vrittis of any kind in Brahman. Brahman is Nirvikara, Nirvikalpa and Nitya Suddha (ever pure). This method is a perfect and powerful one. Vrittis completely die away.

Conquer passion. It will then be easy to subdue anger, which is only one of its followers.

Control anger by love. Anger is a powerful energy that is uncontrollable by practical Vyavaharic Buddhi, but controllable by pure reason (Sattvic Buddhi) or Viveka-Vichara.

When you become angry with your servant when he fails to supply your usual milk on a day, raise a question within yourself: "Why should I be a slave to milk?" Then the wave of anger will at once naturally subside. It will not arise on other occasions also, if you are careful and thoughtful.

Control anger by Kshama (forgiveness), Daya, patience, tolerance, universal love (Visva-Prema), mildness, Viveka, Vichara, Atma-Bhava, Udasinata, Nirabhimanata and such other virtues. Forgive and pity the man who does you harm. Consider censure as a blessing, ornament and nectar. Bear reproach. Develop universal love by service, charity, Brahma-Bhava. Recall any calm and pure state, which when once brought to mind, suppresses the hatred and brings composure. When anger is subdued, rudeness, pride and envy will vanish of themselves. Prayer and devotion will root out anger.

Practise Pratipaksha-Bhavana (entertaining a counter-idea). When you get angry, fill the mind with the idea of love. If you are depressed, fill the mind with the idea of joy and exhilaration.

When you become intensely angry, leave the place immediately for half an hour. Take a long walk. Repeat the sacred Mantra, "OM SANTIH," 108 times. Your anger will subside. I shall tell you another easy way. When you get angry, count from one to thirty. The anger will subside.

When anger tries to exhibit itself, observe silence. Keep quiet. Never utter a harsh word or obscene speech. Try to nip it before it emerges out from the subconscious mind. You will have to be very alert. It tries to come out suddenly. Before anger manifests, there is an agitation (Udvega) in the mind. You must try to extirpate this very agitation in the mind before it assumes a very gross form in the shape of twitching of muscles of the face, clenching of teeth, red eyes, etc. You will have to punish the mind well. You will have to impose self-restraint and punishment on yourself by way of fasting for a day whenever Udvega (agitation) manifests in the mind.

If you strive and make sincere effort to subdue your anger, the hatred subsides. Even then, a slight movement of impatience lingers although the angry feeling has gone. You must eschew this slight disturbance also. For a man who is leading a divine life, this is a very serious drawback.

Irritability is a weakness of the mind. If you are easily irritable, it is likely that you may do injustice to many. Remove this by the practice of patience, Titiksha, tolerance, Karuna (mercy), love, Brahma-Bhava, Narayana-Bhava, etc.

Calmness of mind is a direct means to the realisation of Brahman (or the Highest Self).

Verily a certain man in his behaviour is calm. His calmness is noticed by everyone as he discharges his duties, large and small, beautifully well. Another man is calm in his behaviour, in speech, which is noticed by everyone. For, by nature, he is friendly, sweet in speech, congenial, of a frank countenance, ready at greetings. You should be calm in all the three states. Towards such a one, the development of love is not difficult.

You must have the knack to keep the mind always in balance and in tune. Close your eyes. Dive deep into the Divine Source. Feel His Presence. Remember Him always. Practise His Name. Repeat His Name even while at work. You will gain immense spiritual strength. Meditate early in the morning before you mix with people. You must rise above the thousand and one things which would irritate you easily in the course of your daily life. Then only you can turn out wonderful work daily with harmony and concord.

HATRED AND ITS MODIFICATIONS

Hatred and malice are two formidable passions. They are so deeply implanted in your system that it is very difficult to root them out. Pride is not so fearful as hatred and malice. When a man is placed in a high position and earns much money and is thereby honoured and respected by all, he becomes very proud. When he loses that position and fails to earn money, his pride vanishes. But hatred and malice are two passions which are inveterate and need constant and diligent efforts for their eradication.

Prejudice, intolerance, Ghrina, insolence, impertinence,

scorn, contempt—these Vrittis are all modifications of the emotion of hatred. Suspicion becomes prejudice by repetition. Prejudice develops into ill-will (Ghrina) and intolerance. Ill-will is a mild form of hatred. When repeated, it develops into hatred. Hatred, by successive repetition, becomes malice or extreme enmity.

Prejudice

Prejudice or unreasonable dislike, prepossessions and intolerance are three undesirable Vrittis in the mind. Prejudice makes the mind and brain callous. The mind cannot think truly. Prejudice is a kind of mental sore. If you have prejudice against Mohammedans, you cannot understand the teachings of Mohammed in the Quoran. The brain and the mind will not harmoniously vibrate to receive the spiritual ideas of the Quoran, because the prejudice has rendered the mind callous.

Prejudice is like an open sore on the physical body through which the will-power of the man is leaking. Be liberal or catholic in your views. You must give a place for every school of philosophy and every religion. A particular religion suits a particular nation according to the stage of evolution, temperament and capacity of the people. Arya Samaja, Brahmo Samaja, New Thought Movement, Occultism and cults of various kinds and denominations serve their own useful purpose. Prejudice is only unreasonable dislike. You must remove it by efforts and right thinking.

Intolerance

Intolerance is narrow-mindedness on account of some narrow beliefs, convictions and views. You must be extremely detached and sober in your views. Your mind will be greatly disturbed through intolerance. Even though your views are diametrically opposite to the views of others, you must have perfect tolerance. A man of tolerance has an expanded heart. Tolerance brings lasting peace.

Insolence

Insolence is overbearing nature. It is haughtiness manifested in contemptuous treatment of others. It is arrogant contempt. It is brutal impudence. It is grossly rude or disrespectful nature. Insolence is rude, haughty behaviour in violation of the established rules of social intercourse. The insolent man has utter disregard for the feelings of others. He makes personal attacks either in words or in actions, indicative of either scorn or triumph.

HOW TO ERADICATE HATRED

No Samadhi or union with God is possible when hatred, prejudice, jealousy, anger, lust, etc., exist in the mind. Remove these defects by love, Titiksha, Brahma-Bhavana, Atma-Drishti, Satsanga, Vichara. Love is the greatest power on earth. Karuna is the highest Sadhana. Do not give pain to others and relieve pain where it is; this is Karuna.

He who loves another man, loves himself only. He who gives rupees five as charity to a poor man in distress, gives it to himself. For, there is nothing else save his own self in the universe. He who hurts, hates and abuses another man, hurts, hates and abuses himself only. He digs his own grave.

When thoughts of revenge and hatred arise in the mind, try to control the physical body and speech first. Do not utter evil and harsh words. Do not censure. Do not try to injure others. If you succeed in this by practice for some months, the thoughts of revenge, having no scope for manifesting outside, will die by themselves. It is extremely difficult to control such thoughts from the very beginning without having recourse to control of body and speech first.

Constant Vichara and development of the opposite virtues—Prema, Daya and Karuna (love, compassion, sympathy and commiseration)—will eradicate the two violent passions of hatred and malice.

When hatred manifests, reflect on the blessings of love; it will slowly vanish. The blessings of love are many. Happy he sleeps. Happy he lives. He sees no bad dreams. He is dear to all alike. He is dear to subhuman beings. Devas guard him. Fire, poison and sword cannot approach him. Quickly he concentrates the mind. His complexion is serene. He dies peacefully and goes to Brahma-Loka.

Have no enemies. Do not entertain inimical thought against any person who might have done any wrong to you. If, while you are directing your mind towards your enemy, you recall the offences that have been committed against yourself and hatred arises in you, you should dispel it by repeatedly dwelling on love with him. Imagine again and again that he is your intimate friend and, with effort, raise a strong current of love towards him. Call in the mind affectionate feelings and others that cause love and tenderness. Remember the story of Pavahari Baba and Jayadeva, the author of Gita Govinda in Bhakta Vijaya, who intently prayed to God and got Mukti for his enemy—the robber who had cut off his two hands.

Serve the man whom you hate. Share with him what you have. Give him something to eat. Shampoo his legs. Make prostration sincerely. Your hatred will subside. He will also begin to love you. Gifts and kind words tame the untamed men. Men bow their heads by gifts and kind words.

If you give a blanket to a needy man with unwillingness, it is not Dana (charitable act) at all. It is a selfish act only. The mind will be waiting to take the blanket back when the first chance comes. Give anything willingly.

THE SADHANA OF EQUAL VISION

Serve all. Serve the Lord in all. Love all. Respect all. Develop cosmic love. Have Atma-Bhavana and Atma-Drishti. Have equal vision (Sama Drishti). All kinds of hatred will disappear. The Sadhana of equal vision is extremely difficult, but strenuous and constant efforts will bring about success eventually.

Aspirants who wish to abolish the dividing line should immediately develop love for a very dear person, after him for an indifferent person and then after him for an enemy. And, in doing so, in each compartment they should make the heart tender and loving and should immediately afterwards induce Dhyana (meditation).

You should discriminate between a thief and an honest man, but you should love the thief. A worldly-minded person hates a thief, sees him outside and considers that he is entirely separate from the thief; whereas, a Jnani loves a thief as his own Self and sees him within himself.

When you remember that a savage or a rogue is a saint of the future and has all the divine qualities in a potential form, you will begin to love everybody. Hatred will slowly vanish. It is only a question of time for the rogue or the savage for his evolution and development.

An aspirant who wishes to begin with the development of the four divine states, viz., love, pity, sympathy, and even-mindedness should first, having cut off the impediments, take up the subject of meditation, finish his light tiffin and drive away his drowsiness due to eating, sit comfortably on a seat well-arranged in a secluded spot and think on the evils of hatred and the very many advantages of forbearance. Verily, by means of this practice, hatred will slowly vanish and forbearance will be developed. A man who is overcome with hatred and whose mind is assailed by hatred, kills beings. Patience is the highest virtue. Nothing can excel forbearance. He who is strong in forbearance is, indeed, a divine being.

There is nothing absolutely right or absolutely wrong in this relative universe. Right and wrong are mind-made. Everybody is right from his own point of view. There is a grain of truth in everything. The point of view is the determining factor in the life of each. When the understanding is illumined by wisdom, the point of view is broad and entire. When the understanding is darkened by ignorance, the point of view is narrow, limited and one-sided. Broad view is the sign of expansion of heart. A man of broad view is free from suspicion, prejudice, prepossessions and intolerance of various sorts. Broad view results from foreign travels, good birth, vast study, Satsanga, public service, varied experience, meditation, etc. A man of broad views sees things in their entirety and in their right relations. Broad view creates harmony and concord. Narrow view creates disharmony and discord.

ANTICIPATION AND AVARICE

Memory and anticipation are two kinds of evil Vrittis for a spiritual aspirant, though they are beneficial for worldly-minded persons. Pratyasa (anticipation) and Parigraha (grasping) make you a beggar of beggars and destroy your will-power. Do not anticipate anything. Anticipation fattens the mind and causes restlessness. Do not expect anything. It causes mental disturbance. If you do not expect, you would not have disappointment. Forget everything that pertains to the world. Even if anything that is conducive to luxury comes, reject it at once. You will grow strong. Remember God and God alone. Everything else here is a dream. The world is a long dream.

Destroy avarice by Santosha (contentment), integrity, disinterestedness and charity. Do not entertain hopes. You will not have any disappointment. Santosha is one of the four sentinels of the domain of Moksha. A contented mind is a continual feast. If you have Santosha, you will get help from the other three sentinels, viz., Sama, Vichara and Satsanga. With the help of these four sentinels, you can attain Brahma-Jnana, the ultimate goal of life.

MOHA AND ITS CURE

Moha (delusion) is a strong weapon of Maya. Do not say, my friend, that desire is more powerful than Moha. Moha is as much powerful and dangerous as desire is. Moha does three things. It creates the idea of 'mineness'—my wife, my son, my house, etc. It produces infatuated love and attachment for body, wife, son and property. It creates the 'Nitya-Buddhi' (the idea of stability) in the perishable objects of the world and 'Dehatma-Buddhi'. It makes a false thing appear as true. The world appears as real on account of Moha. The body is mistaken for Atman or pure Self owing to the delusive influence of Moha.

Although you know fully well that the body of a woman is made up of flesh, bone, skin, hair, blood, urine and faeces, yet you passionately cling to the form. Why? Because of the force of Raga, Moha, Samskara, Vasana and Kalpana (imagination). When there is Vasana-Kshaya (annihilation of Vasanas) through Vichara and Viveka, you will not be attached towards a woman.

Get rid of excessive Moha and attachment to wife, money and also children by Sannyasa (external renunciation). If there is external change, internal change must also come. External renunciation is quite necessary.

The mind is generally attracted by brilliant light, beauty, intelligence, varied colours and pleasant sounds. Do not be deceived by these paltry things. Enquire within. What is the Adhishthana or background for all these things? There is one Essence at the back of the mind and all objects of this seeming sense-universe. That Essence is all-full (Paripurna) and self-contained. That Essence is the Brahman of the Upanishads. That Essence verily you are—"*Tat Tvam Asi*"—my dear readers!

PRIDE

Pride is a feeling of superiority over others. It is of nine kinds: (i) physical pride (pride of possessing great physical strength), (ii) intellectual pride (pride of great learning), (iii) moral pride (pride of possessing great moral virtues), (iv) psychic pride (pride of possessing great psychic powers or Siddhis), (v) spiritual pride, (vi) pride of noble birth, (vii) pride of power, wealth and other possessions, (viii) pride of being handsome and (ix) Rajamada (pride of sovereignty). All these varieties of pride should be completely overcome.

Get rid of pride through Viveka. Everything is Anitya. Why are you vainly puffed up with pride?

Arrogance is a form of pride. It is undue assumption of self-importance. It is claiming too much. Darpa is vanity. It is vain display. It is vain show. The man is puffed up even though he actually does not possess anything. A man of pride actually possesses something. That is the difference between pride and vanity. Vanity is a form of exaggerated pride.

Hypocrisy (Dambha) is pretending to be what one is really not. It is feigning. It is concealment of one's true character. It is the opposite of Adambhitva of the Gita (XIII-7). A hypocrite pretends to be what he is really not, in order to extract money, honour, fame or something else from others.

Hypocrisy, falsehood, cheating, avarice and Trishna (avidity) are very closely related. They are members of one family. Hypocrisy is the offspring of avarice. Falsehood is the son of hypocrisy. Hypocrisy co-exists with falsehood. Trishna is the mother of hypocrisy. Hypocrisy cannot live even for a moment without falsehood, the son and avarice and Trishna (father and mother). When there is a craving for objects, greed for money comes in. Without money, there can be no enjoyment. To satisfy the hunger for money, persons have to put on hypocrisy, tell lies and cheat others. The root cause of all this is craving for enjoyment. Deceitful diplomacy and falsehood are old allies of greed and hatred.

Self-sufficiency is a peculiar modification in the mind. It is the effect of vanity, pride and Dambha. It is a Rajoguna Vritti. Remove it by right thinking, Vichara and practice of the opposite virtue, humility.

JEALOUSY AND ITS MODIFICATIONS

Jealousy is a form of continuous anger. Irshya is a form of jealousy. It is a form of hatred. Blaming, accusing, mocking, ridiculing, unjust criticism, censure, cavilling, vilifying, tale-bearing, backbiting, scandalmongering, faultfinding, complaining—all proceed from jealousy, either subtle or gross, a hatred of various sorts. They all indicate lack of proper mental culture and meanness of the person. They should be removed.

Taunting is to censure sarcastically. Teasing is to torment or irritate with jests. Sneering is to show contempt by the expression of the face, as by turning up the nose. Frowning is to wrinkle the brow as in anger. Mocking is to laugh at in ridicule, to mimic in ridicule. Ridiculing is to make a wit exposing one to laughter. It is derision or mockery. It is exposing one to merriment. A joke is a clever insult. You must avoid all these when you move with others, as they cause rupture between friends, heated feelings and a sense of hostility. Words must be soft and arguments hard; if words are hard, they will bring discord. A single harsh word will break the friendship of long years in a minute. Word or sound has got tremendous power. It is Sabda Brahman. It is Sakti.

There is a world of difference between "Just comments" and Ninda (censure). "Just comments" is not Ninda. It is permissible. It is unavoidable too. You can avoid it only when you shut yourself alone in a far-off Himalayan cave. If you have no hatred for a man, if you are not jealous of him and if you point out to your friend in the course of conversation his weaknesses and good virtues also—"Mr. Thomas is an honest, loving, kind, sympathetic man. He is humble. He speaks the truth. But, he is extremely irritable and hot-tempered."—this is not Ninda (censure) at all, although you point out the defect of Mr. Thomas. In Ninda, you vilify a man. You point out his defects only. You exaggerate his weaknesses. You point out the defect to everybody of your own accord without being asked. In your heart of hearts, you are jealous of the man. You want to vilify him.

If you always look into the faults of others, you will actually imbibe those faults by constantly thinking of them. Always look into the bright side of a man. Ignore his defects. Hatred will vanish. Love will increase.

Faultfinding, cavilling and scandalmongering are defects. Defects and weaknesses are two distinct qualities. Anger is a defect. Tea-habit is a weakness. To be over-sentimental is a weakness. Both defects and weaknesses should be removed by substituting the opposite virtues.

HOW TO DESTROY JEALOUSY

There are three ways of destroying jealousy:

(i) Mithya Drishti (Dosha Drishti): "The whole world with its enjoyments, wealth and luxury is quite illusory. What do I gain by being jealous of another?" When anyone thinks like this seriously several times daily, the Vritti of jealousy will slowly die. This Vritti is the root of all miseries. It is deep-rooted.

(ii) Bhratri Bhava (feeling of universal brotherhood). You are not jealous of your intimate friend or loving brother. In these cases, you have become one with your friend or brother. You feel inwardly that all that belong to them is yours. You will have to do this with everybody. You will have to love everybody as your brother or friend. Then you will have no Vritti of jealousy.

(iii) This is a developed stage: Repeat the formula 'I am the all,' 'I am all-in all.' Feel yourself everywhere. Think there is nothing save Atman, your own Self, everywhere. Jealousy will slowly vanish by entertaining this Atma-Bhava. You must always entertain this idea—"*Vasudevah sarvamiti*" (Vasudeva is all). "Vasudeva" means all-pervading. You will have infinite joy which can only be felt. It cannot be adequately described in words.

If you place a big mirror in front of a dog and keep some bread in front, the dog at once barks by looking at its reflection in the mirror. It foolishly imagines that there is another dog. Even so, man sees his own reflection only through his mind-mirror in all the people, but foolishly imagines like the dog that they are all different from him and fights on account of hatred and jealousy.

FEAR—A DIRE DISEASE

Fear is a great human curse. It is a negative thought. It is your worst enemy. It assumes various forms, viz., fear of death, fear of disease, fear of public criticism, fear of losing your property or money, etc. Fear blights many lives, makes people unhappy and unsuccessful.

Some people can bravely face the shell or the shot on the battlefield. But they are afraid of public criticism and public opinion. Some can face a tiger fearlessly in the forest. But they are afraid of the surgeon's knife and bistoury. You should get rid of fear of all sorts.

The power of imagination in the mind intensifies fear. Fear is due to delusion or Moha, attachment to the gross and physical body on account of Avidya (ignorance). Attachment to the body (Moha, Dehadhyasa) is the cause of all fear. He who can throw off the physical sheath (Annamaya Kosha) either by Yoga or Jnana will be free from fear. He who has conquered fear, has conquered everything, has gained mastery over the mind.

Some people faint when they see a copious quantity of blood. Some men cannot see a surgical operation. They faint. These are all mental weaknesses. Some cannot take their food if some faecal or vomited matter is nearby. All mental weaknesses must be eradicated by Vichara.

A calm mind means courage. You may face without fear the trials and difficulties of the spiritual path. It has its root in the recognition of the unity of the Self. "Abhayam" (fearlessness) is one of the Daivi Sampats (divine qualities). Constantly think you are Atman. You will slowly develop immense courage. The one idea that you are the Immortal Self (Atman) can destroy efficiently fear of every description. This is the only potent tonic, the one sure panacea for this dire disease of fear. Think you are immortal (Amrita), fearless (Abhaya) Atman. Slowly the fear will vanish. Develop the positive virtue, namely, courage. Fear will slowly disappear.

DOUBT

Doubt is a great tormentor of mind. It has got a mental world of its own. It again and again troubles a man. There is no end for doubts. If one doubt is removed, another doubt stands ready to take its place. This is the trick of the mind. Cut the knot of doubts by the sword of wisdom. Know him who gets the doubts. No one doubts the doubter. If all doubts vanish through Brahma-Jnana, then the mind will be destroyed.

Thoughts of worry and thoughts of fear are fearful forces within us. They poison the very sources of life and destroy the harmony, the running efficiency, the vitality and vigour; while the opposite thoughts of cheerfulness, joy and courage heal, soothe, instead of irritating and immensely augment efficiency and multiply the mental power. Be always cheerful. Smile. Laugh.

EVIL VRITTIS ARE YOUR REAL ENEMIES—
DESTROY THEM

Who is your real enemy? It is your own Antahkarana (mind) possessed by the evil Vrittis. That mind alone, which is free from attachment, delusion, jealousy, lust, selfishness and anger, can have constant memory of God. If the mirror is dirty, you cannot see your face properly. Even so, if the mind-mirror is dirty through the accumulation of Mala (six passions, Kama, Krodha, etc.), Brahman cannot be reflected in the mind. When it is cleansed thoroughly, when it becomes Sattvic, it is fit (Yogayukta) to reflect Brahman.

Whatever you practise—Karma Yoga or Bhakti Yoga or Raja Yoga or Jnana Yoga—, you must be free from jealousy, hatred, attachment, pride and egoism and you must have control over Indriyas. Chitta-Suddhi—Yama and Niyama—is a common element in all kinds of Yoga. What can a man do in Karma Yoga if he has no self-restraint, if he is extremely selfish? If you want everything for yourself, if you are luxurious and if you have not reduced your wants, how can you spare something for others? You can unite with the cosmos only through love, unselfish service and disinterested charity.

Aspirants should totally abandon all the evil Vrittis described above. These constitute what is known as Asur. Sampat (devilish qualities). Whether you live in a town or in a cave of the Himalayas, it is all the same when you have a ruffled mind. You carry your own thoughts with you even if you remove yourself to a far-off, lonely cave. The mind remains the same. Peace comes from within. Irritation, anger, impatience, revenge, suspicion, prejudice, grudge, dislike, intolerance, restlessness, depression, fired or heated feelings—all these must be totally removed by spiritual Sadhana, by developing Sattvic qualities, by meditation on OM, by constant Vichara. Then only can peace be obtained. By developing Daivi Sampat (divine qualities) such as Karuna, Satya, Ahimsa, Brahmacharya, Daya, etc., the devilish qualities will be overcome.

PRATIPAKSHA-BHAVANA OR
THE METHOD OF SUBSTITUTION

It is the method of substitution, Pratipaksha-Bhavana. When

there is a lustful thought, substitute thoughts of purity. Begin to study the Gita or the Upanishads. Sing Hari's Bhajana on harmonium. Impure thoughts will vanish. When there is hatred, substitute thoughts of love. Think of the good qualities of the man whom you hate. Remember again and again his kind actions. Serve him with sweets, fruits and milk. Talk to him kind words. Laugh with him. Shampoo his legs. Take him to be Lord Siva or Narayana when you serve him. Hatred will disappear. When there is fear, fill the mind with thoughts of courage. When there is irritability, meditate on the virtues of tolerance, patience and self-restraint. The negative thoughts will die of themselves. If you are depressed, fill the mind with the idea of joy and exhilaration. If you are sick, fill the mind with ideas of health, strength, power and vitality. Practise this. Practise this. Herein lies a great treasure for you.

Every thought or emotion or mood produces a strong vibration in every cell of the body and leaves a strong impression there. If you know the method of raising an opposite thought or counter-thought, then only you can lead a happy, harmonious life of peace and power. A thought of love will at once neutralise a thought of hatred. A thought of courage will immediately serve as a powerful antidote against a thought of fear.

Idea creates the world. Idea brings one into existence. Idea develops the desires and excites the passions. So, a contrary idea of killing the desires and passions will counteract the former idea of satisfying the desires. So, when a man will be impressed with this, a contrary idea will help him to destroy his desires and passions.

How can you ignore an evil thought? By forgetting. How can you forget? By not indulging in it again. How can you prevent the mind from indulging in it again? By thinking of something else which is more interesting. IGNORE. FORGET. THINK OF SOMETHING INTERESTING. This is a great Sadhana. Call to mind the sublime ideas contained in the Gita. Remember the ennobling and soul-elevating ideas embodied in the Upanishads and the Yogavasishtha. Argue, cogitate, reflect, ratiocinate within—subjectively. Worldly thoughts, thoughts of enmity, hatred, revenge, anger, lust—all will die.

When there are diseases, discord, disharmony in the cells of the body owing to influence of vicious thoughts, worry-thoughts, fear-thoughts, hatred-thoughts, jealousy-thoughts, lustful thoughts, you can neutralise the poison or canker in these diseased, morbid cells and establish peace, harmony, health, new vigour and vitality by entertaining sublime, soul-stirring, life-giving, soul-awakening, Sattvic, divine thoughts, by vibrations of 'OM' chanting, by repetition of the different Names of the Lord, by Pranayama, Kirtana (singing of the Name of the Lord), study of the Gita and the holy scriptures, by meditation, etc. Think constantly that you are Suddha Sat-Chit-Ananda Vyapaka Atman. All the evil propensities will vanish and the Sattvic virtues will manifest themselves.

Do not exert to destroy the different Vrittis—Kama, Krodha, Dvesha, etc. If you can destroy one Vritti Ahankara, all other Vrittis will die by themselves. Ahankara is the corner-stone of the edifice of Jiva. If the corner-stone is removed, the whole edifice of Jiva will tumble down. This is the secret.

Why are you afraid of Kama, Krodha, etc.? They are your servants. You are Sat-Chit-Ananda Atman. Assert the majesty and magnanimity of the Self.

CHAPTER 29

CULTIVATION OF VIRTUES

Maitri (friendliness), Karuna (compassion), Daya (sympathy), Visva-Prema (cosmic or universal love), Kshama (forgiveness), Dhriti (spiritual patience), Titiksha (power of endurance, forbearance) and tolerance are Sattvic qualities of the mind. They contribute to the peace and happiness of human beings. They should be cultivated to a very high degree.

Love and pity make the mind soft. Pity has the characteristic feature of evolving the mode of removing pain; the property of not being able to bear seeing others suffer; the manifestation of not harming; the proximate cause of seeing the need of those overcome by pain. Its consummation is the suppression of harming; its failure is the production of sorrow.

Patience, tenacity, Utsaha (perseverance) and determination are indispensable for success in Self-realisation. They should be developed to a maximum degree, particularly by spiritual aspirants. When you meditate on OM, when you assert yourself as Brahman in the morning meditation, you will gain a lot of strength. That will help to give you courage that is needed for the progress in the spiritual path. Many difficulties on the path of Truth are to be overcome through the help of fortitude and endurance (Titiksha). These qualities are the forms of courage. Fortitude is mental power of endurance. It is firmness in meeting danger. It is power of resistance.

THE TEN LAKSHANAS OF DHARMA

"Dhritih kshama damo'steyam saucham-indriyanigrahah
Dheer-vidya satyam-akrodho dasakam dharmalakshanam"
(Manusmriti, VI-92)

Patience, forgiveness, control of mind, non-stealing, external and internal purity, control of Indriyas, knowledge of Sastras, knowledge of Atman, truthfulness and absence of anger are the ten Lakshanas of Dharma according to Manu.

Your thoughts must agree with the word. This is Arjava (straightforwardness). Practise this. You will derive wonderful benefits. If you practise Satya for twelve years, you will get

Vak-Siddhi. Whatever you speak will come to pass. Chinta (anxiety) will vanish. You will be free from committing many evil actions by speaking the truth.

Patience, perseverance, application, interest, faith, zeal, enthusiasm, determination are necessary during Sadhana. Sraddha and Bhakti are noble Vrittis that help a man to free himself from bondage. These virtues have to be cultivated. Then only is success possible. Look at the various difficulties that crop up in the way. The spiritual line is, therefore, difficult. Very few take to the path, one in thousands (according to the Gita). Out of them very few succeed. Many give up Sadhana when they are half-way, as they find it difficult to pull on till the end is reached. It is only the Dhira (firm) with Dhriti, Dhairya and Utsaha that reaches the goal of Sat-Chit-Ananda state. Hail, hail, to such rare noble souls!

CHAPTER 30

HOW TO CONTROL THE MIND

"*Manojaya eva mahajayah*—Conquest of mind is the greatest victory."

"*Man jita, jag jita*—If you conquer mind, you have conquered the world."
(*Hindi Proverb*)

In Hindu philosophy, you will always find an esoteric and an exoteric meaning. This is the reason why you need the help of a teacher. It is extremely difficult to comprehend the esoteric, inner meaning. You will find in Hatha Yogic books: "There is a young, virgin widow seated at the junction of the Ganga and the Yamuna." What will you make out of this? It is difficult to understand. The young widow is the Sushumna Nadi. The Ganga is Pingala Nadi. The Yamuna is Ida Nadi.

In Katha Upanishad, you will find a word whose meaning is brick. 'Brick' means here 'Devata' or deity.

THE SECRET OF RAMAYANA

There is also a Rahasya (secret) of Ramayana. The secret of Ramayana is control of mind. Killing the ten-headed monster Ravana of Lanka means the annihilation of the ten evil Vrittis of the mind such as Kama, Krodha, etc. Sita is mind. Rama is Suddha-Brahman. Bringing Sita back from Lanka is concentrating the mind on Rama (Brahman) by withdrawing it from Vishaya (objects) and uniting it with Rama. Sita (mind) unites with Rama (Brahman), her husband in Ayodhya (Sahasrara Chakra). Mind merges in Brahman. This is, briefly, the esoteric meaning of Ramayana. This is the Adhyatmic exposition of Ramayana.

MASTERY OF MIND, THE ONLY GATEWAY TO MOKSHA

On this side is matter; on the other side is pure Spirit (Atman or Brahman). Mind forms a bridge between the two. Cross the bridge (control the mind). You will attain Brahman.

He is a real potentate and a Maharaja who has conquered the mind. He is the richest man who has conquered desires, passions and the mind. If the mind is under control, it matters little whether you stay in a palace or a cave in the Himalayas like Vasishtha-Guha, fourteen miles from Rishikesh, where Swami Ramatirtha lived, whether you do active Vyavahara or sit in silence.

It is, indeed, a rare thing to find a mind that is not affected by its contact with fluctuation. Like heat which is inseparable from fire, fluctuation which debases the mind, is inseparable from it. Devoid of this fluctuation, the mind ceases to exist. It is this fluctuation-potency of the mind that you should destroy through ceaseless Atma-Jnana enquiry.

Mind is the cause of Sankalpa-Vikalpa. Therefore, you must control the mind. You must bind it.

True freedom results from the disenthralment of the mind. Reflection of the Self made upon the mind cannot be perceptible when the mind is not free from its fluctuations, as the reflection of the moon made upon the surface of a turbulent ocean cannot be visible or perceptible. To attain Self-realisation, one must constantly struggle with the mind for its purification and steadiness. It is only the power of the will which can control it and stop its fluctuations. With the triple weapon of strong desire, Sraddha (faith) and strong will-power, you can have sanguine success in any attempt you undertake. If the mind is purged of all its impurities and worldly taints, it will become exceedingly calm. All fluctuations of the mind will cease. Then the supreme Nishtha (meditation) will supervene. Then all Samsaric delusion, attendant with its births and deaths, will come to an end. Then you will get Parama Dhama (supreme abode of peace).

There is no other vessel on this earth on which one can cross the ocean of metempsychosis than the mastery of the antagonistic mind. They alone will reach the world of Moksha who have controlled the serpent of mind replete with desires and impure Vasanas.

To lovers of Moksha, in whom the invincible desires have been destroyed and who try to win their way up to Salvation through their own efforts, the easy abandonment of their dire mind is itself their transcendental path and they then feel as if a great load were off their heads. No other path is truly beneficial.

If you get the mastery over the mind and get true Jnana or illumination after destroying Ahankara and subjugating the

Indriyas (organs), you will be doubtless free from the trammels of births and deaths. The differentiations such as 'I,' 'you,' 'he' will vanish. All tribulations, annoyances, miseries, grief will cease with the destruction of the mind.

WHO CAN CONTROL THE MIND?

The mind can be controlled by untiring perseverance and patience equal to that of one engaged in emptying the ocean, drop by drop, with the tip of a blade of grass.

A bird laid its eggs on the seashore. The waves came in and washed away the eggs. The bird became very angry. It wanted to empty the ocean with its beak. It applied all its energy in emptying the ocean. The king of the birds pitied its condition and came to its help. Narada, the peace-making Rishi, also came and gave some advice to the bird. When the king of the ocean saw all these, he was very much terrified. He brought back all the eggs of the bird and handed them over to the bird with apology and prostrations. Sadhakas (aspirants), who are attempting to control the mind, should have the same asinine patience and untiring perseverance as that of the bird which attempted to empty the ocean with its small beak.

You must have the knack or the pluck or the aptitude to tame the mind. To tame a lion or a tiger is far more easy than taming one's own mind. Tame your own mind first. Then you can take the minds of others quite easily.

MIND IS THE CAUSE OF BONDAGE AND LIBERATION

Mind is the cause of bondage and salvation of man. "*Mana eva manushyanam karanam bandhamokshayoh*"—The mind has two aspects—one is discriminative and the other is imaginative. Mind, in its aspect of discrimination, releases itself from the bondage and attains Moksha. In its aspect of imagination, it binds itself to the world.

It is the mind which binds a man to this world; where there is no mind, there is no bondage. Mind imagines, through indiscrimination and ignorance, that the soul has been confined and located in this body and hence it perceives the soul to be in bondage. Mind exactly identifies itself with the Jivatman and feels itself to be 'I' and hence thinks, 'I am in bondage.' The egoistic mind is the root of bondage. The non-egoistic mind is the root of Moksha.

DESTROY MIND THROUGH MIND

The sovereign specific presented by the wise sages for the eradication of the mind's disease can be had easily through the mind alone. The intelligent cleanse a dirty cloth with the dirty earth only. A murderous Agni-Astra (missile) is counteracted by Varuna-Astra. The venom of serpent-bite is removed by its antidote of an edible poison. So also is the case with Jiva. Having developed discrimination, destroy the delusions of the heterogeneous mind through the one-pointed Manas, like an iron severing another iron.

PURIFY THE MIND

You must be saved from the malformation and the miscarriage of your mind. Mind is like a playful child. The clamant energies of the mind must be bent to become the passive channels for the transmission of truth. The mind must be filled with Sattva (purity). It should be trained to think of Truth or God constantly.

The Yoga system requires us to go through a course of mental and spiritual discipline. The Upanishads also emphasise the practice of austere virtues before the goal can be reached. Tapas destroys sins, weakens the Indriyas, purifies the Chitta and leads to Ekagrata (one-pointedness of mind).

The penances will give you mental quiet and remove the restlessness of the mind which is a great obstacle to knowledge. The life of celibacy (Brahmacharya), where you will have no family attachment to perturb your mind, would enable you to give whole-hearted attention to your spiritual Sadhana. If you practise Satya and Brahmacharya, you will become fearless (Nirbhaya). You will eventually realise Brahman also. Get hold of one thing firmly with leech-like tenacity. Sraddha or faith is necessary.

Arsenic, when purified and administered in proper doses, is a blessing. It removes many diseases. It improves the blood. When it is not purified properly and given in overdoses, it brings about many ill-effects. Even so, when the mind is rendered pure and Nirvishaya, it leads on to Moksha. When it is impure and Vishayasakta (fond of sensual objects), it leads on to bondage.

Blessed are the pure in heart, for they will have Darshan of the Lord. The heart must be pure. The eye also must be chaste in its look. There is a tongue in the eye. A lustful eye wants to taste the different types of beauty for its selection. Lust of the eyes is as much dangerous as lust of the flesh. Beauty of nature emanates from the Lord. Train the eye properly. Let it see Atman everywhere.

The Yogic methods give directions as to how you should purify and refine the mind and improve the mirror and keep it clean by getting rid of the impurities such as lust, anger, greed, vanity, jealousy, etc. The aim of Dana, Japa, Vrata, Tirtha-Yatra, Seva, Daya, Svadhyaya, Agnihotra, Yajna is purification of the mind.

The Sermon on the Mount by Lord Jesus is the essence of Raja-Yogic Yama practice. It is difficult to put the teachings into practice. But, if they are put into practice, mind can be easily controlled.

This is the summary of the Sermon:

(1) "Blessed are the poor in spirit; for theirs is the kingdom of heaven."

(2) "Blessed are they that mourn; for they shall be comforted."

(3) "Blessed are the meek; for they shall inherit the earth."

(4) "Blessed are they who do hunger and thirst after righteousness; for they shall be filled."

(5) "Blessed are the merciful; for they shall obtain mercy."

(6) "Blessed are the pure in heart; for they shall see God."

(7) "Blessed are the peace-makers; for they shall be called the children of God."

(8) "Blessed are they who are persecuted for righteousness' sake; for theirs is the kingdom of heaven."

(9) "Blessed are ye, when men shall revile you, and persecute you, and shall say all manner of evil against you falsely, for my sake. Rejoice, and be exceedingly glad; for great is the reward in heaven; for so persecuted they the prophets which were before you."

(10) "But I say unto you, that ye resist not evil; but whosoever shall smite on thy right cheek, turn to him the other also."

(11) "And if any man shall sue thee in the law and take away thy coat, let him have thy cloak also."

(12) "Love your enemies as thyself, bless them that curse you, do good to them that hate you, and pray for them which despitefully use you, and persecute you."

Before you go to work daily, study once carefully this Sermon of Lord Jesus in the morning and remember the teachings once or twice during the course of the day. In course of time, you will be able to regulate your emotions and moods, cultivate virtue and eradicate vice. You will have immense peace and will-force.

The spiritual path is rugged, thorny and precipitous. Sruti declares: "*Kshurasya dhara nisita duratyaya durgam pathastat kavayo vadanti*,—The path is as sharp as the edge of a razor and impassable; that path, the intelligents say, is hard to go by." The thorns must be weeded out with patience and perseverance. Some of the thorns are internal; some are external. Lust, greed, wrath, delusion, vanity, etc., are the internal thorns. Company with the evil-minded persons is the worst of all the external thorns. Therefore, shun ruthlessly evil company.

DO GOOD AND INTROSPECT

Do always virtuous actions. Watch the mind and see what it is doing. These two methods are quite sufficient to control the mind.

Awaken your spiritual Samskaras by Satsanga, Japa, etc. Protect them. Develop them. Nourish them. Vichara, Sadhana, Nididhyasana, Satsanga will all pave a long way in the control of the mind and the attainment of Moksha.

Introspect. Have an inner life always. Let a portion of the mind and hands do their work mechanically. An acrobat girl, while exhibiting her performances, has her attention riveted on the water-pot she bears on her head although all the time she is dancing to various tunes. So does truly pious man attend to all his business concerns, but has his mind's eye fixed upon the blissful feet of the Lord. This is Karma-Yoga and Jnana-Yoga combined. This will lead to integral development. This is balance. This is synthetic Yoga. Some Vedantins have one-sided development. This is not good.

DO KIRTAN

A serpent is very fond of music. If you sing Punnagavarali tune melodiously, the serpent will come in front of you. Mind also is like a serpent. It likes melodious tunes very much. It can be entrapped very easily by sweet sounds.

Fix the mind on the sweet Anahata sounds that emanate from the heart by closing the ears. It can be controlled quite easily by this method. This is Laya-Yoga. The Ganika Pingala fixed her mind on the "Rama, Rama" sound uttered by the parrot and attained Bhava-Samadhi. Ramaprasad of Bengal, a famous Bhakta, controlled the mind through music. Music exercises a tremendous, soothing influence on a ruffled mind. In America, doctors use music in curing many diseases, particularly of nervous origin. Music elevates the mind also.

Kirtan, which is one of the nine forms of worship (Navavidha Bhakti) causes Bhava-Samadhi (union with God through Bhava or feeling). It is prevalent throughout India. It corresponds to the singing of hymns by Christians. Ramaprasad realised God through Kirtan. His songs are very famous in Bengal. In this Kali-Yuga or Iron Age, Kirtan is an easy way to God-realisation. Sing the Name of Hari constantly. Praise constantly His qualities. You will have Darshan of Hari. Those who can sing well should retire to a solitary place and sing heartily with Suddha Bhava. In course of time, they will enter into Bhava-Samadhi. There is no doubt about it.

ALWAYS THINK OF GOD

CONSTANTLY THINK OF GOD. YOU CAN VERY EASILY CONTROL THE MIND. Even if you think of Lord Vishnu or Siva only once, even if you once form a mental image of these deities, the Sattvic material will increase a bit. If you think a crore of times, your mind will be filled with a large quantity of Sattva. Constant thinking of God thins out the mind and destroys the Vasanas and Sankalpas.

When you fix your mind on Lord Krishna in the lotus of your heart, your attention is fixed on the figure of Lord Krishna. When the attention is fixed, the spiritual current is started. When you meditate, the flow of the current becomes steady and when the meditation gets very deep and intense, 'Union' (Samadhi) takes place. You become one with the Lord. All

Sankalpas and Vikalpas stop. There is complete 'Chitta-Vritti-Nirodha' (restraint of the modifications of the mind).

PRACTISE PRANAYAMA

To bring about control of mind, two things are essential, viz., Prana-Nirodha (control of Prana) and Sanga-Tyaga (renunciation of Sanga or association). By the latter is meant dissociation, not with the world, but only with the longing after or the attraction towards the objects of the world.

Pranayama or control of breath checks the velocity of the mind and reduces the quantity of thinking. It removes the dross (impurities) in the form of Rajas and Tamas from the mind.

For control of the mind, Kumbhaka (retention of breath) is indispensable. You will have to practise Kumbhaka daily. You will have to practise Puraka, Kumbhaka and Rechaka (inhalation, retention and exhalation of breath) regularly and rhythmically. Then the mind will become Ekagra. The period of Kumbhaka will increase by systematic practice, with regulated diet and proper dietetic discipline (light, nutritious, Sattvic food). This is the Hathayogic method. The practice of Kumbhaka must be done under the guidance of a Guru who is a developed Yogin.

PRACTISE SAMA AND DAMA

Uparati of mind (calmness) comes through the practice of Sama and Dama. Sama is calmness of mind induced by the eradication of Vasanas. Vasana-Tyaga (renunciation of desires) through discrimination constitutes the practice of Sama, one of the sixfold virtues (Shatsampatti). If a desire arises in your mind, do not give way to it. This will become the practice of Sama. Sama is keeping the mind in the heart by Sadhana. Sama is restraint of the mind by not allowing it to externalise or objectify. The restraint of the external activities and the Indriyas is the practice of Dama (Bahyavrittinigraha).

If you renounce the desire for eating mangoes, it is Sama. If you do not allow the feet to carry you to the bazaar to purchase the mangoes, if you do not allow the eyes to see the mangoes and if you do not allow the tongue to taste them, it is Dama.

A desire arises to eat sweets. You do not allow the feet to move to the bazaar to purchase the sweets. You do not allow the tongue to eat the sweets. You do not allow the eyes to see the sweets also. This kind of restraint of the Indriyas is termed Dama.

It is termed Sama when you do not allow any thought to arise in the mind concerning sweets by eradication of Vasanas (Vasana-Tyaga). This eradication of the Vasanas can be accomplished through Vichara, Brahma-Chintana, Japa, Dhyana, Pranayama, etc.

Sama is an internal restraint. Dama is a restraint of the Indriyas. Though the practice of Sama includes the practice of Dama, as the Indriyas will not move and work without the help of the mind, yet the practice of Dama is necessary. The practice of Dama should go hand in hand with Sama. Sama alone will not suffice. You must attack the enemy, desire, from within and without. Then alone you can control the mind quite easily. Then alone the mind will be in perfect control.

DEVELOP VAIRAGYA

Those who practise Vairagya are real tamers of their minds. Have no longing for objects. Avoid them. Vairagya thins out the mind. Vairagya is a drastic purgative for the mind. The thief-mind shudders and trembles when it hears the words, 'Vairagya,' 'Tyaga,' 'Sannyasa.' It gets a death-blow when it hears these three terms.

Destroy all the pleasure-centres of the mind such as frequently eating dainty dishes, gossiping, sightseeing, music and company of women slowly and cautiously. Keep up three Sattvic pleasure-centres such as study of books dealing with Atma-Jnana, meditation and service of humanity. When you advance in meditation, give up service and study also for some time. After you have attained Nirvikalpa state, preach, work and distribute divine knowledge (Jnana Yajna of the Gita, XVIII-70).

Whatever object the mind likes much must be given up. Whatever object the mind dwells upon constantly, thinks about very often, must be abandoned. If you like brinjals or apples much, give them up first. You will gain a great deal of peace, will-power and control of mind.

Suppose you like tea, mangoes, grapes and sweets very much. Make it a point to renounce them and even the desire for these objects. After some months, the craving or the hankering will be attenuated and will slowly vanish. You must be devoting three or four hours daily in proper prayer, Japa and meditation of God. The above objects which used to attract you before very much seem very loathsome now. They present the very reverse of your former feelings. They give you intense pain. This is a sign of true Vairagya (dispassion) and destruction of the mind.

If all objects which have an enchanting appearance become eyesores and present the very reverse of the former feelings, then know that the mind is destroyed. When the mind is changed, the objects which gave you pleasure before will give you pain. That is the sign of annihilation of the mind.

Things which used to upset you easily will not touch you now. Occasions which would have made you irritable do not make you so now. You have gained strength, power and endurance, power of resistance, power to deal with troubles. Certain unkind words from other people which used to torment you, no longer give you the trouble now. Even if you become irritable and show signs of anger, you are able now to compose yourself quickly. These are all the signs of your gaining mental strength and will-power. Meditation brings about all these beneficial results.

When there is quiescence in the mind and an indifference in it towards all enjoyments and when the powerful Indriyas are turned inwards and the Ajnana of the mind is destroyed, then and then only all the noble words of the wise Guru will infiltrate and spread in the mind of the disciple, just as rose-coloured water impinges on a perfectly white cloth.

HAVE SANTOSHA

The mind is ease-loving, easy-going and happy-go-lucky. You must check this nature. The desire for ease and comfort is ingrained in the mind. Aspirants should be very cautious and careful. Do not try to fulfil your desires. This is one way of controlling the mind.

You must not take back those things which you have once renounced. Whenever you give up an object, the desire for that particular object becomes keen and strong for a few days. It agitates your mind. Keep quiet. Stand firm. It gets thinned out and dies eventually. Whenever the mind hisses to get back the objects that are rejected, raise the rod of Viveka. It will lower down its hood. It will keep quiet.

You must not give indulgence or leniency to the mind. If you increase your wants even by one article, the articles will begin to swell in number. Luxuries will come one by one. If you allow it to take one luxury today, it wants two tomorrow. Luxuries will increase daily. It will become like an overfondled child. Spare the rod and spoil the child; this also applies to the mind. It is worse than the child. You will have to punish it by fasting for every serious mistake it does. Keep the organs in their proper places. Do not allow them to move an inch. Raise the rod of Viveka whenever an organ hisses to raise its head. By this practice you will get a concentrated mind. Those who, without longing for objects, avoid them can be termed the subjugators of their minds.

Those who are not content with anything that comes in their way are of weak minds only. Santosha (contentment in the mind) is a very great virtue. "Santoshat paramam labham—by contentment, you will have great gain." It is one of the four sentinels of the vast domain of Moksha. If you have this virtue, it will lead to the attainment of Satsanga (association with the wise), Vichara (enquiry of Self) and Santi (peace).

When you do not want to store things for tomorrow, it is called "Asangraha Buddhi." It is the mental state of a true Sannyasin. A Sannyasin has no thought of tomorrow; whereas a householder has, on the opposite, Sangraha Buddhi. We must be as free as a lark which has no "Sangraha Buddhi."

TAKE EVERYTHING AS IT COMES

Take everything as it comes, instead of complaining. By this means, one seizes every opportunity. One develops easily, gains a great deal of mental strength and evenness of mind. Irritability vanishes. Power of endurance and patience will develop.

If you have to live amidst noise, do not complain of it, but profit by it. One may make use of outer disturbances for the practice of concentration. You must develop the power to work undisturbed by whatsoever may happen nearby. The power comes with practice and it is then useful in a variety of ways. To learn to work under different conditions means progress and a great deal of mental control.

HAVE RECOURSE TO SATSANGA

Without being impressed with a clear idea of the nature of the mind, you cannot bridle it. A sublime thought checks the mind and a base idea excites it. It is necessary for a man to keep company with spiritual men and to avoid the company of the dregs of society.

Company of spiritual persons and good environments play a tremendous part in the elevation of the mind. Satsanga helps a long way in the attainment of Moksha. There is no other way. It thoroughly overhauls the mind and changes the current and its Rajasic nature. It removes the old Vishaya-Samskaras and fills the mind with Sattvic Samskaras. It destroys the three fires—Adhyatmic, Adhibhautic and Adhidaivic Tapa—and cools the Antahkarana. It destroys Moha. If you can have Satsanga, you need not go to any Tirtha. It is Tirtha of Tirthas. Wherever there is Satsanga, the sacred Triveni is already there.

Annihilate this mind of Ajnana (ignorance) through the power of constant association with holy men (Satsanga). In the absence of positive good company, have negative good company of books written by realised persons and books dealing with Atma-Jnana (spiritual knowledge) such as Sri Sankara's works, Yogavasishtha, Sri Dattatreya's Avadhuta Gita, the Upanishads, the Brahma-Sutras, Atma-Purana, Sarva-Vedanta-Siddhanta-Sara-Sangraha, Sri Sankaracharya's Aparokshanubhuti, etc., etc.

Study of inspiring books helps spiritual Sadhana but too much study brings about muddy condition of the brain. When you come down from meditation, you can study occasionally for a short time books like Avadhuta-Gita, Yogavasishtha, Katha-Upanishad, Brihadaranyaka-Upanishad. This will elevate the mind.

If you are in the company of Sannyasins, if you read books on Yoga, Vedanta, etc., a mental adhesion takes place in the mind for attaining God-consciousness. Mere mental adhesion will not help you much either. Burning Vairagya, burning Mumukshutva, capacity for spiritual Sadhana, intent and constant application and Nididhyasana (meditation) are needed. Then only is Self-realisation possible.

ANNIHILATE SANKALPAS

The ideas of differentiation of this person or that person or 'I' or 'thou' or of this or that object do pertain to the mind only. Put an end to the mind with the sword of Abhavana (non-thought). Kill the soldiers one by one when they emerge out of the fort. Eventually you can get hold of the fortress. Even so, destroy every thought one by one as it arises in the mind. Eventually you can conquer the mind.

If you can do the extinction of all sorts of Kalpanas (imaginations, thoughts), like thick clouds that are dispersed through stormy gales, the mind will get absorbed into the Source, Chit (Absolute Consciousness). Then you will be free from all sorts of tribulations and worries and miseries. Then only you will have perennial happiness and the wealth of Moksha.

Mind is Maya. If the mind runs towards the sensual objects wildly, Maya takes a stronghold of the man. Maya havocs through the mind. This lower impulsive mind drags you down in all kinds of petty sensual enjoyments and deludes you in a variety of ways. Maya, through her power, raises millions of Sankalpas in the mind. The Jiva becomes a prey to the Sankalpas.

This lower Manas cannot approach those who have a strong Viveka (power of discrimination) between Sat and Asat (the real and the unreal). Maya is very easy to be detected and Self to be realised by men who possess discrimination and strong determination. Through these powers, viz., Viveka and will, it can be controlled.

Slay the lower mind, the enemy of Atman through the higher and Sattvic mind. Use your Vichara, Viveka and pure reason constantly when objects trouble you, delude you. After reason has dispersed the darkness of the illusions of sense which cover the mind, it still returns to those things which are deceitful as the appearance of water on sandy deserts. Again and again, exercise your reason till you are established in knowledge. The power of Avidya is great, indeed.

Renounce desires; renounce Sankalpas of objects. Cultivate Vairagya. Give up this little false 'I.' All the Sankalpas encircle and envelop this 'I.' Do not pay much heed to the body. Think of the body and its wants as little as possible.

Have no Sankalpa. The fluctuating mind will die by itself. It will melt in Brahman (Arupa Manonasa). Then you will have the

Sakshatkara (Beatific vision of Atman). When the mind dies, 'I,' 'you,' 'he,' 'this,' 'that,' time, space, Jiva, Jagat, all will dwindle into nothing. Idea of inside and outside will vanish. There will be only one experience of the One, Akhanda (the indivisible) Chidakasa which is Paripurna (all-full). All the doubts and delusions will disappear through the Jnana in the heart.

DESTROY THE EGO

You should try to destroy not only the thoughts (Sankalpas), but the mind itself and the Aham Vritti that identifies with the body and the Vyavaharic Buddhi that creates the Jiva-Bhava and differences in the world. Then you will be established in Svarupa (Sahaja-Sat-Chit-Ananda-Nirvikalpa) state. That is the real Mouna state or Advaita Brahmanishtha. Control of mind includes control of Buddhi and the annihilation of the little 'I,' the false self-arrogating personality.

Lord Jesus says, "Empty thyself and I will fill thee." The meaning is: "Destroy your egoism. You will be filled with God." This emptying means "Yogas-chittavrittinirodhah—restraining all the mental modifications." This emptying process or "making the mind blank" is, no doubt, a trying discipline. But, continued practice of an intense type will bring success. There is no doubt about this. It is only through the rigorous discipline that you can rise to that height of strenuous impersonality from which the gifted souls of the world see distant visions and enjoy a higher, divine life.

If the mind is divested of all the Sankalpas of 'I,' then, through meditation of Atman after being initiated by a Guru and having known the real significance of the Vedas, the mind can be turned back from various pains and made to rest on the subjective blissful Atman.

PRACTISE BRAHMA-VICHARA

Do not wrestle or struggle with the mind. It is wastage of energy. It is great strain and drain on the will-force. Do not fight with the mind. Live in Truth. Live in OM. Live in Atman through Vichara, Brahma-Bhavana and Nididhyasana. All obstacles, all disturbing factors, all emotions will vanish of themselves. Try, practise, feel and realise the usefulness of the Vichara method. Perfect control of mind can be effected only through

Brahma-Vichara. Pranayama, Japa and various other methods are only auxiliaries.

DO NOT LET FAILURES DISCOURAGE YOU

Do not let failures discourage you, but go on doing your best. Do not brood over your faults and failures. Only look at them to see the reason why you failed and then, try again. So doing, you will starve out the tendencies which led you into them; whereas, thinking about them only gives them new strength. Do not make too much fuss about little failures. Do not sit down and brood over failures.

There are some people who have got the habit of trying to do one thing while thinking of another. These people always fail in undertakings. The thinking part of the mind should work in harmony with the acting part of the mind. While attending to any one object, our thoughts ought not to wander on another. While you are reading, think of reading only. Do not think of cricket match. While you are playing in a cricket match, do not think of studies. The frequent cause of failure is striving to think of more than one thing at a time.

Whenever you observe Niyama (religious observances) do it to the letter rigidly. Do not say, "I will do it as far as possible." This term 'as far as possible' will give leniency to the mind. The mind will be simply waiting for an opportunity and it will yield to the first temptation quite readily, whenever the first chance arises. Be strict, therefore.

CHECK THE WANDERING HABIT OF THE MIND

The mind in the vast majority of persons has been allowed to run wild and follow its own sweet will and desire. It is ever changing and wandering. It jumps from one object to another. It is fickle. It wants variety. Monotony brings disgust. It is like a spoiled child who is given to much indulgence by its parents or a badly trained animal. The minds of many of us are like menageries of wild animals, each pursuing the bent of its own nature and going its own way. Restraint of the mind is a thing unknown to the vast majority of persons.

This wandering habit of the mind manifests itself in various ways. You will have to be alert always to check this wandering habit of the mind. A householder's mind wanders to cinema, theatre, circus, etc. A Sadhu's mind wanders to Varanasi, Vrindavana and Nasik. Many Sadhus do not stick to one place during Sadhana. The wandering habit of the mind must be controlled by rendering it chaste and constant by Vichara. The mind must be trained to stick to one place for five years during your meditative life, to one method of Sadhana, to one path of Yoga—either Karma, Bhakti or Vedanta—to one spiritual objective and to one guide. "A rolling stone gathers no moss." When you take up a book for study, you must finish it before you take up another. When you take up any work, you must devote your whole-hearted attention to the work on hand and finish it before you take up another work. "One thing at a time and that done well is a very good rule as many can tell." This is Yogin's way of doing. This is a very good rule for success in life.

Do not have a goat's mind or a prostitute's heart. A goat grazes for a few seconds in one patch of green grass and then immediately jumps to a far distant patch, even though there is plenty of grass to eat in the first patch. Even so, a wavering mind jumps from one Sadhana to another Sadhana, from one Guru to another Guru, from Bhakti Yoga to Vedanta, from Rishikesh to Vrindavana. This is extremely deleterious for the Sadhana. Stick to one Guru, one place, one form of Yoga, one kind of Sadhana. Be steady and firm. Then only, you will succeed. Have a steady, resolute mind.

Discipline the mind. Tell the mind, "O Mind! Be steady. Be fixed on one idea. Absolute is the only Reality." If it wanders, if it wavers, go to a lonely place, give two or three sharp slaps on your face. Then the mind will become steady. Self-punishment helps a lot in checking the wandering mind. Frighten the mind as if you will beat it with a whip or rod, whenever it wanders from the Lakshya, whenever it entertains evil thoughts.

Mind tempts and deceives you through object. Distance lends enchantment to the view. Until you attain the object, it will seem to you as a pleasurable object from a distance. When you actually get it, it becomes a source of vexation and pain. Desire is mixed with pain. Objects are so delusive that they often deceive even the wise in this way. He is a really wise man who can detect the illusive nature of these objects.

Mind always tempts you to have various sightseeing. It is all vain trick of the mind to divert you from the goal. Use your Viveka always. Address the mind thus: "O foolish mind, have you not seen before, various places and scenery? What is there in sightseeing? Rest in Atman within. It is self-contained. You can see everything there. It is Purnakama; it is Purnarupa. (It contains all forms; it is Beauty of beauties). What are you going to see outside? Is it not the same sky, the same earth, the same passions, the same eating, the same gossiping, the same sleeping, the same latrines, the same urinals, the same cemeteries everywhere?"

In the beginning, I used to give a long rope to my mind. It will whisper to me, "Let me go to Allahabad Kumbha Mela." I would say, "My dear friend, my mind! You can go now." As soon as I return, I would ask, "O mind, are you satisfied now? What did you enjoy there?" It would hide itself and drop down its head in utter shame. Gradually, it left off its old habits and became my true friend, guide and Guru through true counsels it imparts in the way of obtaining the highest goal.

Do not allow the mind to wander here and there like the strolling street dog. Keep it under your control always. Then alone you can be happy. It must be ever ready to obey you, to carry out your behests. If the mind says to you, "Go eastward," then go westward. If the mind says to you, "Go southward," then march northward. If the mind says to you, "Take a hot cup of tea in winter," then take a cup of icy cold water. Swim like fish against the mental current. You will control the mind quite easily.

Order the mind to do a thing which it does not relish and it will revolt. Coax and it will obey.

If the mind is deprived of its pleasure-centres of all sense-objects, it clings to Vairagya and Tyaga and must naturally move towards Atman. Renounce everything mentally and destroy the mind through the attainment of Atma-Jnana. Rest in the self-existent Brahmic seat. It is only through dauntless energy that the painless wealth of Moksha can be acquired.

CHANGE THE HABITS

Mind is a bundle of habits. Bad habits and prejudices hidden in one's nature will necessarily be brought to the surface of the mind when the proper opportunity comes. If you change the habits, you can also change your character. You sow an act; you reap a habit. You sow a habit; you reap a character. You sow a character; you reap a destiny. Habits originate in the conscious mind. But, when they become established by constant repetition, they sink down into the depths of the unconscious mind and become 'second nature.'

Though habit is second nature, it can be changed by a new healthy, agreeable habit of a stronger nature. You can change any habit by patient efforts and perseverance. Habits of sleeping in the daytime, late rising, loud talking, etc., can be gradually changed by developing new habits.

By new practice, you can change the manner of your handwriting. So also, by a new mode of thinking, you can change your destiny. When you draw water with a rope and bucket from a well with a brick parapet, a definite groove is formed along the brick and the rope readily runs along the groove. Even so, the mental force (the mind) runs easily or flows readily along the grooves in the brain made by continuous thinking on certain lines. Now you are thinking, 'I am the body.' Think, 'I am Brahman.' In course of time, you will be established in Brahmic consciousness.

By spiritual Sadhana, Vichara, meditation, Pranayama, Japa, Sama and Dama an entirely new mind is formed in a Sadhaka with new feelings, new nerve-channels, new avenues and grooves in the brain for the mind to move and walk about, new nerve-currents and new brain-cells, etc. He will never think about affairs that tend to self-aggrandisement and self-exaltation. He thinks for the well-being of the world. He thinks, feels and works in terms of unity.

Do not be a slave to one idea. Whenever you get new healthy ideas, the old ideas must be given up. The vast majority of persons are slaves of old outgrown ideas. They have not got the strength to change the old habits in the mind and the old ideas. When you hear a new and striking news, you are startled. When you see a new thing, you are startled. It is natural. It is much more so with new ideas. The mind runs in ruts—in its old, narrow grooves. It is directly or indirectly attached to some pleasing or favourite ideas. It unnecessarily sticks to one idea like glue and never gives it up. It is a great ordeal for the mind to take up a new idea. Whenever you want to introduce any new, healthy idea in the mind and eschew any old outgrown idea, the mind fights against it and rebels with vehemence. Place the idea near the ruts. It will slowly take it. It may revolt furiously to take it up in the beginning. Later on, by coaxing and training, it will absorb and assimilate it.

In the mind, there is an internal fight that is ever going on between Svabhava (nature) and will, between old worldly habits and new spiritual habits in the case of the aspirants, between old Vishaya-Samskaras and new spiritual Samskaras, between Subha Vasanas and Asubha Vasanas, between Viveka and instinctive mind and Indriyas. Whenever you try to change an evil habit and establish a new habit, there will ensue an internal fight between Will and Svabhava. If you try to drive away anger, lust, etc., they say and assert, "O Jivas! You have given us permission to stay in this house of flesh and body for a long time. Why do you want to drive us now? We have helped you a lot during times of your excitements and passions. We have every right to remain here. We will persist, resist all your efforts to drive us; we shall disturb your meditation and recur again and again." The Svabhava will try its level best to get back to its old habit. Never yield. The will is bound to succeed in the end. Even if you fail once or twice, it does not matter. Again apply the will. Eventually, will—pure, strong and irresistible—is bound to succeed. There is no doubt about this. When your reason grows, when you become wiser and wiser by study, contact with the wise and meditation, your mind must be well prepared to take up at any moment new, healthy, rational ideas and eschew old, morbid ones. This is a healthy growth of the mind.

MIND IS YOUR TOOL ONLY: HANDLE IT NICELY

Mind is your tool or instrument only. You must know how to handle it nicely. When emotions, moods, sentiments, arise in the mind, separate them, study their nature, dissect and analyse them. Do not identify yourself with them. The real 'I' is entirely distinct from them. It is the silent Sakshi. Master your impulses, emotions and moods and rise from the position of a slave to a spiritual king who can rule over them with force and power. You are eternal, all-pervading Atman in reality. Shake yourself from the tyranny of the mind that has oppressed you for so long, domineered over you and exploited you uptil now. Rise up boldly like a lion. Assert the magnanimity of your Self and be free.

      Become an expert driver of the subtle, powerful 'machine-mind.' Use all the mental faculties to your best advantage. Mind will become quite a good, willing servant when you know how to tackle with it ably. Use the subconscious mind also; pass on orders to work for you while you are asleep and even while you are conscious. It will sort, analyse and rearrange all facts and figures for you in the twinkling of an eye.

The mind is very plastic if you know the secret of its manipulation. You can bend it any way you like. You can create a dislike for the things you like best now and a liking for the articles which now you dislike most.

Do a thing which the mind does not want to do. Do not do a thing which the mind wants to do. This is one way of developing the will and controlling the mind.

MAINTAIN A POSITIVE ATTITUDE

Try to acquire the power of closing yourself against detrimental or undesirable influences by making yourself positive by a particular attitude of the mind. By so doing, you may be receptive to all higher impulses of the soul within and to all higher forces and influences from without. Make a suggestion to yourself, "I close myself; I make myself positive to all things below and open and receptive to all higher influences, to all things above." By taking this attitude of the mind, consciously, now and then, it soon becomes a habit. All the lower and undesirable influences from both the seen and the unseen side of life are closed out while all higher influences are invited and, in the degree that they are invited, they will enter.

In the mind there is doubt; there is reality also. A doubt arises whether there is a God or not. This is termed Samsaya-Bhavana. Another doubt crops up whether I can realise Brahman or not. Then another voice yells: "God or Brahman is real. He is a solid, concrete Reality as an Amalaka fruit in my hand. He is a mass of Knowledge and Ananda (Prajnanaghana, Chidghana, Anandaghana). I can realise!" We have clearly understood something and these ideas are well-grounded and ingrained. Some ideas are hazy and not firm. They come and go. We will have to cultivate ideas and ground them till they are firmly fixed and implanted. Clarification of ideas will remove perplexity and confusion in the mind.

When a doubt arises, "whether there is God or not, whether I will succeed in Self-realisation or not," it must be dispelled by well-directed suggestions and affirmations such as: "It is true; I will succeed. There is no doubt of this." In my dictionary, in my vocabulary, there are no such words as 'can't,' 'impossible,' 'difficult,' etc. Everything is possible under the sun. Nothing is difficult when you strongly make up your mind. Strong determination and firm resolution will bring sanguine success in every affair or undertaking.

THE POWER OF THE HELPING FORCES

Inside, there are helping forces also to act against the hostile forces of demoniacal nature. If you once repeat 'Om' or 'Rama' ten times, if you once sit in meditation for five minutes, the Samskara of this will force you to repeat the Mantra again many times, to sit again in meditation for some time though you forget all about spirituality owing to the force of Maya or Avidya. The hostile forces, e.g., lust, anger, etc., will try to bring you down; the spiritual currents, the force of Sattva and Subha Vasanas will try to take you up to God. If evil thoughts enter your mind once in a month instead of thrice weekly (remember that evil thinking is the beginning of adultery), if you become angry once in a month instead of once weekly, that is a sign of progress, that is a sign of your increased will-power; that is a sign of growing spiritual strength. Be of good cheer. Keep a diary of spiritual progress.

A mind always hopeful, confident, courageous and determined on its set purpose and keeping itself to that purpose, attracts to itself, out of the elements, things and powers favourable to that purpose.

SOME GUIDE-LINES IN MIND-CONTROL

Mind is so framed that it runs to extremes. Through Sadhana or spiritual practice, it should be brought to a balanced state (Samata). It is one-sided by its very nature. It is through mental drill or training that integral development must be achieved.

Make a vigorous and earnest search within. Do not trust the mind and the Indriyas. They are your enemies. Women and wealth are your bitter foes. These are two great evils.

Mind exercises its sovereignty over man through the force of attachment, craving, Samskara and Vasana (tendency, latent desire, will to possess and enjoy, world-desire). It does various tricks. When you once know its ways, it lurks like a thief. It will no longer trouble you.

In controlling the mind, you have to do seven things: (1) You must get rid of all desires, Vasanas and Trishnas. (2) You must control your emotions. You must control the temper so that you may feel no anger or impatience. (3) You must control the mind itself so that the thought may always be calm and un-ruffled. (4) You must control the nerves through the mind so that they may be as little irritable as possible. (5) You must give up Abhimana. Abhimana strengthens the mind. It is the seed of the mind. When you have become a Nirabhimani, how can criti-cisms, taunts and censure affect you? (6) You must destroy all attachments ruthlessly. (7) You must give up all hopes and prejudices.

The following will bring you peace of mind undoubtedly. (1) Avoid the company of evil persons. (2) Live alone. (3) Re-duce your wants. (4) Do not argue. Arguing creates sense of hostility. It is a sheer waste of energy. (5) Do not compare your-self with others. (6) Do not lend your ears for public criticism. (7) Give up the idea of name and fame.

According to Patanjali Maharshi, Maitri (friendship be-tween equals), Karuna (mercy towards inferiors), Mudita (com-placency towards superiors), Upeksha (indifference towards rogues), will bring about Chittaprasada or peace of mind.

You should, through your higher Sattvic mind, avoid the mind which runs in the direction of objects and, progressing higher up, should, without any despondency of heart, accumu-late wealth of Tapasya for acquiring that imperishable Supreme Seat (Parama Pada). Like an emperor who brings under his sway all kings on earth, the fluctuating mind should be brought under the perfect control of the non-fluctuating mind and then, the latter reaches its own state which is the Supreme One.

CHAPTER 31
CONCENTRATION

"*Tatpratishedhartham-ekatattvabhyasah* — To remove this (tossing and various other obstacles which stand in the way of one-pointedness of mind), the practice of concentration on one thing alone (should be made)." *(Patanjali Yoga Sutras, I-32)*

CONCENTRATION, THE KEY TO PEACE

Worldly pleasures intensify the desire for enjoying greater pleasures. Hence, the mind of worldlings is very restless. There is no satisfaction and mental peace. Mind can never be satisfied, whatever amount of pleasure you may store up for it. The more it enjoys the pleasures, the more it wants them. So, people are exceedingly troubled and bothered by their own minds. They are tired of their minds. Hence, in order to remove these botherations and troubles, the Rishis thought it best to deprive the mind of all sensual pleasures. When the mind has been concentrated or made extinct, it cannot pinch one to seek for further pleasure and all botherations and troubles are removed for ever and the person attains real peace.

There is an externalising or objectifying power in the mind. This leads to Bahirmukha Vritti. The mind is drawn towards various objects. There is dissipation of mental energy, the powers of the mind, in various directions. The rays of the mind are like the rays of light, scattered in the case of worldly-minded persons. When the rays of the mind are scattered over diverse objects, you get pain. When the rays are gathered and concentrated by practice, the mind becomes concentrated and you get Ananda (happiness) from within.

When you see your dear friend after six years, the Ananda that you get is not from the person, but from within yourself. The mind becomes concentrated for the time being and you get happiness from within your own self.

When you are in Kashmir, when you are enjoying the picturesque scenery of Muttan, Gulmarg, Sonamarg, Chashmashahi and Anantanag, your mind will be suddenly upset by shock, if you receive a telegram which brings the unhappy tidings of the untimely demise of your only son. The scenery will no longer interest you. They have lost their charm for you. There is ejection of attention. There is depression. It is concentration and attention that gives you pleasure in sight-seeing.

For purposes of concentration, you will have to gather the scattered rays of the mind patiently through Vairagya and Abhyasa, through Tyaga (renunciation) and Tapas and then march boldly with indefatigable energy towards God or Brahman. Through constant Sadhana (spiritual practice), the mind must be checked from externalising. It must be made to move towards Brahman, its original home. When the mental rays are concentrated, illumination begins.

ILLUSTRATIONS OF THE NATURE OF MIND

Mind is compared to quicksilver, because its rays are scattered over various objects. It is compared to a monkey, because it jumps from one object to another object. It is compared to moving air, because it is Chanchala. It is compared to a furious, rutting elephant, because of its passionate impetuosity. Mind is known by the name 'Great Bird,' because it jumps from one object to another object just as a bird jumps from one twig to another, from one tree to another. Raja Yoga teaches us how to concentrate the mind and then how to ransack the innermost recesses of our own mind.

DIFFERENT DEGREES OF CONCENTRATION

Kshipta, Mudha, Vikshipta, Ekagra and Niruddha are the five Yogic Bhumikas. The Chitta or mind manifests itself in five different forms. In the Kshipta state, the rays of the mind are scattered on various objects. It is restless and jumps from one object to another. In the Mudha state, the mind is dull and forgetful. Vikshipta is the gathering mind. It is occasionally steady and, at other times, distracted. By practice of concentration, the mind struggles to gather itself. In the Ekagra state, it is one-pointed. There is only one idea present in the mind. The mind is under perfect control in the Niruddha state. Dharana is practised for stopping the modifications of the mind.

THE POWER OF CONCENTRATION

By manipulating the mind, you will be able to bring it under your control, make it work as you like and compel it to concentrate its powers as you desire. He who has learnt to manipulate the mind will get the whole of Nature under his control. There is no limit to the power of the human mind. The more concentrated it is, the more power is brought to bear on one point. A scientist concentrates his mind and invents many things. Through concentration, he opens the layers of the gross mind and penetrates deeply into higher regions of the mind and gets deeper knowledge. He concentrates all the energies of his mind into one focus and throws them out upon the materials he is analysing and so finds out their secrets.

CONCENTRATION, MAN'S FOREMOST DUTY

Sri Sankara writes in the commentary on Chhandogya Upanishad (VII-xx-1) that a man's duty consists in the control of the senses and concentration of mind. So long as the thoughts of one are not thoroughly destroyed through persistent practice, he should ever be concentrating his mind on one truth at a time. Through such unremitting practice, one-pointedness will accrue to the mind and instantly, all the hosts of thoughts will vanish. Concentration is opposed to sensuous desires, bliss to flurry and worry, sustained thinking to perplexity, applied thinking to sloth to torpor, rapture to ill-will.

You are born to concentrate the mind on God after collecting the mental rays that are dissipated on various objects. That is your important duty. You forget the duty on account of Moha for family, children, money, power, position, respect, name and fame.

Concentration of the mind on God after purification can give you real happiness and knowledge. You are born for this purpose only. You are carried away to external objects through Raga and Moha (attachment and infatuated love).

Fix the mind on Atman. Fix the mind on the all-pervading, pure Intelligence and self-luminous effulgence (Svayamjyotis). Stand firm in Brahman. Then will you become 'Brahma-samstha,' established in Brahman.

HOW TO CONCENTRATE

Practise concentration of mind. In trying to concentrate your mind or even project a thought, you will find that you require naturally to form images in your mind. You cannot help it. Fix the mind on one object, on one idea. Withdraw the mind, again and again, when it runs away from the Lakshya and fix it there. Do not allow the mind to create hundreds of thought-forms. Introspect and watch the mind carefully. Live alone. Avoid company. Do not mix. This is important. Do not allow the mind to dissipate its energy in vain on vain thoughts, vain worry, vain imagination and vain fear and forebodings. Make it hold on to one thought-form for half an hour by incessant practice. Make the mind to shape itself into one shape and try to keep the shape for hours together through constant and incessant practice.

WHAT IS CONCENTRATION?

"*Desabandhas-chittasya dharana*—Concentration is holding the mind to one form or object steadily for a long time" (Yoga Sutras, III-1). "Dharana is fixing the mind on an external object or an internal Chakra or one abstract idea as *Aham brahmasmi*" (Yoga Sutras, III-1).

CONCENTRATION ON THE INTERNAL CHAKRAS

A Raja Yogi concentrates on the Trikuti (Ajna Chakra, the space between the two eyebrows) which is the seat of the mind in the waking state. You can easily control the mind if you can concentrate on this region. Meditation and concentration on the Ajna Chakra lead to control of mind very easily. Light is seen during concentration in this region very quickly, even in a day's practice, by some persons. He who wants to meditate on Virat and he who wants to help the world should select this region for his concentration.

A Bhakta or devotee should concentrate on the heart, the seat of emotion and feeling. He who concentrates on the heart gets great Ananda. He who wants to get Ananda should concentrate on the heart.

A Hatha Yogi fixes his mind on the Sushumna Nadi, the middle path in the spinal canal and on a specified centre, viz., the Muladhara or the Manipura or the Ajna Chakra. Some Yogis ignore the lower Chakras and fix their mind on the Ajna Chakra only. Their theory is that by controlling the Ajna Chakra, all the lower Chakras can be automatically controlled. When you concentrate on a Chakra, a thread-like connection is formed in the beginning between the mind and the Chakra (centre of spiritual energy). Then the Yogi ascends along the Sushumna from Chakra to Chakra. The ascent is made gradually by patient efforts. Even a mere shaking of the opening of Sushumna causes a great deal of Ananda (bliss). You become intoxicated. You will entirely forget the world. When the opening of Sushumna is shaken a bit, the Kula-Kundalini Sakti tries to enter Sushumna. Great Vairagya comes in. You will become fearless. You will behold various visions. You will witness the splendid "Antarjyotis." This is termed "Unmani Avastha." You will get different Siddhis, different types of Ananda and you will get different kinds of knowledge by controlling and operating on different Chakras. If you have conquered the Muladhara Chakra, you have conquered the earth-plane already. If you have conquered the Manipura Chakra, you have already conquered fire. Fire will not burn you. Panchadharana (five kinds of Dharana) will help you to conquer the five elements. Learn them under a Guru who is a developed Yogi.

A NOTE OF CAUTION

If you get headache or pain by concentrating on the Trikuti (the space between the two eyebrows) by turning the eyes upward, give up the practice at once. Concentrate on the heart. If you find it difficult to concentrate on your heart or the space between the two eyebrows (Trikuti) or top of the head, if you experience headache or pain in the skull, shift your centre of concentration to any object outside the body.

CONCENTRATION ON EXTERNAL OBJECTS

It is easy to concentrate the mind on external objects. The mind has a natural tendency to go outwards. You can concentrate on the blue sky, light of the sun, the all-pervading air or ether or sun, moon or stars.

TRAINING IN CONCENTRATION

Train the mind in a variety of ways in concentration in the beginning. Concentrate on the Anahata sounds of the heart by closing the ears. Concentrate on the breath with Soham repetition. Concentrate on any concrete image. Concentrate on the blue sky. Concentrate on the all-pervading light of the sun. Concentrate on the various Chakras of the body. Concentrate on the abstract ideas of Satyam (Truth), Jnanam (Wisdom), Anantam (Infinity), Ekam (One), Nityam (Eternal Essence), etc. Lastly, stick to one thing only.

AIDS TO CONCENTRATION

Faith

Though any subject has been established by means of arguments and valid authorities, still people's minds being entirely taken up with gross external objects, any clear conception of subtle ultimate truths is almost impossible without proper faith. When there is faith, the mind can be easily concentrated on the subject to be understood; and then the understanding quickly follows.

Control of Breath

Remove the Rajas and Tamas that envelop the Sattva of the mind by Pranayama, Japa, Vichara and Bhakti. Then the mind becomes fit for concentration. Pranayama or control of breath removes the veil of Rajas and Tamas that envelops Sattva. It purifies the nerves (Nadis). It makes the mind firm and steady and thereby renders it fit for concentration. The dross of the mind is cleansed by Pranayama, just as the dross of gold is got rid of by melting. A Hatha Yogi tries to concentrate his mind by having his breath controlled through Pranayama.

A Raja Yogi tries to concentrate his mind by "Chitta-Vritti-Nirodha" (restraining the various modifications of the Chitta), by not allowing the mind to assume various shapes of objects. He does not care for control of breath. But, his breath becomes necessarily controlled when his mind is concentrated. Hatha Yoga is a branch of Raja Yoga.

Avadhana or Attention

Attention (Avadhana) plays a very great part in concentration. It is the basis of will. When it is properly guided and directed towards the internal world for purposes of introspection (Antarmukha Vritti), it will analyse the mind and illumine very many astounding facts for you.

The force wherewith anything strikes the mind is generally in proportion to the degree of attention bestowed upon it. Moreover, the great art of memory is attention and inattentive people have bad memories. Power of attention becomes weakened in old age.

Attention is focussing of consciousness. It is one of the signs of trained will. It is found in men of strong mentality. It is a rare faculty. Brahmacharya wonderfully develops this power. A Yogi who possesses this faculty can even fix the mind on an unpleasant object for a very long time. Attention can be cultivated and developed by persistent practice. All the great men of the world who have achieved greatness have risen up through this faculty.

It is through the power of attention that mind carries out all its activities. Attention is the basis of will-force. Therefore cultivate the power of attention.

Attention may be either subjective or internal on an idea or objective or external on any object. Throw your entire attention into whatever you happen to be doing at the moment. It is easy to fasten the mind on an object which the mind likes best. Practise attention on unpleasant tasks, from which you have been shrinking before on account of their unpleasantness. Throw interest upon uninteresting objects and ideas. Hold them on before your mind. Interest will slowly manifest. Many mental weaknesses will vanish. The mind will become stronger and stronger.

AN ILLUSTRATION OF SINGLE-MINDED CONCENTRATION

There was a workman who used to manufacture arrows. Once he was very busy at his work. He was so much absorbed in his work that he did not notice even a big party of a Raja with his retinue passing in front of his shop. Such must be the nature of your concentration when you fix your mind on God. You must have the one idea of God and God alone. No doubt, it takes some time to have a complete Ekagrata of mind. You will have to struggle very hard to have a single-minded concentration. Sri Dattatreya made the above arrow-maker as one of his Gurus.

A COMMON BLUNDER

Some medical students leave the medical college soon after joining it as they find it disgusting to wash the pus in ulcers and dissect the dead bodies. They make a serious blunder. In the beginning, it is loathing. After studying Pathology, Medicine, Operative Surgery, Morbid Anatomy, Bacteriology, the course will be very interesting in the final year. Many spiritual aspirants leave off the practice of concentration of mind after some time as they find it difficult to practise. They also make a grave mistake like the medical students. In the beginning of practice, when you struggle to get over the body-consciousness, it will be disgusting and troublesome. It will be a physical wrestling. The emotions and Sankalpas will be abundant. In the third year of practice, the mind will be cool, pure and strong. You will derive immense joy. The sum total of pleasures of the whole world is nothing when compared to the Ananda derived from the meditation. Do not give up the practice at any cost. Plod on. Persevere. Have patience (Dhriti), Utsaha (cheerfulness) and Sahasa (tenacity, application). You will succeed eventually. Never despair. Find out by serious introspection the various impediments that act as stumbling blocks in your concentration and remove them with patience and efforts one by one. Do not allow new Sankalpas and new Vasanas to crop up. Nip them in the bud through Viveka, Vichara and Dhyana.

Know that you are progressing in Yoga and that the Sattva is increasing, when you are always cheerful, when the mind is even and concentrated.

CHAPTER 32

MEDITATION

"*Achintaiva param dhyanam*—To be thoughtless is the highest form of meditation." *(Sri Sankaracharya)*

"*Dhyanam nirvishayam manah*—When the mind becomes Nirvishaya (free from thinking of sense-objects and their enjoyments), it is meditation." *(Patanjali Yoga Sutras)*

WHAT IS MEDITATION?

In Vedanta or the path of Jnana, the terms "Manana" (reflection) and "Nididhyasana" are very frequently used. Manana-Vritti-Tiraskara is driving away all the thoughts of worldly objects and Svajatiya-Vritti-Pravaha is increasing the thought-currents of God or Brahman like a steady stream. Nididhyasana is meditation of Atman. It is deep and intense contemplation. It is Anatma-Vritti-Vivadana-Rahita Atmakara-Vritti-Sthiti. The mind is perfectly established in the Absolute. No worldly thoughts will intrude now. The contemplation is like a steady flow of oil (*Tailadharavat*).

INDISPENSABILITY OF MEDITATION FOR GOD-REALISATION

Mind feels tired after hard and protracted work. It cannot therefore, be Atman. Atman is the store-house of all powers (Ananta-Sakti). Mind is only an instrument of Atman. It should be properly disciplined. Just as you develop the physical body through gymnastics and various kinds of physical exercises, you will have to train the mind through mental training, mental culture or mental drill. In meditation and concentration, you will have to train the mind in a variety of ways. Then only the gross mind will become subtle (Sukshma).

Put a piece of iron rod in the blazing furnace. It becomes red like fire. Remove it. It loses its red colour. If you want to keep it always red, you must always keep it in fire. Even so, if you want to keep the mind charged with the fire of Brahmic wisdom, you must keep it always in contact or touch with the Brahmic fire of knowledge through constant and intense meditation. You must keep up an unceasing flow of the Brahmic consciousness. Then you will have the Sahajavastha (natural state).

Leading a virtuous life is not by itself sufficient for God-realisation. Concentration of mind is absolutely necessary. A good, virtuous life only prepares the mind as a fit instrument for concentration and meditation. It is concentration and meditation that eventually lead to Self-realisation.

God has hidden Himself in this world (immanent) and is seated in the cavity of the lotus of your heart. He is an absentee landlord. You will have to seek Him through concentration and meditation with a pure mind. This is a real play of hide and seek.

All the visible things are Maya. Maya will vanish through Jnana or meditation on Atman. One should exert himself to get rid of Maya. Maya havocs through the mind. Destruction of the mind means the annihilation of Maya. Nididhyasana is the only way for conquering Maya. Lord Buddha, Raja Bhartrihari, Dattatreya, Akhow of Gujarat—all had conquered Maya and mind through deep meditation only. Enter the silence. Meditate. Meditate. Solitude and intense meditation are two important requisites for Self-realisation.

Make the mind blank. It is the only medium for these severe strokes of grief. It is difficult to suppress thought and, after it is once suppressed, a new succession of thoughts arises which overpowers the mind. Fix the mind on some tranquil object. You will succeed in checking the mind. Collect your thoughts in the Spirit (Atman), as a person cools himself by going into a pool of water in the hot season. Meditate continually on Hari, who is of an azure hue and who wears an invaluable necklace and is adorned with ornaments on His arms, in His ears and on His head.

PREREQUISITES FOR MEDITATION

For meditation, you want a properly trained instrument (mind). You must have a calm, clear, pure, subtle, sharp, steady and one-pointed Buddhi to understand the Brahma-Tattva or Brahma-Vastu. Then and then only is realisation possible. Brahman is pure and subtle and you need a pure and subtle mind to approach Brahman.

Only a trained mind which utterly controls the body can inquire and meditate endlessly so long as life remains, never for a moment losing sight of the object of its search and contemplation (the Brahman), never for a moment letting it to be obscured by any terrestrial temptation. All physical activities should be completely suspended, all attachments should be ruthlessly cut asunder completely for five or six years, if you want to practise Dhyana Yoga, if you want to realise God through concentration of mind. Newspaper-reading and correspondence with friends and relatives should be completely stopped, as they cause distraction of mind and strengthen the world-idea. Seclusion for a period of five or six years is indispensable.

For purposes of meditation, everything must be rendered Sattvic. The place of meditation must be Sattvic. The food must be Sattvic. The wearing apparel must be Sattvic. The company must be Sattvic. Talking must be Sattvic. The sound that you hear must be Sattvic. Thinking must be Sattvic. Study must be Sattvic. Everything must be Sattvic. Then only good progress in Sadhana is possible, particularly with the beginners (neophytes).

A solitary place with spiritual vibratory conditions, a cool, Sattvic place with temperate climate as at Uttarkashi, Rishikesh, Lakshmanjhula, Kankhal or Badrinarayan is indispensably requisite for concentration of mind and meditation, because the brain gets hot during meditation. The banks of the Ganga or Narmada, Himalayan scenery, lovely flower-gardens, sacred temples—these are the places which elevate the mind in concentration and mediation. Have recourse to them.

Of course, the ideal condition cannot always be obtained as this is a relative plane. All places combine advantages and some disadvantages also side by side. You must select a place which has the maximum of advantages and minimum of disadvantages. You must do the best you can. You must try to put up with some difficulties. You must overcome them. You should be alone with yourself. You should be able to abstract yourself from the distracting causes.

There must be good, Sattvic, substantial light, nutritious food. Meditation is possible only when the mind is full of Sattva-Guna. The stomach should not be loaded. There is an intimate connection between the mind and the food. A heavy meal is harmful. Take a full meal at 11 a.m. and half a seer of milk at night. The night meal should be light for those who meditate.

There must be capacity for Sadhana. Then only meditation will go on steadily with happiness. Asana (posture) steadies the body. Bandhas and Mudras make the body firm. Pranayama makes the body light. Nadi-Suddhi effects Samyavastha of the mind. Having acquired these qualifications, you will have to fix the mind on Brahman.

When Sushumna Nadi is working, i.e., when the breath flows through both the nostrils, meditation goes on with ease and joy. The mind then is calm. There is an increase of Sattva Guna when Sushumna is operating. Sit for meditation the moment Sushumna begins to flow.

You can meditate only when the mind is beyond all anxieties. Retire to a quiet room or place where you do not fear interruption so that your mind may feel secure and at rest. Sit in a comfortable posture and be, so far as possible, free from external disturbing influences. Drive off negative thoughts. Become positive always. Positive overpowers negative. You can do nice meditation when you are positive.

There must be firm Vairagya, burning Mumukshutva and strong Viveka in you. There must be a good, spiritual teacher (Anubhava Guru) to guide you.

You must have an intellectual grasp, intellectual conviction and comprehensive understanding of Brahman first through the purified mind.

Many do not get the above favourable conditions for spiritual Sadhana. That is the reason why they do not make any spiritual progress.

SAGUNA AND NIRGUNA FORMS OF MEDITATION

When you see the concrete figure of Lord Krishna with open eyes and meditate, it is the concrete form of meditation. When you reflect on the image of Lord Krishna by closing your eyes, it is also concrete form of meditation, but it is more abstract. When you meditate on the infinite abstract light, it is still more abstract meditation. The former two types belong to Saguna form of meditation, the latter to Nirguna form.

Even in Nirguna meditation, there is an abstract form in the beginning for fixing the mind. Later on, this form vanishes and the meditator and the meditated become one. Meditation proceeds from the mind only. The help of the mind is always needed either for perception of an object or for the understanding of Brahman. When you read a book with absorbing interest and attention, your mind gets fixed to the ideas. Even so, in Nirguna meditation of Brahman (formless Dhyana), the mind is fixed on one idea, viz., that of Atman.

EXERCISES IN SAGUNA MEDITATION

Sit on Padmasana in a solitary room. Close your eyes. Meditate on the effulgence in the sun, splendour in the moon, glory in the stars, beauty in the sky. This is one kind of meditation for beginners.

Meditate on the Himalayas. Imagine that the river Ganga takes its origin from the icy region of Gangotri, near Uttarkashi, flows through Rishikesh, Haridwar, Varanasi and enters the Gangasagar in the Bay of Bengal. Himalayas, Ganga and the sea—these three thoughts only should occupy your mind. First, take your mind to icy Gangotri, then along the Ganga and finally to the sea. Then, again take it to the icy Gangotri. Rotate the mind in this manner for 15 minutes. This is another kind of meditation.

Imagine that there is a fine garden with lovely flowers. In one corner, there are jasmine flowers. In another corner, there are beautiful cabbage roses. In the third corner there is the 'lady of the night.' In the fourth corner, there are Champaka flowers. Now, meditate on these four varieties of flowers. First meditate on jasmine. Then take the mind to rose, then to the 'lady of the night' and finally to the Champaka. Again rotate the mind as above. Do this again and again for fifteen minutes. Gross meditations like these will prepare the mind for finer abstract meditation on subtle ideas.

Meditate on the magnanimity of the ocean, its infinite nature. Compare the ocean with the Infinite Brahman, the waves, foams and blocks of ice to the various names and forms. Identify yourself with the ocean. Become silent. Expand. Expand.

EXERCISES IN NIRGUNA MEDITATION

There is a living, universal Power that underlies all these names and forms. Meditate on this Power which is formless.

This will form an elementary Nirguna meditation without any form (formless Dhyana).

"There is no world. There is neither body nor the mind. There is only one Chaitanya (pure consciousness). I am that pure consciousness."—This is Nirguna meditation (without attributes).

Sit on Padmasana. Open the eyes. Gaze steadily on the formless air only. This is also another method of formless meditation. Concentrate on the air. This will lead to the realisation of the nameless and formless Brahman, the One Living Truth.

Imagine that there is a Parama, Ananta, Akhanda Jyotis (supreme, infinite effulgence) hidden behind all the phenomena with an effulgence that amounts to the blaze of crores of suns together. Meditate on That. That is also another form of Nirguna meditation.

Concentrate and meditate on the expansive sky. This is also another kind of Nirguna, Nirakara meditation. By the previous methods in concentration, the mind will stop thinking of finite forms. It will slowly begin to melt in the ocean of Peace, as it is deprived of its contents, viz., forms of various sorts. It will become subtler and subtler also.

MEDITATION ON 'OM'

Have the figure OM in front of you. Concentrate on this. Do Trataka also with open eyes (steady gazing without winking till tears flow profusely). This is both Saguna and Nirguna meditation (with and without attributes). Keep a picture of OM in your meditation room. You can do Puja for the symbol of Brahman. Burn incense, etc. Offer flowers. This suits the modern educated persons.

MEDITATION ON MIND

Mind is Brahman or God in manifestation. Mind is God in motion. As Brahman is approachable by means of the mind, it is only proper to meditate upon the Mind as Brahman. "The mind should be adored as Brahman; this is intellectual worship." (Chhandogya Upanishad, III-18). This is Upasana Vakya.

THE MEDITATION ROOM

The meditation room should be regarded as a temple of God.

Talks of profane nature should never be indulged in the room. No vicious thoughts of rancorous jealousy, avarice are to be entertained there. Admittance should ever be sought in it with a pious and reverent mind. For, what we do, what we think and what we speak of leave their impressions on the ether of the room and, if no care is taken to avoid them, they will exert their influence on the aspirant's mind and, rendering his mind perverse and restive, make him incapable of attending to the devotion. The words uttered, the thoughts cherished, the deeds done are not lost; they are always reflected on the subtle layers of ether encircling the room where they are done and affect the mind invariably. As much as possible effort should be made to overcome them. This is to be done for a few months only; when the habit is changed, everything will be all right.

HOW TO MEDITATE

Sit in a lonely place on Padma, Siddha or Sukha Asana. Free yourself from all passions, emotions and impulses. Subjugate the senses. Withdraw the mind from objects. Now the mind will be calm, one-pointed, pure and subtle. With the help of this trained instrument, disciplined mind, contemplate on that one Infinite Self. Do not think of anything else. Do not allow any worldly thought to enter the mind. Do not allow the mind to think of any physical or mental enjoyment. When it indulges in these thoughts, give it a good hammering. Then it will move towards God. Just as the Ganga flows continuously towards the sea, thoughts of God should flow continuously towards the Lord. Just as oil, when poured from one vessel to another, flows in an unbroken, continuous stream, just as the harmonious sound produced from the ringing of bells falls upon the ear in a continuous stream, so also the mind should 'flow' towards God in one continuous stream. There must be a continuous divine Vritti-Pravaha, Svajatiya-Vritti-Pravaha, from the Sattvic mind towards God through continuous Sadhana.

You must have a mental image of God or Brahman (concrete or abstract) before you begin to meditate. When you are a neophyte in meditation, start repeating some sublime Slokas or Stotras (hymns) for ten minutes as soon as you sit for meditation. This will elevate the mind. The mind can be easily withdrawn from the worldly objects. Then stop this kind of thinking also and fix the mind on one idea only by repeated and strenuous efforts. Then Nishtha will ensue.

In Nididhyasana (meditation), you will have to develop the Svajatiya-Vritti-Pravaha. Make the thoughts of Brahman or Divine Presence flow like inundation or flood. Do Vijatiya-Vritti-Tiraskara. Renounce the thoughts of objects. Drive them away with the whip of Viveka and Vichara. There is struggle in the beginning. It is trying indeed. But, later on, as you will grow stronger and stronger and as you grow in purity, Brahma-Chintana becomes easy. You rejoice in the life of unity. You get strength from Atman. Inner strength grows when all the Vishaya Vrittis are thinned out and the mind becomes one-pointed (Ekagra).

When you start a fire, you heap up some straw, pieces of paper, thin pieces of wood. The fire gets extinguished quickly. You blow it again several times through the mouth of the blow-pipe. After some time it becomes a small conflagration. You can hardly extinguish it now even with great efforts. Even so, in the beginning of meditation in neophytes, they fall down from meditation in their old grooves. They will have to lift up their minds again and again and fix on the Lakshya. When the meditation becomes deep and steady, they get established in God eventually. Then the meditation becomes Sahaja (natural). It becomes habitual. Use the blow-pipe of Tivra Vairagya and intense meditation to kindle the fire of meditation.

During meditation, note how long you can shut out all worldly thoughts. Watch the mind very carefully. If it is for twenty minutes, try to increase the period to thirty or forty minutes and so on. Fill the mind with the thoughts of God again and again.

Allow the one Brahmic idea to flow gently and continuously. Constantly think of God. The mind should always move towards God. Fasten the mind with a fine silk thread to the lotus feet of Lord Siva or Hari. Drive out foreign or extraneous (worldly) ideas gently. Try to keep up the Brahmakara Vritti by repeating OM or "Aham Brahmasmi" mentally very often. The idea of infinity, the idea of an ocean of light, the idea of all-knowledge and all-Ananda should accompany the mental repetition of OM. If the mind wanders, repeat verbally six times the long (Dhirga) Pranava with $3\frac{1}{2}$ Matras. This process will remove the Vikshepa and all other obstacles.

When you begin to sweep a room that was kept closed for six months, various kinds of dirt come out from the corners of the room. Similarly, during meditation, under pressure of Yoga, through the Grace of God, various kinds of impurities float about on the surface of the mind. Bravely remove them one by one by suitable methods and counter-virtues with patience and strenuous efforts. The old vicious Samskaras revenge when you try to suppress them. Do not be afraid. They lose their strength after some time. You have to tame the mind just as you tame a wild elephant or a tiger. Do not indulge in vicious thoughts which serve as food for the mind. Make the mind Antarmukha (self-introspective). Substitute good, virtuous, sublime thoughts. Feed the mind with ennobling aspirations and ideals. Old vicious Samskaras will be gradually thinned out and eventually obliterated. Now the Brahmakara Vritti will dawn. Coupled with Brahma-Jnana, this is the destroyer of Avidya. Allow the Brahmakara Vritti to flow steadily like Tailadhara (continuous flow of oil). Now Niratisayananda (infinite bliss) will flow. At this state, the whole universe will appear as Sat-Chit-Ananda only. This thought also will die. You will then enter Sahajananda state (Advaita-Avastharupa Samadhi).

SOME USEFUL HINTS

In meditation, do not strain the eyes. Do not strain the brain. Do not struggle or wrestle with the mind. It is a serious mistake. Many neophytes commit this grave error. That is the reason why they get easily tired soon. They get headache and they have to get up very often to pass urine during the course of meditation owing to the irritation set up in the micturition centre in the spinal cord.

Make no violent effort to control the mind. Do not wrestle with it with force. It is a mistake to do so. But, rather allow it for a while and let it run and exhaust its efforts. The mind will jump now like an untrained monkey first. Gradually, it will slow down. Then you can fix the mind on your Lakshya either on a concrete form or on an abstract idea.

Get up at 4 a.m. (Brahma Muhurta). Sit comfortably in the Padma, Siddha, Sukha or Svastika Asana. Keep the head, neck and trunk in one straight line. Relax the muscles, nerves and brain. Calm the objective mind. Close the eyes. Do not struggle with the mind. Do not voluntarily and violently drive away intruding thoughts. Gently allow the divine thoughts to flow. Steadily think of the Lakshya (point of meditation). Have sublime, Sattvic thoughts. Vicious thoughts will, by themselves, vanish.

Even if the mind runs outside during your practice in meditation, do not bother. Allow it to run. Slowly try to bring it to your Lakshya (centre). By repeated practice, the mind will be finally focussed in your heart, in the Atman, the Indweller of your hearts, the final goal of life. In the beginning, the mind may run out 80 times. Within six months, it may run 70 times; within a year, it may run 50 times; within 2 years, it may run 30 times; within 5 years, it will be completely fixed in the Divine Consciousness. Then, it will not run out at all even if you try your level best to bring it out, like the wandering bull, which was in the habit of running to gardens of different landlords for eating grass, but which now eats fresh gram and extract of cotton seeds in its own resting place.

If there is much strain in meditation, reduce the number of hours for a few days. Do light meditation only. When you have regained the normal tone, again increase the period. Use your common-sense all throughout Sadhana. I always reiterate on this point.

Those who meditate for four or five hours at one stretch can have two Asanas, either Padma and Vajra or Siddha and Vajra, in the beginning. Sometimes, the blood accumulates in one part of the legs or thighs and gives a little trouble. After two hours, change the Asana from Padma or Siddha Asana to Vajrasana or stretch the legs at full length. Lean against a wall or a pillow. Keep the spine erect. This is the most comfortable Asana. Join two chairs. Sit on one chair and stretch the legs on another chair. This is another contrivance.

Pose or Asana is really mental. Try to have a mental Padma or mental Siddha Asana. If the mind is wandering, you cannot have a steady body or a steady physical pose. When the mind is steady or fixed in Brahman, steadiness of the body automatically follows.

Have the one all-pervading Bhavana (feeling). Deny the finite body as a mere appearance. Try to keep up the feelings always. Whatever elevates you, you can take it up for your advantage just to elevate the mind and then continue your prolonged meditation.

You must daily increase your Vairagya, meditation and Sattvic virtues such as patience, perseverance, mercy, love, forgiveness, purity, etc. Vairagya and good qualities help meditation. Meditation increases the Sattvic qualities.

Just as you conserve the energy by observing Mouna (vow of silence), so also you will have to conserve the mental energy by stopping useless thinking. Then you will save abundant reserve energy for meditation.

Remember these three word-images: PURIFICATION, CONCENTRATION, ABSORPTION. Repeat them mentally during meditation. This is a triplet. Remember this triplet. Purify the mind. Get rid of Mala (impurities such as Kama, Krodha, etc.). Perform selfless, desireless actions. This will purify the mind. Practise Upasana, Pranayama, Trataka and Rajayogic "Chitta-Vritti-Nirodha." This will help Ekagrata. Then practise constant and deep meditation. The mind will be absorbed eventually.

"Pranavo dhanuh saro hyatma brahma tallakshyam uchyate;
Apramattena veddhavyam saravan tanmayo bhavet."

"Om is the bow, mind is the arrow and Brahman is the mark to be aimed at. Brahman is to be hit or pierced by him whose thoughts are concentrated. Then he will be of the same nature (Tanmaya) as Brahman, as the arrow becomes one with the aim when it has pierced it." (Mundakopanishad, II-ii-4)

Sit on Padma or Siddha Asana. Close the eyes. Concentrate the gaze on the Trikuti (space between the two eyebrows). Now, chant Dhirga Pranava (long OM) forcibly for five minutes. This will remove Vikshepa or tossing of the mind. Concentration will ensue. Now repeat OM mentally with Brahma-Bhavana. Whenever the mind begins to wander, again chant OM verbally. As soon as the mind gets calm, mentally repeat OM again. The same process can be adopted for Saguna meditation also.

Those who have knowledge of the flow of the five Tattvas in the nostrils can very rapidly advance in meditation. There is an intimate connection between the mind and the five Tattvas. When Agni-Tattva flows through the nostrils, mind is much agitated and meditation is interrupted. During the flow of the Akasa-Tattva, meditation is very favourable. A knowledge of

"Svara-Sadhana" or "Svarodaya" as it is popularly termed is an indispensable necessity for those who take up to meditation.

Just as a very skilful archer, in shooting at a bird, is aware of the way in which he takes his steps, holds the bow, the bow-string and the arrow at the time when he pierces the bird—"Standing in this position, holding thus the bow, thus the bow-string and thus the arrow, I pierce the bird"—and ever afterwards would not fail to fulfil these conditions that he might pierce the bird, even so should the aspirant note the conditions such as suitable food thus: "Eating this kind of food, following such a person, in such a dwelling, in this mode, at this time, I attained to this meditation and Samadhi."

As a clever cook, in serving his master, notes the kind of food that he relishes and hence forward serves it and gets gain, so the aspirant too notes the conditions such as nourishment, etc., at the moment of attaining meditation and Samadhi and, in fulfilling them, gets ecstasy again and again.

MEDITATION WITH EYES OPEN

In the beginning, when you are a neophyte, you can close your eyes to remove the distraction of mind, as you are very weak. But, later on, you must meditate with eyes open, even during walking. You must keep your balance of mind even when you are in the bustle of a city. Then only you are perfect. Why do you close your eyes during meditation? Open your eyes and meditate. Think strongly that the world is unreal, that there is no world, that there is Atman only. If you can meditate on Atman even when the eyes are open, you will be a strong man. You will not be easily disturbed.

BENEFITS OF MEDITATION

Agni (fire) is of two kinds, viz., Samanya Agni (ordinary fire) and Visesha Agni (special fire). Samanya Agni is hidden in all trees and woods. It is of no use for burning purposes. Visesha Agni that is formed by rubbing a match or rubbing two pieces of wood is useful for cooking and other purposes. Similarly, there is Samanya Chaitanya (ordinary intelligence or consciousness) that is pervading everywhere. There is also Visesha Chaitanya (special intelligence). Samanya Chaitanya cannot destroy the ignorance or Avidya of men. It is only the special intelligence—Atmakara Vritti or Avichhinna Visesha Chaitanya that can destroy the Mula Ajnana, the primitive ignorance that envelops the Svarupa (Brahman or Existence). This special intelligence is developed when a man meditates on the Infinite with a pure heart.

In contemplation, you are in spiritual contact with the unchanging Light. You are cleansed of all the impurities. This Light cleanses the soul which touches it. The sun-glass is exposed to the light of the sun and the straws that are underneath catch fire. So, within yourself, if you have an open heart devotedly lifted up to God, the Light of His purity and love, illumining this open soul, will consume all your shortcomings in the fire of Divine Love. The Light brings enhanced energy and great comfort.

This purifying process leads to a deeper insight into Truth. This is the action of Grace of the Lord upon the soul in meditation. In this inflowing Grace, there forthwith arises that Light of the mind into which God is sending a ray of His unclouded Splendour. This Light is vastly potent.

If you can meditate for half an hour, you will be able to engage yourself with peace and spiritual strength in the battle of life for one week through the force of this meditation. Such is the beneficial result of meditation. As you have to move with different minds of a peculiar nature in your daily life, get the strength and peace from the meditation and you will have no trouble and worry then.

All actions, whether internal or external, can be done only when the mind is united with the organs. Thought is the real action. If you have control over the mind by steady practice, if you can regulate your emotions and moods, you will not do foolish and wrong actions. Meditation will help a lot in checking various emotions and impulses.

Meditation acts as a powerful tonic. It is a mental and nervine tonic as well. The holy vibrations penetrate all the cells of the body and cure the diseases of the body. Those who meditate save doctor's bills. The powerful, soothing waves that arise during meditation exercise a benign influence on the mind, nerves, organs and cells of the body. The divine energy freely flows like Tailadhara (flow of oil from one vessel to another) from the feet of the Lord to the different systems of the Sadhakas.

Considerable changes take place in the mind, brain and

the nervous system by the practice of meditation. New nerve-currents, new vibrations, new avenues, new grooves, new cells, new channels are formed. The whole mind and the nervous system are remodelled. You will develop a new heart, a new mind, new sensations, new feelings, new mode of thinking and acting and a new view of the universe (as God in manifestation).

The fire of meditation, annihilates all foulness due to vice. Then suddenly comes knowledge or Divine Wisdom which directly leads to Mukti or final emancipation.

Real peace and Ananda (bliss) manifest only when the Vasanas are thinned out and Sankalpas get extinguished. When you fix the mind either on Sri Krishna or Siva or Atman even for five minutes, Sattva Guna is infused into the mind. Vasanas are thinned out and Sphurana of Sankalpa becomes less and less. You will feel peace and bliss during the five minutes. You can compare this Ananda from meditation with the transitory sensual pleasures. You will find that this Ananda from meditation is a million times superior to sensual pleasure. Meditate and feel this Ananda. Then you will know its real value.

You will get the full Ananda of the divine glory only when you merge deep into silent meditation. When you are on the border-land of divinity of God, when you are at the threshold of God, when you are in the outer skirts, you will not get the maximum peace and bliss.

These are the benefits that are derived by the Yogic students who practise meditation systematically. They are Santi (peace), Santosha (contentment), Abhaya (fearlessness), peculiar spiritual Ananda (bliss), unruffled state of mind in worldly difficulties, Nischala Sthiti (steadiness), inspiration, intuitive perception, Sattvic qualities and absence of anger (Akrodha), egoism and Raga-Dvesha (like and dislike).

Develop the Prakamya, the divine vision (Divine Drishti), Jnana-Chakshus by concentration, purification and meditation.

HOW TO DEVELOP VIRTUES BY MEDITATION

Examine your character. Pick some distinct defect in it. Find out its opposite. Let us say that you suffer from irritability. The opposite of irritability is patience. Try to develop this virtue by meditation on the abstract virtue of patience. Regularly, every morning, sit down at 4 a.m. in Padma or Siddha Asana in a solitary room for half an hour and begin to think on patience, its value, its practice under provocation, taking one point one day, another on another day and thinking as steadily as you can, recalling the mind when it wanders. Think of yourself as perfectly patient, a model of patience and end with a vow: "This patience which is my true self, I will feel and show from today."

For a few days, probably, there will be no change perceptible. You will still feel and show irritability. Go on practising steadily every morning. Presently, as you say an irritable thing, the thought will flash into your mind, unbidden: "I should have been patient." Still go on in practice. Soon, the thought of patience will arise with the irritable impulse and the outer manifestation will be checked. Still go on practising. The irritable impulse will grow feebler and feebler until you find that irritability has disappeared and patience has become your normal attitude towards annoyances. In this manner, you can develop various virtues as sympathy, self-restraint, purity, humility, benevolence, nobility, generosity, etc.

CHAPTER 33

EXPERIENCES AND OBSTACLES IN MEDITATION

WHAT HAPPENS DURING MEDITATION

In meditation, new grooves are formed in the brain and the mind moves upwards in the new spiritual grooves. When the mind becomes steady in meditation, the eyeballs also become steady. A Yogi whose mind is calm will have a steady eye. There will be no winking at all. The eyes will be lustrous, red or pure white. When you enter into very deep, silent meditation, the breath will not come out of the nostrils. There may be occasional slow movement of the lungs and the abdomen. During normal exhalation the air comes out 16 digits. When the mind gets concentrated, it will become less and less. It will come to 15 then 14, 13, 12, 10, 8 and so on. From the nature of the breathing, you can infer the degree of concentration of an aspirant. Watch the breath very carefully.

Man tries to grasp the abstract through forms. After the mind has been purified, an abstract image is formed in the purified mind by Sravana (listening to spiritual discourses and holy scriptures) and Brahma-Chintana. This abstract image melts later on into deep Nididhyasana. What is left behind is Chinmatra or Kevala Asti (pure Existence alone).

In Nididhyasana or profound and continued meditation, thinking ceases. There is only one idea of "Aham Brahmasmi." When this idea also is given up, Nirvikalpa Samadhi or Sahaja Advaita-Nishtha ensues. Just as salt melts in water, the Sattvic mind melts in silence in Brahman—its Adhishthana (substratum).

EXPERIENCES IN MEDITATION

Various persons get various spiritual experiences. There cannot be a common experience for all. It depends upon the temperament, mode of Sadhana, place of concentration and various other factors. Some hear melodious sounds in the ears. Some see lights. Some get Ananda (spiritual bliss). Some get both Prakasa and Ananda. During meditation, you may experience that you are rising from your seat. Some experience that they fly in the air.

Lights

The Divine light comes not through open doors, but only through narrow slits. The aspirant sees the Divine Ray as a sunbeam passing through a chick into a dark room. It is like a 'flash of lightning.' This sudden illumination chokes all sounds of words. The aspirant is spell-bound in ecstasy and awe. He trembles with love and awe, just as Arjuna did when he had the Virat-Visvarupa-Darsana of Lord Krishna. So bright and glorious is the Light environing the Divine that the initiate is dazzled and bewildered.

During meditation, the colour of lights that you see varies according to the Tattva that flows through the nostrils. If there is Agni-Tattva, you will see red-coloured lights. If Akasa-Tattva flows, you will have blue-coloured lights. If Apas-Tattva (water) prevails, you will see white-coloured lights. If there is Prithvi-Tattva, you will have yellow lights. If there is Vayu-Tattva, you will see black colour. You can change the Tattva by various ways. But the best way is by thought. "As you think, so you also become." When the Agni-Tattva flows, think intently of Apas-Tattva. Apas-Tattva will begin to flow soon.

Rapture

During meditation, you get rapture or ecstasy. It is of five kinds viz., the lesser thrill, momentary rapture, flooding rapture, transporting rapture and all-pervading rapture. The lesser thrill is only able to raise the hairs of the body (like the goose skin). The momentary rapture is like the productions of lightning, moment by moment. Like waves breaking on the seashore, the flooding rapture descends rapidly on the body and breaks. Transporting rapture is strong and lifts the body up to the extent of launching it into the air. When the all-pervading rapture arises, the whole body is completely surcharged, blown like a full-bladder.

Crossing the Body-Consciousness

Aspirants are eager to get spiritual experiences soon. As soon as they get them, they are afraid. They are awfully alarmed when they go above the body-consciousness. They entertain a passing wonder whether they will come back again or not. Why should they be afraid at all? It does not matter much whether they return to body-consciousness or not. All our attempts are mainly directed towards getting over this body-consciousness. We are used to certain limitations. When these limitations suddenly drop away, we feel that there is no definite base left to stand upon. That is the reason why we are afraid when we go above the body-consciousness. That is a novel experience. Courage is needed. Bravery is an indispensable requisite. Sruti says, "*Nayam-atma balahinena labhyah*—This Atman can hardly be attained by weak (timid) persons." All sorts of forces have to be encountered on the way. A dacoit or an anarchist can easily realise God, because he is fearless. A push in the right direction is only necessary for him. How Jagai and Madhai, rogues of the first water, became very good saints! They pelted stones at Nityananda, the disciple of Lord Gouranga. Nityananda won them by pure divine love. Dacoit Ratnakara became Sage Valmiki.

Visions of Spirits

Sometimes, bad spirits will trouble you. They may have ugly, fierce faces with long teeth. Drive them with your strong will. Give the word of command: "Get out." They will go away. They are vampires. They are elementals. They will not do any harm to the Sadhakas. Your courage will be tested here. If you are timid, you cannot march further. Draw power and courage from the Atman within, the inexhaustible Source (Avyaya). You will come across very good spirits also. They will help you a lot in your onward march.

There is a kind of vision one occasionally gets during meditation. You may behold a dazzling light with abrupt motion. You may behold a head of marvellous form, of the colour of a flame, red as fire and very awful to look at. It has three wings of marvellous length and breadth, white as a dazzling cloud. At times they would beat terribly and again would be still. The head never utters a word, but remains altogether still. Now and again, there is beating with its extended wings.

During meditation, some of the visions that you see are your own materialised thoughts, while some others are real, objective visions.

BREAK VEIL AFTER VEIL

If you get experiences of the glimpses of Self during intense meditation, if you see a blazing light during meditation and if you get spiritual visions of angels, archangels, Rishis, Munis, Devatas and any other extraordinary spiritual experiences, do not fall back in terror. Do not mistake them for phantoms. Do not give up the Sadhana. Plod on. Persevere diligently. Break veil after veil.

If there is any error in Sadhana (meditation), at once consult the senior Sannyasins or realised souls and remove the mistake. If your general health is sound, if you are cheerful, happy and strong, physically and mentally, if the mind is peaceful and unruffled, if you get Ananda in meditation and if your will is growing strong, pure and irresistible, think that you are improving in meditation and everything is going all right.

March on boldly. Do not look back. Cross the intense void and darkness. Pierce the layer of Moha. Melt the subtle Ahankara now. Svarupa will shine by itself. You will experience the Turiya (Arudha state).

OBSTACLES TO MEDITATION

Obstacles to meditation are really from within. Environments are from within; you create your own environments. Try to be happy in whatever situation you are placed. Do not complain. Bear sufferings. You can conquer Nature. Maya is Tuchha (nothing) or Alpa (small or non-entity) for a Brahma-Jnani.

The obstacles to meditation are only from within. Sleepiness, passions, confused state of the mind, Manorajya (building castles in the air) are the chief obstacles that stand in the way of fixing the mind on God or Brahman. The five hindrances to meditation, viz., sense-desire, ill-will, sloth-torpor, flurry-worry and perplexity should be removed. For, when these are not removed, meditation cannot arise. The mind that lusts after many things through sense-desire is not concentrated on one object; or being overcome by sense-desire, it does not enter upon the progress of meditation in order to put away the sensuous element. The mind that is harassed by ill-will concerning an object does not proceed at once. The mind that is overcome by sloth and torpor is unwieldy. Obsessed by worry and flurry, it does not repose, but flirts about. Struck by perplexity, it does not go on the path that leads to the attainment of meditation and Samadhi. Obstacles to meditation are thus really from within. They are not from without. Train the mind properly.

Laya (sleep), Vikshepa (tossing of mind from one object to another), Kashaya (memory of sensual pleasures) and hidden Vasanas and Rasasvada (the happiness derived from Savikalpa Samadhi) are four stumbling blocks in meditation.

Tandri and Manorajya

When the mind has been withdrawn from objects through Vairagya and Uparati, do not allow it to go into sleep or Manorajya (fancies and wild imagination). When you constantly contemplate on the meaning of the Mahavakya 'Aham Brahmasmi' or 'Tat Tvam Asi' through the process of Mahavakyanusandhana, all the Vishayas (seeing, hearing, touching, tasting and smelling) will stop. But, owing to the force of Samskaras, Manorajya (building castles in the air) will continue. Mind builds castles in the air. This is termed Manoratha in Sanskrit. This is a serious obstacle to meditation. It should be stopped by Vichara. Sometimes, during the course of meditation, the mind suddenly slips into its old grooves for sleeping. People think that they are meditating, while they are actually sleeping. A mixture of drowsiness (Tandri) and Manorajya (building castles in the air, reverie) is mistaken by aspirants for deep meditation and Samadhi. The mind appears to be established in concentration and free from Vikshepa (distraction). This is a mistake. Alasya and Stabdhata (stupefaction arising from fear or wonder, mental restlessness and mental depression) are other disturbing factors in meditation.

Closely watch the mind. Make it Ekagra (one-pointed) and allow it to rest on the Svarupa Brahman). Be thoughtful, careful and vigilant. Stand up for ten minutes and dash cold water on the face and head, if drowsiness comes in. Remove the two serious obstacles of Tandri and Manorajya by Vichara, Pranayama and light, Sattvic diet. Tandri and Alasya are removed by Pranayama, Sirshasana, Sarvangasana and Mayurasana and light, Sattvic diet. Find out the disturbing causes and remove them. Avoid the company of those whom your mind dislikes. Do not argue. Do not contradict. Do not try to convince persons who are unreasonable and undeveloped. Talk little. Observe Mouna. Live alone. In this way, you can avoid all sorts of excitements. Have constant Satsanga. Study elevating books such as the Yogavasishtha, the Upanishads, etc. Have Brahma-Bhavana. Repeat OM with meaning and feeling. All depressing thoughts will melt away.

If you are alert and if by protracted efforts and incessant, vigilant Svarupa-Chintana (meditation on Brahman), you get over the obstacles of sleep, Manorajya, etc., the steady Brahmakara Vritti and Brahma-Jnana will dawn in no time. Ajnana will vanish. You will be established in Sahaja Paramananda state. All Sanchita (accumulated) Karmas will be burnt up in the fire of wisdom.

Dreams in Meditation

Various sorts of fantastic dreams trouble some aspirants very much. Sometimes, there is a mixture of meditation and dreams. The presence of dreams denotes that you are not yet well-established in deep meditation, that you have not removed Vikshepa (tossing of the mind) and that you have not done constant, intense Sadhana. As the phenomenon of dreams is very peculiar and inexplicable, it is very difficult to control dreams unless you wipe out all the Samskaras in the Karana Sarira (causal body) and control all thoughts. As you grow in purity, Viveka and concentration, dreams will decrease.

Depression

Very often, depression comes in meditation in neophytes owing to previous Samskaras, influence of astral entities, evil spirits, bad company, cloudy days, bad stomach owing to indigestion and loaded bowels in constipation. It must be removed quickly by cheerful thoughts, a brisk walk, singing, laughing, prayer, Pranayama, etc.

Vikshepa

Scents, soft beds, novel-reading, dramas, theatres, cinemas, vulgar music, dancing, flowers, company of women, Rajasic diet—all these excite passions and cause disturbance of the mind. Too much salt, too much chillies, too much sweets cause intense thirst and disturb meditation. Too much talking, too much walking and too much mixing disturb the mind in meditation.

Impulses disturb meditation. All obscure subconscious impulses should be controlled by the intellect and will. Sex-impulse and ambition are two real disturbing factors in meditation.

They carry on guerilla warfare. They attack the Sadhakas again and again. They appear to be thinned out for some time. They get revived often. They should be extirpated by great efforts, Vichara, Viveka (power of discrimination between Atman and Anatman, Self and non-Self) and Sivoham-Bhavana.

It is the sound that sets the mind in motion. It is the sound that makes the mind to think. Sound disturbs the mind a great deal in meditation. A sound with meaning disturbs more than a sound without meaning. A continuous sound as the silent murmur of a river is not so disturbing as an abrupt, sudden, sharp, broken sound. The mind does not feel a sound when it is used to it. You feel only when the clock stops.

Tushnimbhuta Avastha

Tushnimbhuta Avastha is a quiet state of the mind wherein there is neither attraction nor repulsion for objects for a short time. It occurs in the Jagrat state. It is a neutral state of the mind. It is an obstacle to meditation. It should be avoided. It is mistaken by ignorant Sadhakas for Samadhi.

Kashaya

Kashaya means colouring. Raga, Dvesha and Moha are the Kashaya or colouring of the mind. Kashaya is the subtle influence in the mind produced by enjoyment and left there to fructify in time to come and distract the mind from Samadhi. This is a serious obstacle to meditation. It does not allow the Sadhaka to enter into Samadhi-Nishtha. It induces the subtle memory of pleasures enjoyed. It is hidden Vasana. From the Samskara, Vasana originates. Samskara is the cause and Vasana is the effect. It is a kind of Mala (impurity of mind). Constant Vichara coupled with Brahma-Bhavana is the only potent remedy to eradicate this dire malady Kashaya.

Sattvic Vrittis

During meditation, when your mind is more Sattvic, you will be inspired. The mind will be composing fine poems and solving some problems of life. Stamp out these Sattvic Vrittis also. This is all dissipation of mental energy. Soar higher and higher to Atman only.

Savikalpa Samadhi

Even the happiness of Savikalpa Samadhi is an obstacle, because it prevents you from entering into the Nirvikalpa state. It produces false Tushti (contentment) and you stop your further Sadhana.

The mind should be freed from all these obstacles. Then only will you enter into pure Advaita Nirvikalpa state. Vichara and Brahma-Bhavana are the only helps to attain this highest state.

MEDITATION AND WORK

He who meditates is not able to work. He who works is not able to meditate. This is not balance. This is not equanimity. The two principles, meditation and action, must be well-balanced. You must be able, if you are ready to follow the divine injunction, to take up whatever work you are given—even a stupendous work—and leave it the next day, with the same quietness with which you took it up and without feeling that the responsibility is yours. You must be able to work hard in the world with tremendous force and, when the work is over, you must be able to shut yourself up in a cave as an absolute recluse for a long time with great peace of mind. That is balance, that is real strength. Then only you have gone beyond the qualities (Gunatita). "He, O Pandava, who hateth not radiance (Sattva) nor outgoing energy (work), nor even sloth and slumber (Moha) when present, nor longeth after them when absent—he is said to have crossed over the qualities" (Gita, XIV-22).

When you advance in the spiritual practice, it will be very difficult for you to do meditation and office work at the same time, because the mind will undergo double strain. Those who practise meditation will find that they are more sensitive than the people who do not meditate and, because of that, the strain on the physical body is enormous. The mind works in different grooves and channels with different Samskaras during meditation. It finds it very difficult to adjust to different kinds of uncongenial activities. As soon as it comes down from the meditation, it gropes in darkness. It gets bewildered and puzzled. The Prana (energy) which moves inward in different grooves and channels and which is subtle during the meditation has to move in new, different channels during worldly activities. It becomes very gross during work. It has to work in different grooves and channels. When you again sit for meditation in the evening, you will have to struggle hard to wipe out the newly acquired Samskaras you have gathered during the course of the day and get calm and one-pointedness of mind. This struggle sometimes brings in headache.

It behoves, therefore, that advanced Grihastha Yogic students (householders) will have to stop all the worldly activities when they advance in meditation, if they desire to progress further. They themselves will be forced to give up all work, if they are really sincere. Work is a hindrance in meditation for advanced students. That is the reason why Lord Krishna says in the Gita, "For a sage who is seeking Yoga, action is called the means; for the same sage who is enthroned in Yoga (state of Yogarudha), serenity (Sama) is called the means." Then, work and meditation become incompatible like acid and alkali or fire and water or light and darkness.

REASONS FOR FAILURES IN MEDITATION

Some practise meditation for a period of 15 years and yet they have not made any real progress at all. Why? This is due to lack of earnestness, Vairagya, keen longing for liberation and intense, constant Sadhana. There is always a complaint amongst the aspirants, "I am meditating for the last 12 years. I have not made any improvement. I have no realisation." Why is it so? What is the reason? They have not plunged themselves in deep meditation into the innermost recesses of their hearts. They have not properly assimilated and saturated the mind with the thoughts of God. They have not done regular, systematic Sadhana. They have not disciplined the Indriyas perfectly. They have not collected all the outgoing rays of the mind. They have not made the self-determination, "I will realise this very second." They have not given the full 100% of the mind or 16 annas of the mind—their full mind—to God. They have not kept an increasing flow of Divine Consciousness like the flow of oil (Tailadharavat).

You will have to note very carefully whether you remain stationary in the spiritual path even after many years of spiritual practice or whether you are progressing. Sometimes, you may go downwards also, if you are not very vigilant and careful, if your Vairagya wanes and if you are slack in meditation. Reaction may set in.

Just as the man who foolishly runs after two rabbits will not catch hold of any one of them, so also a meditator who runs after two conflicting thoughts will not get success in any one of the two thoughts. If he has divine thoughts for ten minutes and then worldly conflicting thoughts for the next ten minutes, he will not succeed in anything, in getting at the Divine Consciousness. You must run after one rabbit only with vigour, strength and one-pointedness. You are sure to catch it. You must have only divine thoughts at all times. Then you are sure to realise God soon.

You must not be too hasty in longing for the fruits at once, when you take to meditation. Haste makes waste. A young lady perambulated an Asvattha tree (*Filicus religiosa*) 108 times for getting an offspring and immediately touched her abdomen to see whether there was a child or not. It is simply foolishness. She will have to wait for some months. Even so, if those who read works dealing with Atma-Jnana and who do take delight therein will not be hasty in longing for the fruits at once, but will meditate regularly and gradually upon them, then the mind will, by degrees, be ripened and, in the end, the endless Atman will be reached; and they will get Atmasakshatkara (Self-realisation).

You will have to exert in the beginning to get an equilibrium of mind. Later on, you will have a habitual balanced state of mind. So is the case with meditation. After some years of practice, meditation becomes habitual.

CONDITIONS FOR SELF-REALISATION

Just as you saturate water with salt or sugar, you will have to saturate the mind with thoughts of God and Brahman, with divine glory, Divine Presence with sublime soul-awakening spiritual thoughts. Then only you will always be established in the Divine Consciousness. Before saturating the mind with thoughts of Brahman, you will have to assimilate the divine ideas first. Assimilation first and then saturation. Then comes realisation, at once, without a moment's delay. Remember the triplet always: "Assimilation—Saturation—Realisation."

Free yourself from the base thoughts of the mind, the various useless Sankalpas (imaginations). Just as you render the turbid water pure by the addition of clearing nut (strychnos potatorum), so also you will have to make the turbid mind, filled with Vasanas and f*alse Sankalpas, pure* by Brahma-Chintana (thinking and reflecting on the Absolute). If the mind constantly dwells on sensual objects, the conception of the reality of the universe will surely increase. If the mind ceaselessly thinks of Atman (Absolute), the world appears like a dream. Mark the word "ceaseless." This is important. Then only there will be true illumination. Then only there will be dawn of spiritual knowledge. The Jnana-Surya (the Sun of Knowledge) will rise in the firmament of Chidakasa (knowledge-space).

You will find very often these terms in the Gita: "*Ananya-chetah*" "*Matchittah*" "*Nityayuktah*" "*Manmanah*" "*Ekagra-manah*" "*Sarvabhavah.*" These terms connote that you will have to give your full mind, entire 100% mind to God. Then only you will have Self-realisation. Even if one ray of mind runs outside, it is impossible to attain God-consciousness.

It is the actions of the mind that are truly termed Karmas. True liberation results from the disenthralment of the mind. Those who have freed themselves from the fluctuation of their minds come into possession of the supreme Nishtha (meditation). Should the mind be purged of all its impurities, then it will become very calm and all the worldly delusion, with its births and deaths, will be soon destroyed.

Mind exists on account of "I." "I" exists on account of mind. "I" is only an idea in the mind. "Mind" and "I" are identical. If "I" vanishes, mind will also vanish; and if mind vanishes, "I" will vanish. Destroy the mind through Tattva-Jnana. Destroy the "I" through "Aham Brahmasmi Bhavana," through constant and intense Nididhyasana. When mind vanishes or thoughts cease, Nama-Rupa will cease to exist and the Goal is reached.

CHAPTER 34

SAMADHI

CHARACTERISTICS OF SAMADHI

When the mind is completely absorbed in one object of meditation, it is termed Samadhi. The mind identifies itself with the object of meditation. In Samadhi, there is neither Dhyana nor Dhyata (neither meditation nor meditator). The meditator and meditated, the thinker and the thought, the worshipper and the worshipped become one or identical. The Triputi (triad) vanishes. The mind loses its own consciousness and becomes identical with the object of meditation. The meditator has dissolved his personality in the sea of God, drowned and forgotten there till he becomes simply the instrument of God. When his mouth opens, it speaks God's words without effort or forethought through direct intuition and, when he raises his hand, God flows again through that to work a miracle.

In Samadhi, there is neither seeing nor hearing. There is neither physical nor mental consciousness. There is only spiritual consciousness. There is only Existence (Sat). That is your real Svarupa. When the water dries up in a pool, the reflection of the sun in the water also vanishes. When the mind melts in Brahman, when the mind-lake dries up, the reflected Chaitanya (Chidabhasa) also vanishes. The Jivatman (personality) goes away. There remains Existence alone.

Turiya is the spiritual condition where there is no play of mind, where the mind is dissolved in Brahman. It is the "fourth dimension," where there is infinite Brahmic bliss. It is not a condition of inertia, forgetfulness or annihilation. It is a state of absolute consciousness which baffles all attempts at description. It is the final goal of all. It is Mukti. It is Moksha.

Generally, when you have what you call dreamless sleep, it is one of two things; either you do not remember what you dreamt of or you fell into absolute unconsciousness which is almost death—a taste of death. But, there is the possibility of a sleep in which you enter into an absolute silence, immortality and peace in all parts of your being and your consciousness merges into Satchidananda. You can hardly call it sleep, for there is perfect "awareness." In that condition, you can remain for a few minutes or hours or days; but, these few minutes give you more rest and refreshment than hours of ordinary sleep. You cannot have it by chance. It requires a long training.

Samadhi is not a stone-like inert state as many people imagine. A life in the spi rit (Atman or Divine) is not annihilation. When the self is bound down to its empirical accidents, its activities are not fully exercised and, when the limitations of the empirical existence are transcended, the universal life is intensified and you have enrichment of Self. You will have a rich inner life. You will have an expanded cosmic life and supra-cosmic life, too.

THE DIFFERENT KINDS OF SAMADHI

A Raja Yogi gets Nirodha-Samadhi through Chitta-Vritti-Nirodha (by restraining the mental modifications). A Bhakta gets Bhava-Samadhi through Prema of the Lord. A Vedanti gets Bheda-Samadhi through Mithyatva-Buddhi and concentration on the idea of the Asti-Bhati-Priya (the Anvaya method).

It is only the Raja Yogi who attempts the annihilation of the Vrittis, the Nirodha Samadhi ("*Yogaschittavrittinirodhah*"— Patanjali Yoga Sutras, I-2). A Vedanti has always Atma-Bhava, Brahma-Bhava whenever he comes across objects. So he does not try to annihilate the Vrittis. There is no Pratyahara for him. There is no Bahirmukha Vritti for him. He rejects Nama-Rupa and takes Asti-Bhati-Priya (Bheda-Samadhi). A Bhakta sees Narayana or Krishna in all objects. He also does not check the Vrittis. He, like the Vedanti, changes his mental attitude. It is the mind that creates all the differences and separateness. The world is all Ananda, only if you change your angle of vision, your mental attitude. You will find heaven on earth.

You can bring down to normal objective consciousness a Raja Yogi or Bhakti Yogi or Jnana Yogi by mere shaking of the body or blowing a conch. Chudalai brought down her husband Sikhidhvaja from Samadhi by shaking his body. Lord Hari brought Prahlada down from his Samadhi by blowing His conch.

SAMADHI THROUGH HATHA YOGA

A Hatha Yogi draws all his Prana from the different parts of his body and takes it to the Sahasrara Chakra (thousand-petalled lotus) at the top of the head. Then he enters into Samadhi (superconscious state). Therefore it is very difficult to bring him down to objective consciousness by merely shaking his body. Hatha Yogis have remained buried underneath the earth in Samadhi for years together. They plug the posterior nostrils through Khechari Mudra (a kind of Hatha Yogic Kriya) with their long tongues.

Prana and Apana that move in the chest and anus respectively are united by the Yogic processes of Jalandhara, Mula and Uddiyana Bandhas and the united Prana-Apana is driven into the Sushumna Nadi of the spinal canal. The Pranas, when thus driven, draw up the mind also along the Sushumna Nadi which is otherwise known as Brahma Nadi. During the ascent in the Sushumna Nadi, the three Granthis or knots, viz., Brahma-Granthi at Muladhara-Chakra, Vishnu-Granthi at Manipura-Chakra and Rudra-Granthi at Ajna-Chakra should be cut asunder by strenuous efforts. These knots prevent the ascent of Kundalini. Bhastrika Pranayama breaks down these knots. When Kula-Kundalini Sakti that lies dormant in the Muladhara-Chakra in the form of a coiled serpent with $3\frac{1}{2}$ curves or turns, with the face downwards is awakened by spiritual Sadhana, it ascends upwards towards Sahasrara Chakra or the thousand-petalled lotus in the crown of the head and takes along with it the mind and Prana also. When the mind is in the Sushumna, the Yogi is shut out from the objective, physical consciousness of the world. He is practically dead to the world, sees various visions and moves in the mental, ethereal space (Chidakasa). Samadhi starts.

SAMADHI THROUGH RAJA YOGA

Deep meditation leads to Samadhi or oneness with God. If you can fix the mind for ten seconds steadily on a particular object or Murti, it is Dharana (concentration). Ten such Dharanas become Dhyana (meditation). Ten such Dhyanas form a Samadhi. The mind is filled with Atman or God. Mind loses its own consciousness and becomes identified with the object of meditation (Tatchitta, Tanmaya, Tadakara). Just as a toy made of salt melts in water, even so, the mind melts in Brahman in

Nirvikalpa Samadhi. A sudden stroke of mystic illumination puts an end to all the empirical existence altogether and the very idea or remembrance of such a thing as this world or the narrow individuality of the spirit in this world absolutely leaves the Self.

In trained Yogis, you cannot say where Pratyahara (abstraction) ends and Dharana (concentration) begins; where Dharana ends and Dhyana (meditation) begins; where Dhyana ends and Samadhi (superconscious state) begins. The moment they sit on the Asana, all the processes occur simultaneously with electric or lightning speed and they enter Samadhi at their conscious will. In the neophytes, Pratyahara first takes place. Then Dharana begins. Then Dhyana slowly commences. Before Samadhi manifests, their minds, getting impatient and tired, drop down. Constant and intense Sadhana, with light but nutritious food, will bring about sanguine success in getting Samadhi.

YOGIC SAMADHI AND VEDANTIC SAMADHI

There is a difference between the Nirvikalpa state of a Yogi and the Nirvikalpa state of a Vedantin. The former concerns the mind. The latter concerns the pure Atman or Brahman only. In Yogic Samadhi, Dhyeya remains. Dhyeya means the object of meditation. In Vedantic Samadhi, Kevala Asti (Existence alone) remains.

SAVIKALPA SAMADHI AND NIRVIKALPA SAMADHI

The ground floor represents the life of passion in the sense-universe. The first storey corresponds to Savikalpa Samadhi. The second storey is tantamount to Nirvikalpa Samadhi. The third storey represents the Sahajavastha or a Jivanmukta. The moving of a bullock cart can be compared to Savikalpa Samadhi. It stops. This is Nirvikalpa Samadhi. The bulls are detached. This is Sahajavastha. When the Yogi has reached the last perfect stage of meditation and Samadhi, the fire whereof burns surely all the residue of his actions, he at once gets Liberation (Jivanmukti) in this very life.

In Savikalpa Samadhi, there is Triputi or the triad—Dhyata (the meditator), Dhyana (meditation) and Dhyeya (object of meditation). In Nirvikalpa Samadhi, this Triputi vanishes (Triputirahita). Nirvikalpa means "free from all sorts of modifications and imaginations." The mind completely melts in Brahman. The happiness or bliss that you get in Savikalpa Samadhi is termed Rasasvada. This is also an obstacle (Pratibandha or Vighna) for further spiritual progress. It makes you stop here. It cannot liberate you. You must further march onwards to attain the highest Nirvikalpa state wherein lies your whole freedom.

ADVANTAGES OF BHAKTI YOGA SADHANA

The practices of Hatha Yoga and Raja Yoga are not suited to the majority of men in this age, while they have always an irresistible charm for such practices because of their apparent concreteness and promise of speedy rewards. A vast majority of persons have no good physique and robust constitution. They are weaklings. In this age, children beget children. There are baby mothers. Devotion or Bhakti Yoga is, therefore, easy and safe. Any man can repeat the Name of God. Anyone can sing His praise. Without a mother, you cannot have a son. Even so, without Ananya Bhakti (one-pointed or single-minded devotion), you cannot have Jnana. When Bhakti is fully ripe, Brahma-Jnana dawns of itself, without much effort on the part of the Sadhaka.

Any Mantra is very powerful. It purifies the mind. It induces Vairagya. It causes Antarmukha Vritti. Every Mantra has a Rishi who gave it; a Devata as its informing power; the Bija or seed, a significant word which gives it a special power; a Sakti or energy of the form of the Mantra, i.e., the vibration-forms set up by its sounds; the Kilaka or the pillar, that which supports and strengthens the Mantra. Kilaka is a sort of plug which conceals the Mantra-Chaitanya. By constant and prolonged repetition of the Mantra with Bhava (feeling or right mental attitude) and concentration, the Mantra-Chaitanya is awakened. Then the Sadhaka gets Mantra-Siddhi. There is a spiritual current in all Mantras. A Mantra takes the devotee's soul first to one centre and then to another and so on, till access is gained to the goal or final region. Dhruva had Darshana of Lord Hari by repeating the Dvadasakshara (consisting of twelve letters) Mantra 'Om Namo Bhagavate Vaasudevaya' given by Rishi Narada. Prahlada had Darshana of Mahavishnu by repeating the "Narayana" Mantra. Valmiki realised God by repeating "Mara-Mara" (which becomes Rama-Rama during the course of repetition). Tukaram of Maharashtra became one with Lord

Krishna by chanting always "Vittala-Vittala," the name of the reputed image of Sri Krishna at Pandharpur.

CONTEMPLATION—FILLING—IDENTIFICATION

Mark the three processes that take place in the mind during meditation. These are: CONTEMPLATION, FILLING, IDENTIFICATION. This is another triplet. Remember these three word-images. Repeat them mentally while doing Sadhana. It will help you a lot really.

Contemplate on Atman. Fill the mind with Atman. Then the mind becomes identified with Brahman in accordance with what is known as the Bhramarakitanyaya (analogy of wasp and caterpillar). As you think, so you become. Think you are Brahman; Brahman you will become.

When the mind is withdrawn from the objects and deep reflection sets in, the objective consciousness is shut up; Savitarka Samadhi commences. Ratiocination, analysis and synthesis (a priori and a posteriori ways of reasoning), investigation and abstract reasoning take place. This is Samadhi with reasoning. Evil thoughts cannot enter now. The mind is Sattvic.

Deep study of philosophical works with Chitta Suddhi is itself a form of Samadhi. The mind here is free from worldly thoughts.

When your meditation becomes deep, you generally operate through the subtle Karana Sarira only. The Karana-Sarira consciousness becomes your normal consciousness. Yogis have a normal Karana-Sarira consciousness. Bhaktas like Lord Gouranga, Tukaram, Tulasidas identified themselves with their Karana Sarira and had a normal Karana-Sarira consciousness. A Bhakta of Karana-Sarira consciousness is an occupant of Brahma Loka even when living in the fleshy tabernacle. He is one with Brahman or Hiranyagarbha. He has Divine Aisvarya; yet he has a thin ethereal body. He keeps up his individuality. A whirlpool is one with the whole mass of the water. It has a separate existence also. Similar is the case with the Bhakta who has a life with his Karana-Sarira in Isvara.

HOW TO ATTAIN SAMADHI THROUGH VEDANTA

Purify the mind by Japa, Pranayama, Satsanga, Svadhyaya, Dana, Yajna, Tapas and selfless service. Then fix it on God.

Destroy Sankalpa-Vikalpa of the mind. Unite the currents of the mind with the spiritual current. Abandon the idea or notion of "I," "he," "thou," Ghata (pot), Pata (cloth), i.e., Nana-Bhava, Dvaita-Bhava. Have Brahma-Bhavana instead. Then Samadhi or superconscious state will supervene automatically. There are four ways of destroying the ego or Ahankara, viz., two Advaitic methods (positive and negative), one Bhaktas' method of ungrudging, unreserved, absolute self-surrender (Atmanivedana) and the fourth, complete self-sacrifice of Nishkama Karma Yogis.

The negative Vedantic method is denial: "I am not the body, I am not the mind." "Brahma satyam jaganmithya jivo brahmaiva na-aparah:—Brahman alone is real. The world is unreal. Jiva is identical with Brahman." World includes the body. Meditate on this idea. Aham will vanish. The positive method is that everything is Self only: "Sarvam khalvidam brahma—All is Brahman. There is nothing but Brahman."

INTELLIGENT MODERATION IN SADHANA INDISPENSABLE FOR SAMADHI

Should you hold communion with Brahman, devoid of mental fancies and modifications, then the great bondage of the mind will cease, all doubts will vanish and all Karmas will perish:

"Bhidyate hridayagranthih chhidyante sarvasamsayah
Kshiyante chasya karmani tasmin drishte paravare"

The stupid bee, knowing that flowers are blossoming in a certain tree and setting out with a terrific speed, passes it; and, in turning back, reaches it when the juice is finished. Another stupid bee, setting out with a low speed reaches it when the juice is finished. A clever bee, on the other hand, setting out with just the necessary speed, easily reaches the bunch of flowers, takes the juice to its heart's content and, turning it into honey, enjoys its taste.

Similarly, among the students of surgery who are practising surgical work on a lotus-leaf placed in a vessel of water, one stupid student, letting fall the knife with speed, either cuts the lotus-leaf into two or sinks it in the water. Another stupid one, out of fear of cutting or sinking, dare not touch it with the knife. The clever one, on the other hand, makes the stroke with the knife with uniform force, finishes his course and earns money by doing similar work when occasion arises.

To take another instance: on an announcement from the King, "He who brings a cobweb four fathoms long gets 4,000 coins," a stupid man draws the cobweb in haste and cuts it here and there. Another stupid man, through fear of cutting it, dare not even touch it with his fingers. The clever man, on the other hand, rolls it from one end on a stick with mild force, brings it and gets the reward.

To take a fourth instance, a stupid sailor, who goes full sail when the wind is strong, causes the boat to rush off her course. Another stupid man, who lowers the sails when the wind is low, makes the boat remain in the same place. The clever one, on the other hand, goes full sail when the wind is low and half sail when the wind is strong and reaches his destination in safety.

Again, when the teacher announces to his pupils, "He who fills the tube without spilling the oil gets the reward," a stupid student, greedy of gain, filling with haste, spills the oil. Another stupid one, through fear of spilling oil, dare not attempt the task. A clever one, on the other hand, fills the tube with calm and steady force and gets the reward.

Even so, when the sign appears, an aspirant makes strong efforts, saying: "I will quickly attain Samadhi"; but, his mind, through excessive strain, becomes distracted and he is not able to attain ecstasy or Samadhi. Another person, seeing fault in excessive strenuousness, gives up the effort, saying: "What is the use of Samadhi to me now?" His mind, through over-slackness of energy, becomes idle and he too is not able to attain Samadhi. But, he who releases with an intelligent, calm, uniform force the mind that is slack ever so little from slackness and the distracted mind from distraction, drives it towards the goal or Lakshya (i.e., Brahman) and attains Nirvikalpa Samadhi (Advaita-Nishtha). Become like such a one.

Be silent. Know thyself. Know That. Melt the mind in That. Truth is quite pure and simple.

CHAPTER 35

MANONASA

Mind, through ignorance and indiscrimination, considers its false personality to be true and thinks it is the doer of all Karmas and thus becomes egoistic. It imagines that it is in bondage. It identifies itself with the Jivatman; it becomes Jivatman itself and takes the responsibility upon itself for doing good or bad Karmas and enjoying or suffering from their fruits. Hence is mind the doer of Karmas (actions) and responsibility for the Karmas, therefore, rests with it.

Mind is the stealer of Atman. It is a thief. Mind drags the Jivatman into Vishayas (sensual enjoyments). Jivatman is the Abhasa of Chaitanya or reflected intelligence in mind. Mind and Jivatman always live together. They cannot be separated. Slay the mind, the stealer of Atman, through Vichara, Manana and Nididhyasana (constant and profound meditation) on Brahman.

Mind has the potency of creating or undoing the whole world in the twinkling of an eye. Therefore, slay this mind, the slayer of Atman, whether through the destruction of Vasanas (latent subtle desires) or the control of Prana or Brahma-Vichara and Mahavakya-Chintana. The best means of disposing of this great danger of Maya involving all in pains is the destruction of mind. With the destruction of the mind, all the three periods of time vanish into nothing. With the destruction of mind, Atman begins to dawn.

The extinction of Vasanas (Vasana-Kshaya), Manonasa (annihilation of the mind) and Tattva-Jnana (understanding of the Reality), when practised together for a long time are regarded as fruitful. They should be practised at a time. So long as these three are not equally practised again and again, the Supreme Seat (Parama Pada) cannot be attained even after a lapse of hundreds of years. Through the practice of these three for a long time, the firm knots of the heart are cut without doubt, like the breaking of the threads in a lotus-stalk rent in twain.

THE MEANING OF MANONASA

Destruction of the mind does not mean annihilation of the Self. The Vedantins divide the mind into the higher and the lower, of which the lower one leading to desires is asked to be destroyed.

Destruction of desires, annihilation of Ahankara, destruction of Sankalpa—all mean control of mind or annihilation of mind (Manonasa or Amanaskata). Destruction of egoism, Raga-Dvesha (attraction and repulsion for objects) and all Vasanas alone is Manonasa. Manonasa comes through the destruction of the Vasanas. Manonasa does not mean that you should take a sword and cut the mind to pieces.

Manonasa means the death of the present form of the mind (i.e., the instinctive mind of emotions and passions), the form which perceives differences where none exists, which identifies the Self with the body. Its death really means its transformation into and, therefore, the birth of cosmic consciousness.

Vast majority of persons live in Annamaya Kosha only. Their thoughts are directed towards eating, cleansing the body and putting on neat dress. That is all. Even the so-called educated persons live in Annamaya Kosha only. Sometimes, they live in Manomaya Kosha (mental sheath). A spiritual aspirant and a Vivekin live in Vijnanamaya Kosha (Buddhi sheath). The Vijnanamaya Kosha is developed by abstract thinking and reasoning, by systematic meditation, Brahma-Chintana, study of the Upanishads, the Yogavasishtha and the Brahma-Sutras. You must all develop the Vijnanamaya Kosha by the study of Vedantic literature and pure thinking. Then you are safe. Mind will stop to deceive and torment you.

LAYA-CHINTANA OF ANTAHKARANA

Mind is absorbed in Mahat or Buddhi. Individual Buddhi is absorbed in the Cosmic Buddhi; Cosmic Buddhi in Avyakta; Avyakta in Brahman. This is the Laya-Chintana of Antahkarana or Mind.

Sambhavi Mudra, Bhrukuti-Drishti (looking at the spot midway between the two eyebrows), Nasikagra-Drishti (looking steadily at the tip of the nose), Nadanusandhana (hearing the sounds of the ear)—all belong to Laya-Yoga. By these practices the mind gets Laya soon. The Unmani state super-venes rapidly. The Unmani Avastha of Laya-Yogis corresponds to the Bhava-Samadhi of Bhaktas. In Sambhavi Mudra, the eyes are open but the mind is fixed on the Lakshya. The eyes do not see the external objects.

When the mind and senses are thinned out and eventually controlled, Karanendriya-Vyapara (the various activities of Antahkarana and senses) ceases. Jivatva (personality-notion and sensation) vanishes. Brahmatva (existence) remains. This is Kevala Asti.

THE TWO KINDS OF MANONASA

Manonasa is of two kinds, viz., (i) Svarupa Manonasa, destruc-tion of the Svarupa of mind, as in the case of the Jivanmukta and (ii) Arupa Manonasa, destruction of the very form of the mind, as in the case of Videhamuktas, when they leave off their physical bodies. The first is termed "destruction of the mind with form." The second is termed "destruction of the mind with-out form."

HOW TO BRING ABOUT MANONASA

There are five ways of effecting Manahkshaya (destruction of the mind). Two are Yogic methods. Three ways concern Jnana Yoga. (i) When a thought arises, drive it out. Say unto yourself, "Neti, Neti—not this thought, not this thought. I do not want this thought." (ii) Pratipaksha Bhavana—substitute a counter-idea, love for hatred, courage for fear, etc. (iii) Have Brahma-Bhavana. All Sankalpas will die. (iv) Be a Sakshi of the mind. Be indifferent (Udasina). (v) Make the enquiry, "Who am I?" constantly. All thoughts will die. For a man of Vichara (enquiry), the mind dwindles into an airy nothing. This is easier and more effective than the "Neti, Neti" or "Pratipaksha Bhavana" method.

Sankalpa, desire, Raga, Dvesha, Ahankara and mind are the six bricks of the mansion of Jiva. They are the six links of the chain which constitutes the personality—Jiva. Destruction of one brick or one link brings about the destruction of the whole edifice or whole chain.

Therefore, cut off daily the branches of Sankalpa from this dire tree of Manas and ultimately destroy the tree of mind at its root completely. The cutting off the branches is only secondary. The eradication of the tree by removal of 'I' is the primary thing. Therefore, if through virtuous actions you destroy the idea of 'I' which forms the very root of the tree of mind, then it will not spring up again.

Power, possessions, money and knowledge strengthen the Abhimana, i.e., the idea of 'I.' They thicken the mind also. They should be given up in order to thin out the 'I' and the mind. It is through Vairagya and Tyaga that you will have to thin out the mind. When the mind becomes thread-like through the thinning process, it is termed Tanumanasi.

The mind can be controlled either through the control of Prana (Hatha Yogic method) or the arrest of the fluctuation of the mind (Raja-Yogic method—"Yogas-chittavrittinirodhah" of Maharshi Patanjali). Control of mind leads to stoppage of breath and control of breath leads to stoppage of mind, because Prana and mind are under one Sambandha. During meditation, the breathing becomes very slow. Those who practise meditation may be aware of this fact. This goes to show that when the mind is concentrated, Prana stops by itself without any effort.

Pranayama cannot bring about Manonasa (annihilation of the mind). The Vrittis are quietened only temporarily.

Constant and pure thought of Paramatman in our heart would bring about the natural Kumbhaka and absorption of the mind in the heart, the ultimate state and the state which the sages long for. Absorption of the mind in itself is Eternal Bliss (Salvation). Through direct perception of Atman, the mind will be destroyed and will generate infinite Bliss. In such a perception, the seer, sight and the seen become one.

MANONASA AND MANOLAYA

Manolaya is a temporary absorption of the mind in the object of meditation. When you meditate on the form of Bhagavan Sri Krishna, the mind becomes absorbed in the form of Bhagavan Sri Krishna temporarily.

Manolaya takes place during sleep. The mind gets involved into its cause, the Mula Avidya.

Manolaya is not sufficient for attainment of Jnana. In Manolaya, the mind is prone to revive. Manolaya cannot save you from bondage. Manolaya cannot give you Mukti. It is only

Manonasa (annihilation of the lower mind) that can give you liberation. In Manonasa, the mind revives not and is dead. Manonasa is brought about by Brahma-Jnana.

CHAPTER 36

THE MIND COMPARED

RESTLESS LIKE A GHOST

The mind is like a ghost which is restless. Once, a Brahmin Pundit, through Mantra-Siddhi, had control over a ghost. The ghost said to the Pundit, "I can do any work for you in a minute. You must always be giving me some work. If you leave me even for a second without work, I will at once devour you." The Brahmin agreed. The ghost dug a tank for the Brahmin, ploughed the fields and did various sorts of work in a short time. He was not able to give the ghost any further work. The ghost threatened the Brahmin, "Now there is no work for me. I will devour you." The Brahmin was quite puzzled. He did not know what to do. He went to his Guru and explained to him his whole situation. His teacher said, "O Chela, use your common-sense or Yukti (Buddhi). Install a big, stout, soft, wooden post in front of your house. Apply castor oil, wax and other greasy substances to the post. Ask the ghost to get up and get down the whole day and night." The disciple acted accordingly and controlled the ghost. The ghost became very helpless. Even so, you must give always some kind of work or other to the mind, e.g., Japa, meditation, Svadhyaya, service, Kirtan, prayer, Pranayama. You must keep it fully occupied. Then only the mind can be easily controlled. You can be established in physical and mental Brahmacharya.

SCATTERS LIKE MERCURY

The activity of the mind is compared to the mobile mercury. If you place a small quantity of mercury on the ground, it will split into several small pieces and run in various directions. You cannot collect them again. Even so, the rays of the mind are scattered in various directions, in sensual objects. It becomes difficult to collect the dissipated mental rays. Vairagya and Abhyasa will help in making the mind one-pointed.

SHAMELESS AS A STREET DOG

The mind can be compared to the shameless, wandering street-dog with so many wounds on the body. The dog goes to the door of a house. Someone throws a stone at it and it runs away. It goes to another house. There also, it gets a good hitting and thrashing. Then it comes back again to the first house wherefrom it received a pelting of stone. Someone again throws a big stone and it gets another wound. The dog will never leave off its wandering habit in spite of the repeated bad wounds it receives. Even so, this mind always runs towards sensual objects, even though it experiences immense miseries, griefs and sorrows, pains and tribulations. It will never leave off its old habits. You will have to thrash this shameless mind and take it to its source, Brahman, by chanting OM with feeling again and again. Let it taste the Ananda, the Infinite Bliss of Atman. Then alone it will find its rest in OM, its original Abode of Eternal Peace.

JUMPS LIKE A TENNIS BALL

When you play tennis, the ball goes very high in the sky and the next second, it comes down to the ground. Even so, the mind jumps high to the divine glory, dwells on Sattvic divine virtues for a very short time in the beginning of meditation in neophytes and, at once falls down into its old rotten grooves, nasty ruts, foul avenues, stinking channels and dwells on useless, abominable thoughts. The developing soul, the new flame shudders and quivers at the sight of these shocking thoughts. It does not matter; you need not worry. Just as you raise the ball again to the sky by a good, fresh cut or twist or gentle beating, so also, you will have to raise the mind again with effort to the heights of divine glory and divine consciousness.

REFLECTS LIKE A MIRROR

The mind of a man is compared to a mirror in which Reality (Brahman) is reflected. The extent you know about Reality depends upon the state of your mind—whether it corresponds to the full wealth of Reality or not. Colours are not revealed to the blind nor music to the deaf nor philosophical truths to the feeble-minded: "Nayam-atma balahinena labhyah." The revelation will be imperfect or distorted if there is any taint or imperfection. The selfish desires and passions get between the instrument of mind and the Reality to be revealed. Hidden subtle desires (Gupta Vasanas) attack the Sadhakas (aspirants) in a variety of ways. Sadhakas should be ever watching the mind through serious introspection. When the personality of the subject affects the nature of the instrument, the reflection becomes blurred.

Again, if you place a big mirror in front of a dog and keep some bread in front, the dog at once barks by looking at its reflection in the mirror. It foolishly imagines that there is another dog. Even so, man sees his own reflection only through his mind-mirror in all persons, but foolishly imagines like the dog that they are all different from him and fights on account of hatred, malice and jealousy.

OSCILLATES LIKE A PENDULUM

In a clock, the pendulum moves to the right and thence to the left. When the children play on a swing, the swing moves high to one side and at once rises high to the other side. Even so, in the case of aspirants who are not established or well settled in deep meditation, their minds also resemble the pendulum or the swing. They sometimes think of Karma Yoga, enter the world and do actions; while, at other times, they run to the Himalayas for leading a contemplative life. There is struggle inside whether to take up Karma Yoga or Dhyana Yoga. You must decide it once for all and be firm in practising Karma Yoga or in shutting yourself up in a room or cave for some years in the practice of meditation. To run for work into the world for six months and then again into the forest for six months for meditation is no good. Decide one way or the other. Cut asunder the Gordian Knot. Work till you get Chitta-Suddhi. Then meditate till you realise. This is the wisest course.

DROPS DOWN LIKE A TENNIS BALL

If you allow a tennis ball to drop from the highest stair-case, it will not stop at any of the middle steps in the stair-case. It will come down to the ground floor at once. Even so, if you do not take the proper precautions, if you mix with the worldly-minded persons, you will get a quick downfall like the tennis-ball. The mind that you elevated by spiritual practices in six or eight years will become tainted with various sorts of impurities. Beware, therefore, O aspirants!

MISCELLANEOUS COMPARISONS

Mind is compared to a SMALL VESSEL which contains small articles, because mind also contains Vasanas, Trishnas, Samskaras, Vrittis, ideas, Gunas, etc.

Mind is compared to a DHARMASHALA or public resting place, because the Vrittis such as lust, greed, anger, pride, hypocrisy, egoism, etc., take their rest in the mind. Mind is Dharmashala for those Vrittis.

Mind is compared to a PUBLIC ROAD. In a public road, anybody can walk. All sorts of people are moving in a public road. Similarly, all sorts of thoughts are moving in this mind.

Mind is compared to the HOUSE OF A PROSTITUTE, because mind is attached to one object this moment, to another object the next moment, like the prostitute. It has a liking for one object at one time, for another object at another time.

Mind is compared to a DEER, because it is unsteady. It is compared to a MONKEY, because it jumps from one object to another. It is compared to a BIRD, because it flies like a bird. It is compared to the WIND, because it is impetuous, like the wind. Mind is compared to a Ghost, because it behaves like a devil.

Mind is compared to a CHILD, because it needs caning.

Mind is compared to an ENGINE, because it works when the food-fuel is supplied.

Mind is compared to a GARDEN. There are beautiful flowers in a garden. You can cultivate several kinds of flowers in a garden. Even so, you can cultivate the flowers of peace, equal vision, contentment, etc., in the garden of mind.

Mind is compared to a TEMPLE (Mano-Mandira). When the mind is purified, when the evil Vrittis such as lust, greed, etc., are destroyed, the Lord takes His seat in the mind and so it becomes the temple of the Lord.

Mind is also compared to a FLOWER, because it is offered to the Lord by the devotee.

Mind is compared to REINS according to Upanishads. He who holds the mind-reins tight can reach the abode of Bliss.

CHAPTER 37
ESSENCE OF JNANA YOGA

WHAT IS JNANA?

Tattva-jnana is the release from the trammels of one's own mind. Such a release alone leads to the attainment of Moksha. The mind becomes of the nature of Jnana by dint of the efforts towards spiritual direction; but becomes of the nature of the universe through Ajnana. If the mind is bathed in the water of Jnana and cleansed of all its impurities, then the shining Moksha will disclose itself in its native effulgence to those who strive after it. The real bliss is that which arises when the mind, divested of all desires through the eternal Jnana, destroys its subtle form.

THE GLORY OF JNANA YOGA

A Hatha Yogi starts his Sadhana with the body and Prana. A Raja Yogi starts his spiritual practice with the mind. A Jnana Yogi starts his spiritual Sadhana with the Buddhi and Will. To be more accurate a Jnana Yogi starts directly with Brahman. He repeats constantly: "Aham Brahmasmi." He who is attempting to fix the mind on Brahman is really doing the highest Karma Yoga, highest Yajna, highest duty and highest charity. He need not visit Tirthas. He need not distribute charity.

QUALIFICATIONS FOR THE STUDENT OF JNANA YOGA

A complete detachment from the outward things, the manifold objects of sense, together with a capacity for metaphysical abstraction and concentration on inward things are demanded from a spiritual aspirant or an earnest seeker after Truth. The voice of the pure spirit cannot be heard till all superficial organs cease to exist.

For the aspirant in the Jnana-Yogic path, you have the Four Means of Salvation, Sadhana-Chatushtaya, in Vedantic preliminary practice. One of the four means is Shatsampat (six-fold virtues). Of these six virtues, Sama, Dama and

Samadhana are really Yogic practices to control the mind. Sama represents the Chitta-Vritti-Nirodha of Raja Yogis by Vasana-Tyaga, Dama corresponds to Pratyahara. Samadhana is Ekagrata of Yogis. Yoga and Jnana are the two wings of the Hamsa bird (Moksha).

Sama (calmness of mind through Vasana-Tyaga) and Dama (restraint of the Indriyas) are two important items of Shatsampat. Sama and Dama are really Yogic Kriyas. When this Sadhana is over, you will have to take recourse to Sravana and Manana. When you take to deep Nididhyasana, seclusion is necessary for three years.

The purification of the mind will not, by itself, bring about Brahma-Jnana. The purified mind is rendered fit to receive the transcendental light and Ananda. You will have to take refuge in Sravana, Manana and Nididhyasana after purifying the mind.

Sravana, Manana and Nididhyasana (hearing of Srutis, reflection and then meditation on Brahman) are the three Vedantic processes for the attainment of Jnana (Jnanadvaita-Nishtha). This is the ladder with three rungs through which the Vedanti ascends to Brahman. If you do Sravana or hearing of the Srutis once, you must do Manana ten times (reflection of what you have heard) and a hundred times or a thousand times Nididhyasana (profound and constant meditation). Then only real fruit is attained.

A man with Antarmukha Vritti, changed angle of vision, Vairagya and Mumukshutva is alone fit for the study of Vedanta and the practice of OM and Jnana Yogic contemplation. Such a man only will be really benefited. When a man gets a firm conviction that names and forms are unreal and the Adhishthana at their back is real, then it is said that his angle of vision is changed.

It is only through your dauntless energy and own indefatigable efforts that you can get Brahma-Jnana. Guru and Sastras can show you the path and remove your doubts. Anubhava of Aparoksha kind (direct, intuitive knowledge) is left for your own experience. A hungry man will have to eat for himself. He who has a severe itching will have to scratch for himself.

MIND AND BRAHMAN

The capacity of the mind to think exists, because it is enlight-

MIND—ITS MYSTERIES AND CONTROL

ened by the Brahman or Atman shining within and it is by that the mind is capable of activity. Those who have realised the Self say that the mind is pervaded by Brahman. "He who dwells in the mind, is within the mind, whom the mind does not know, whose body is the mind, who from within rules the mind is thy Self, the Inner Ruler, immortal." (Brihadaranyaka Upanishad, III-vii-20). "That which one cannot think with the mind, but that by which they (wise sages) say the mind is made to think, know that alone to be Brahman" (Kena Upanishad, 5). Mind is a mere beggar. It borrows its light and intelligence from the Inner Ruler, the Atman that is self-effulgent. Just as a piece of iron moves in front of a magnet, so also, this mind moves in front of the Inner Ruler. It plays, thinks, feels and imagines before the Divine Presence, just as a prime minister plays and works before the presence of the king. The mind shines in its borrowed feathers. It appears like Chaitanya (pure consciousness). How can the mind which gropes in darkness, which changes in every minute, which has a birth from Mahat and also death (dissolution) in Prakriti be termed as pure consciousness?

The thoughts are various and changing. Now good thoughts manifest. Five minutes later, vicious thoughts appear. The mind is very fickle and changing. It cannot, therefore, be the changeless Atman or Kutastha-Nirvikalpa (unchanging, rock-seated) Brahman.

JADA AND CHAITANYA

Mind, Buddhi, Indriyas and all other things are Jada. That thing which has no knowledge of itself and of other things also is called Jada. Brahman only is Chaitanya-Vastu. Chaitanya or Chit or Chetana is Svayamprakasha (self-luminous) and Sarva-Prakasha (illuminating everything). It illuminates the mind, Buddhi and all Indriyas internally; and externally the sun, the moon, the stars, lightning, fire, etc.

BRAHMAN IS CHAITANYA

Who sees the defects in the sun—whether it shines brightly or whether it is obscured by clouds? It is the eye. Who sees the defects in the eye whether it is a cataract or Timira or not? It is the Buddhi (intellect). Who sees the defects in the Buddhi—whether there is confusion or clarity in it? Who illumines the Buddhi? It is Aham (Infinite 'I'). This Aham is the Kutastha or Atman or Brahman, illuminator of everything. Who illuminates in dreams? There is no other light there. The mind is not self-luminous. It is Jada. It is Brahman who illuminates the objects in the dream.

Suppose there is a blazing light at night. You stand at a distance. Something stands between you and the light as an obstruction and you cannot see the light. But you can clearly see the objects that are illuminated by the light. Though you cannot see the light directly, you clearly conclude that there must be a big light through the perception of the objects. So also, there must be a self-luminous illuminator behind this Nature. That illuminator, the "Light of lights" (*Jyotisham-api tajjyotih*) is the Adhishthana (support) for this illusory world.

If you sit down and realise that you only think by virtue of the one Life and that the mind, animated by the one Life into the act of thinking, is a part of the whole which is God, then you will argue that your mind is out of existence as a separate entity and the result is that mind and body physically (so to speak) disappear and the only thing that remains is Being—Existence which is not explicable in words.

BRAHMAN IS SAKSHI

Raga, Dvesha, pleasure and pain, Kartritva (agency), Bhoktritva are the Dharmas of the mind only. Atman is Sakshi (perceiver) and Asanga (unattached). Like a crystal (Sphatika) which, though tinged with the seven colours is yet unaffected by them, Atman too is not affected by the actions of the mind.

The very idea of creation suggests that there must be a creator. The very idea of matter suggests that there must be a spirit. The very idea of changing phenomenon suggests that there must be an unchanging noumenon. The very idea of a changing mind suggests that there must be an unchanging Sakshi and controller (Niyamaka) for the mind. He is Kutastha Brahman that clearly understands everything and is a Sakshi or silent witness of the Jiva and his activities.

You are able to see the objects only. But the Sakshi or Kutastha Brahman sees the mind, its modifications, the Jivatman or reflected consciousness and the various objects of the universe.

BRAHMAN IS AKHANDA

Time, space and Vastu (substance) are the three categories of the mind. Every object has three kinds of limitations (Pariccheda). Grapes, for instance, are obtainable in a certain season only and in certain places only. So grape has got Desa-Kala-Pariccheda (limitation by space and time). It has got Vastu-Pariccheda also. You cannot find grape on a mango tree. But, the existence of Brahman or Satchidananda is free from these three kinds of Pariccheda (Trividha-Pariccheda-Rahita), because He is eternal, infinite and the essence and Adhishthana for all substances.

An Englishman is different from an Indian. There is Svajatiya Bheda. A tree is different from a stone. There is Vijatiya-Bheda. There is difference between a fruit, flower and leaves in the tree. There is difference between a hand, arm, leg, foot, etc. This is Svagata-Bheda. Brahman has not got these three kinds of Bheda. There cannot be another Brahman, because Infinity is One. So there is no Svajatiya-Bheda in Brahman. The world has emanated from Brahman. It is illusory. So it cannot bring Vijatiya-Bheda for Brahman. World is Brahman Himself. Sat-Chit-Ananda are not three entities. They are one. It is only Sabda-Bheda, like water, Pani, Jala. Sat is Chit. Chit is Sat. Chit is Ananda. So there is no Svagata-Bheda in Brahman. Bheda is a mental creation produced by space, colour, size, etc.

If anything is free from the three kinds of Pariccheda (limitation) of Desa, Kala, Vastu and three kinds of Bheda as described above, then it is termed Akhanda. You can ascribe Akhanda-Lakshana to that substance. That Lakshana can be attributed to Brahman only.

ENQUIRY OF 'WHO AM I?'

Moksha (release from the Samsaric wheel of birth and death) comes through Jnana (knowledge of Atman or God). Jnana comes through Vichara (right enquiry) of 'Who am I?' or understanding and thinking of the right essential significance of the Mahavakya, "Tat Tvam Asi" (Thou art That) of the Upanishads. Enquiry of 'Who am I?' and understanding of 'Tat Tvam Asi' are one and the same.

Brahma-Jnana, which enquires into the true nature of 'I' is

the fire which destroys the mind. It is the 'Jnanagni' referred to in the Gita (IV-37): "*Jnanagnih sarvakarmani bhasmasatkurute tatha*—The fire of wisdom reduces all actions (and the false 'I') to ashes."

When any thought arises in the mind, enquire: Why has this Vritti (modification) arisen? Whom it concerns? Who am I? All the thoughts will die eventually. All mental activities will cease. The mind will turn inward. It will rest on Atman. This is Vedantic Sadhana. You will have to persist constantly in the Sadhana whatever stray thoughts arise. The one thought 'Who am I?' will destroy all other thoughts of worldly nature. That thought will die by itself. Ego will vanish. Balance left is Kevala Asti; Chinmatra; Kevala Suddha Chaitanya; Chidakasa-Matra which is Nama-Rupa-Rahita (free from all names and forms), Vyavahararahita, Mala-Vasana-Rahita, Nishkriya, Niravayava, which is Santa-Siva-Advaita of the Mandukya Upanishad. That is Atman. That is to be known.

THE SAKSHI BHAVA

It is the Vritti (modification in the mind) that binds you with the object. You identify yourself with the Vritti and, through the Vritti, with the object. That is the secret. Be a Sakshi (silent witness to the activities of the mind) of the Vrittis of the mind. There will be no longer bondage. Be the seer of the mind's dramatic performances and be not involved with the mind itself.

When you see a man suffering from appendicular colic, you do not feel yourself any pain. But when you get the same colic, you cry out and experience intense agony. Why? Because of egoism (Ahankara) you identify yourself with the body. If there is absence of Ahankara, you will not feel any pain. This absence of Ahankara can come only when you become impersonal, when you become the Sakshi, when you identify yourself with Brahman (Absolute).

"I am neither Prana nor the senses. I am quite distinct from these. I am Sakshi (witness) for these and their activities. I am Sat-Chit-Ananda Svarupa." This alone is sufficient for the Vedantic Nirguna meditation (formless meditation without any attribute). At once you will be elevated to the highest pinnacle of glory. This is the best formula.

If you have a strong Nischaya (determination) only on the above formula, it is termed Paroksha Jnana (indirect knowledge of Brahman). If you have actual Anubhava through meditation, it is termed Aparoksha Jnana (direct intuitive knowledge of Brahman) or Atmasakshatkara.

If you go above body-consciousness, if you can abandon the body-idea and if the mind rests on Atman or the Self, then, doubtless, you are Sukhi, Santa and Mukta (happy, peaceful and free).

Mind has got a reflexive power of looking up into its own depths. A Raja Yogi develops this power. Introspection helps to cultivate this Yogic faculty. Enter into silence now from today in a dark quiet room. Watch the mind carefully. Be patient. Do not identify yourself with the mind. Be a Sakshi or a silent witness. Separate yourself. You can directly perceive the various mental states.

SOHAM DHYANA

The effort to keep the mind always concentrated on Atman or Brahman is what is called Atma-Vichara.

Till the blissful Jnana dawns on you, you should do constant and intense Sadhana. You must not stop thinking of Brahman (Brahma-Chintana) even for half a second, even for the time taken for one winking. You must become Nididhyasana-Parayana (one whose sole refuge is meditation on OM with feeling and meaning). Then only Brahma-Jnana is possible.

You will have to destroy the Jiva-Bhavana by entertaining the opposite 'Aham Brahmasmi' Bhavana. The Jiva-Bhavana is created by the Vyavaharic Buddhi. You will have to destroy this kind of Vyavaharic Buddhi by developing the Suddha Buddhi or pure reason.

Although you see your body and the world, they really exist not. Never move a fraction of an inch from your established position in Atman. Constantly think that you are the all-pervading Atman (Chidakasa). Even if you are in the mouth of a machine-gun, repeat "Soham"—"Soham"—"Aham Brahma Asmi." Roar like a lion. Fear comes only when you identify yourself with this perishable, fleshy body. If you identify yourself with the infinite, eternal immortal Atman, you will become at once absolutely fearless. Fear is an imaginary modification of the mind of an Ajnani.

Find out your centre. Rest in your centre or equilibrium.

That centre is Atman or Brahman or the One Truth that is shining in your heart from eternity to eternity. If you can rest in your centre, neither trouble nor tribulation, neither loss nor disappointment, neither grief nor sorrow can affect you and throw you off the balance.

If you can keep yourself up in tune with the Infinite, you will have a poised and balanced mind. Nothing can hurt you. You will be always in joy, because you are identifying yourself with Atman. You are resting on the Highest Self. Even though Mansoor and Shams Tabriez the great Sufi Jnanis, were flayed alive, they never felt any sort of pain. They simply uttered 'Analhaq' (I am He). Every drop of blood that fell down also uttered 'Analhaq.' They were always in the bliss of Atman. Look at this marvel. These are the real Jnanis. They showed their power and knowledge of Atman.

A small fishing boat is tossed about severely hither and thither even by ordinary waves of a river. But, a big steamer remains unshaken even though violent waves dash against it with tremendous impetuosity. Even so, a man of the world with a fickle mind is tossed about hither and thither even by the small waves of Raga-Dvesha of the mind; whereas a saint or a Jivanmukta with a balanced and serene mind remains in the world quite steady without being in the least affected by the stormy waves of troubles, tribulations, miseries, afflictions, etc. He is always resting peacefully in the perpetual calm of Atman or the Absolute Self.

Whenever you are much worried, whenever you get heavy depression, whenever you get severe attacks of pain, think you are Atman, full of Ananda. Withdraw the mind from objects and worldly thoughts and fix it on Atman. Enter a solitary room and assert: "I am Anandamaya Atman. How can there be pain there? Pain belongs to the mind. It is a mental creation. I am above mind. Atman is an ocean of Ananda. Atman is a storehouse of Ananda, power and knowledge. I feel that I am Suddha Chaitanya, all-pervading consciousness which is at the back of all these forms, at the back of mind. I am Atman. I am all Ananda." You will derive immense joy, power and exhilaration by this practice.

Strangle every thought of deficiency, imperfection, weakness, inferiority. Even if you have nothing to eat, no cloth to wear, even if you suffer from a terrible incurable disease, cling tenaciously to the ideas, "I am God. I am perfect. I possess everything. All health I am. All joy I am." Remember that to be your right mental attitude. What you habitually think prepares a pattern which the life-processes are constantly weaving, outpicturing in the life.

"I am that Atman or Brahman which is Eka (One), Chidakasa, Akhanda (without parts, indivisible), the Self of all beings (Sarvabhutantaratma)." Try to get established in this Bhava with all efforts (Prayatna). Then the Chanchalata of the mind will vanish. Then you will get eternal bliss. You will become a Jivanmukta. There is not an atom of doubt on this point.

Imagine that you hold the whole world in your womb, in the physical ether which is again supported in your own Svarupa (Chinmaya) body (Chidakasa, Jnana-Vigraha). Then the ideas of externality and separateness will vanish. There is nothing outside you. There is nothing outside Brahman.

APAVADA-YUKTI OF VEDANTA

The toy-elephant made of wood has hidden the reality WOOD when you take it for an elephant. Even so, these names and forms have concealed the Reality BRAHMAN behind these names and forms. Get rid of the Bhranti (illusion) in the mind, that is deep-rooted from Anadikala (beginningless time). This is wood. This is not elephant. So also this is Brahman. This is not world. This is Atman. This is not body. This is Apavada-Yukti in Vedanta. Take out the balance left that is true after throwing off the false thing, viz., elephant, wood, body, etc.

Duality is the very nature of the mind. It can never think in terms of unity. It is through Chitta-Suddhi and Vedantic Sadhana that it should be trained to think in terms of unity.

Clay is the only reality in all the three periods of time. Pot is an unreal thing: "*Vacharambhanam vikaro namadheyam mrittiketyeva satyam*"—Clay only is the reality. The modifications such as jar, pot, etc., are in speech only like ornaments (Chhandogya Upanishad). Similarly, Brahman or Atman is the only real thing, eternal Vastu which has no beginning, no end, no change. The modifications, body, mind, Indriyas and world are all totally false. They are in name only. See the clay in all earthenware vessels. See Atman in all objects (Atma-Drishti).

The cows are different. They differ in colour and various

other particulars. But, milk is the same. Man minus customs, manners, mode of dress and eating, is the same throughout the world. His passions and feelings are the same throughout the world. The languages are different in various districts and climes, but the idea behind all languages is the same. This is oneness behind variety, duality and multiplicity. There is one essence or one Rasa in sleep. All feel alike. There is no Nanabhava in sleep. Similarly, there is one homogeneous substance behind the objects. That is Atman. That is Brahman. That is your real Self.

There is a coconut made of sugar only. It has got marks, lines, external shell, ridges, eyes and everything. But, you have got internal Bhava (feeling) in the mind that it is only sugar. Similarly, even though you see the different objects of the universe, you must have a Bhava and Nischaya (determination) of the Atman that is at the bottom of all these objects, which is the ultimate reality and essence of everything.

Why do you look into the leaves, twigs, flowers, fruits of the mango tree? Look into the source, the seed. The cloth is only cotton and thread. Take the cloth as cotton only. Even so, take the world as Atman or Brahman.

When you see any person or object, think and feel that he or it is Atman or Narayana. By incessant practice, the Nama-Rupa, (name and form) will vanish. Atman or Narayana will shine. The world-idea will vanish. It takes a long time. It demands strenuous efforts. You will see and feel Atman or Narayana everywhere. During the course of the practice, your old Samskaras will trouble you. They are your real enemies. Fight against them boldly. This is the practice of Samyag Jnana. You will have Samyag Darshan of Atman. You will transmute all objects into Atman. Think and feel that all actions are Atma-Puja. Idea of inferiority and idea of menial service will disappear as you see Narayana or Atman everywhere.

THE DAWN OF JNANA

Just as you know the flowering of mango trees that you will get mango fruits shortly, so also you can know that you will get Abheda-Jnana (knowledge of identity of Atman and Paramatman) when the flower of Santi blossoms in your mind.

Just as the six tastes—sourness, bitterness, astringency, sweetness, saltishness and pungency—are rendered full and enjoyed completely only when the Saktis of tastes and the mind join together, so also the plenum (All-full Brahman) arises when all these articles of worship as contentment, equal vision, etc., are combined with Santi (sweet patience or quiescence of mind).

Santi or peace of mind is of two kinds—Sadharana Santi (ordinary peace) and Parama Santi (supreme peace). Ordinary Santi comes when the Vrittis (modifications in the mind) are controlled and the Vikshepa (tossing of mind) is removed. Parama Santi manifests when you get Jnana (Knowledge of Brahman or the Absolute).

DESCRIPTION OF THE JNANA STATE

The Jnana state is a state very difficult to be comprehended. It is a tremendously high state wherein all the Tattvas drop by themselves and Chidakasa only—like the vast, infinite ocean of 'Vyoma' or 'ethereal space' or 'Gagana'—shines by itself. It is the state of pure knowledge which transcends the pleasures of natural scenery and beauties. The beauties of pleasure-gardens, rivers, lakes, snow-clad mountains, green forests, etc., are the creations of Maya. It veils our eyes and prevents us from experiencing the infinite Sahaja (natural) beauty of Atman. The melodious music of birds is also a creation of Maya. It prevents us from hearing the natural Nada of OM—the sweetest Pranava Dhvani. That Nirvana state which transcends all nature is Jnana state.

Jnana-Mouna is that state wherein the mind remains merged in Brahman or Atman or Svarupa. In this state, there is not the slightest trace of the notion of 'I.' As there is no mental activity and as there is no doer, all the Karmas are burnt in the Jnanagni (fire of wisdom). The Jiva feels that he is entirely different from the five Koshas or sheaths, as he identifies himself with the Atman.

In Jnana (Absolute), there is neither East nor West, neither dawning nor setting, neither increase nor decrease, neither sitting nor standing, neither life nor death, neither waking consciousness nor dream state, neither talking nor lecturing, neither thinking nor knowing, neither light nor darkness. The three—actor (Karta), action (Karma) and instrument (Karana)—will shine as one in the Self of Jnanis. What an exalted state it is! It is simply marvellous. It is wonderful. One becomes speechless. It can never be adequately described in words.

I sat on Padmasana. I meditated on Atman. I forgot myself and the surroundings. I saw something which I had never seen upto this time. I heard a Nada which I had never heard upto this time. There was a sensation and knowledge that I was absolutely free from all sorts of attachment. I had an experience of new knowledge. The thought of Atman continued for some time. I had a novel experience of pure bliss. It is a void full of Light and Knowledge and Bliss free from vicissitudes of this world.

When the Self is once recognised and realised, it can never be forgotten. The impression of the recognition of the Self, if once made, can never be obliterated from the mind. It sticks to the mind always.

MUKTI

Mukti is for the mind only. Mukti is for Prakriti. It is not for the Jiva. Jiva is already Brahman. Jiva is ever free. He is identical with Brahman. When the water dries up, the reflection of the sun in water also vanishes. Even so, when the mind-lake dries up by extirpation of all Sankalpas and Vasanas, the reflection of intelligence, Chidabhasa in the mind-lake, also vanishes. The name Jivatman disappears. Ego goes away.

CHAPTER 38

THE MIND IN A JIVANMUKTA

"Dehabhimane galite vijnate paramatman
Yatra yatra mano yati tatra tatra samadhayah"

"With the disappearance of the attachment of the body and with the realisation of the Supreme Self, to whatever object the mind is directed, one experiences Samadhi."

Amana is a Sanskrit term which means 'without mind.' "Amanaskata" is a condition where there is no mind. It is mindlessness. You will find this in Jivanmuktas or liberated sages.

RESIDUAL SATTVA

Jivanmukta is a sage free (from the trammels of births and deaths) while living. Even in the case of a Jivanmukta, though the instinctive mind with low desires is destroyed, the spiritual Sattvic mind does not perish. Like flowers and fruits latent in a seed, a residue of Sattva, the cause of intelligence, rests always in the heart. If you say that his mind is completely annihilated as soon as he attains Jnana, Jivanmukti state is impossible. How will he be able to do Vyavahara (worldly dealings) without an instrument viz., the mind? A Jnani identifies himself with the all-pervading Brahman and uses his mind and body as His instruments for Vyavahara (worldly activities); an Ajnani identifies himself with his body. There have been cases of Jivanmuktas like Raja Janaka who attained Jnana and who utilised mind and body in this manner for the well-being of the humanity at large.

Sri Rama and Sri Krishna were ever resting on Brahman even when they were ruling their kingdoms. They were ever very conscious of their essential Sat-Chit-Ananda Brahmic nature, even though they assumed human forms. They utilised their minds and bodies as their instruments when they were doing various activities.

EMPIRICAL EXISTENCE AND EXISTENCE-REALITY

Even this world does not disappear as absolutely as is supposed in Jivanmukti state. Empirical world, in fact, ceases to exist. But, this does not mean annihilation. It merely means that existence changes its form and colour, as it were, for the Absolute. It is empirical existence and not all-existence which vanishes. Existence-Reality remains, but its limited forms vanish. Externality has to go; spatial and temporal views of things must go; causal determination of one thing by another must go; many-ness and oneness must go. This is inevitable. But, the universe with all its reality will not go even for the liberated soul. It will merely change its form, meaning and significance. Nothing will disappear except a false view, a limited horizon, erroneous idea and a circumscribed vision. Fact, Reality, Existence, however, will remain as fundamental as ever; but the viewpoint will change.

The mind of the Jnanis cannot be termed as a mind, but only as Tattva (Reality). That which gets differentiated through diverse objects is the mind. The mind of a Jnani, on the other hand, becomes stainless, like copper transmuted into gold by alchemic process. The mind of a Jnani is Sattva itself, while persons without Jnana will follow the path chalked out by their minds. When a Jnani sees outside, he may simply see, but the Vritti may not assume Vishayakara as in the case of worldly-minded persons. Just as the mind is free from any Vishayakara in deep-sleep state in all, it is free from any Vishayakara in the waking state also in a Jnani. The world appears to him as a mere dream. He dwells in Brahman even while working. In those that have cognised their Self, the pure Vasanas with which they perform Karmas will not entail them rebirths. The mind of such a Jnani is called Sattvic, but a mind without Jnana is generally termed Manas.

THE PERFECTLY BALANCED MIND

Now, mark the nature of the mind of a Jivanmukta. It is perfectly balanced under all circumstances. His mind is always cool and unaffected by the Dvandvas (pairs of opposites). His mind is free from Harsha and Soka (elation and depression). It is neither elated by enjoyments nor depressed by sorrow and grief. Without being affected by the pleasures or pains of enjoyments though moving in them, the mind of a Jivanmukta will become inured to them. Through internal contentment and freedom from pains, there will arise in the Jnani an equanimity of mind in all circumstances and at all places. Even when pains and the rest attaching themselves to his body exhibit themselves on his face, his mind never writhes under them or their antithesis. It is free from impure Vasanas. There will be no anger or desire. There will not arise any evil impulse of Kama in such a mind. There is not the least longing for objects. His mind is above worldly things. He is not affected by the world. He need not have a separate room or Asana. He need not close the eyes. He need not do any Pratyahara of the senses.

A mind which, though apparently enjoying the diverse objects, does not, in reality, enjoy them, may be stated to be Brahman itself.

DUAL CONSCIOUSNESS

An occultist learns through self-control and discipline to work on two planes at once, that is, to be partly out of his body at the same time when he is working on the physical plane; so that, while he is writing or speaking, he may be doing other things with his astral body. When such is the case with an occultist, little need be said of a full-blown Jnani who is resting on his own Svarupa. A Jnani has dual consciousness. He has consciousness of Brahman as well as consciousness of the world. He sees the world as a dream within himself. A Jnani is always in Samadhi. There is no 'in Samadhi' and 'out of Samadhi' for a Jnani like that of a Raja Yogi.

When you play on the harmonium, you adjust the tune first. It may be fixed either on the second reed or the fourth reed according to the strength and power of your voice. Then you begin to play on the various reeds. The Sapta Svaras are pronounced now. You can play now various Raga-Raginis. He who is aware of the main Sruti can be compared to a Jnani who knows the Atman or support for this universe. He who is aware of the Sapta Svara only without knowing the fundamental Sruti is like an Ajnani who is unaware of the Atman, but who has knowledge of the sense-objects only.

When you see an object with your eyes, you know that it is through the light of the sun that you are able to see it. You have a double Drishti. Similarly, a Jnani has always a double Drishti when he does Vyavahara. Even when he works, he knows he is not working; he is unattached. Even though he sees the world, it is all Brahman and Brahman for him.

SAMA BHAVA AND SAMA DRISHTI

There is a slight difference between Sama Bhava and Sama Drishti. The former is the condition of the mind (as balanced in pleasure and pain, gain and loss, heat and cold, victory and defeat). The latter is the condition of knowledge. The Jnani sees the Atman alone in a scavenger and a king.

When you are expecting to meet a friend of yours at the railway station, the mind tries to see him in several other persons with a like physiognomy (Sadrisya), because the mind is engrossed with the one idea of meeting a particular friend at a particular time. The mind is very eager to see him. A lustful young man sees a woman in a pillar tied with a woman's cloth, in fact, everywhere. The mind is charged with very powerful and lustful thoughts. A God-intoxicated man, on the contrary, sees God in a tree, a stone, boy, child, girl, cow, dog—in fact, in everything. *"Sarvam khalvidam brahma."*

A Jivanmukta, though he has infinite powers, cannot express all his Siddhis through his finite mind.

CHAPTER 39

THE POWERS OF A YOGI

SIDDHIS AND RIDDHIS

There are nine Riddhis and eight Siddhis (major) and eighteen Siddhis (minor). The eight Siddhis are Anima (atomic size), Mahima (colossal size), Garima (excessive bulk), Laghima (extreme lightness), Prapti (attainment of whatever you desire), Prakamya (unhampered will), Isatva (lordliness) and Vasitva (control over all senses). Riddhi means affluence. It is inferior to Siddhi.

BHUTAJAYA

A Raja Yogi gets conquest over the mind (Manojaya) through Nirvikalpa or Nirbija (without seeds or Samskaras) Samadhi and, through Manojaya, gets Bhutajaya also (conquest over the five elements). Fire will not burn such a Yogi. Water will not drown him. Sri Trailinga Swami of Benares and Sri Jnanadeva of Alandi (near Poona) had various Siddhis. Sri Jnanadeva made his house move to receive Changdeva who was coming on the back of a tiger. He made the Masjid walk. Trailinga Swami used to live for six months underneath the Ganga.

KNOWLEDGE OF THE PAST

The Yogi has got the power to plunge deep into the depths of his subconscious mind wherein the Samskaras are embedded and to have direct vision and understanding of the Samskaras of different births through his new Yogic eye. "*Samskara-sakshatkaranat purvajatijnanam*" (Patanjali Yoga-Sutras, III-18). He makes the Yogic Samyama (Dharana, Dhyana and Samadhi) on these latent Samskaras which are only the past experiences in a subtler form. Thus he gets the knowledge of his past life.

ASHTAVADHANA AND SATAVADHANA

An untrained mind can only see or hear at a time, but a perfected mind can see and hear at the same time. It can be linked to several organs, to one or to none. It can be manipulated in any way the Yogi likes. It can do eight things at a time. This is called Ashtavadhana. It can do hundred things at a time. This is Satavadhana.

SEPARATION OF ASTRAL BODY FROM PHYSICAL BODY

A Yogi separates his astral body from the physical body, travels to different parts of the world, as well as to higher planes, in the twinkling of an eye and returns to this physical body like a bird returning to its prison of a cage. A slender thread of Prana connects the physical and the astral bodies. The moment he gets out of the body, the Yogi sees with his astral vision his physical body as a cast-off slough. The process is a very simple one when you know the Yogic technique of separating yourself from the physical body.

PSYCHIC SIDDHIS—A SOURCE OF GREAT DANGER TO SPIRITUAL SADHAKAS

A man may have psychic powers and Siddhis through concentration of the mind. But, he may not have mental purity. Mental purity is of paramount importance for Self-realisation.

Do not think too much of psychic Siddhis. Clairvoyance and clairaudience are not worth having when far greater illumination and peace are possible without the Siddhis than with them.

Why do you care for psychic Siddhis? They are absolutely useless. Shun them ruthlessly even when they try to manifest. They will mislead you and cause your downfall. Beware, Lord Buddha shunned Mara (temptations and Siddhis). Try to get Brahma-Jnana. Then you will have everything. All spiritual Siddhis will welcome you with outstretched hands. You cannot have a downfall then.

A Jnani never cares for psychic powers, for he does not need them in his daily life. Through his Sat-Sankalpa, a Jnani does whatever a Raja Yogi does through his Yogic Samyama. He simply wills. Whatever he desires, then and there it materialises.

CHAPTER 40

NECESSITY FOR A GURU

"Learn thou this by prostration, by investigation and by service. The wise, the seers of the essence of things, will instruct thee in wisdom."
(Gita, IV-34)

Guru or a spiritual preceptor is necessary for aspirants. Some do the practice for some years, independently. Later on, they feel acutely the necessity for a Guru. They come across some obstacles on the way. They do not know how to proceed and how to obviate these impediments. Then they begin to search for a master. This particularly happens in Yogic practice.

It is the duty of the Guru to set each of his disciples upon that path of spiritual development which is best suited to the Chela, one on one path, one on another, according to the Guru's insight into the innate tendency of each.

Isvara is Guru of Gurus. He removes the veil of ignorance and blesses the ignorant Jivas. The aspirant should regard his immediate Guru in the physical form as an incarnation of that Guru of Gurus and should have equal devotion to him also. Guru in the physical form is the main source and embodiment of all good and happiness that can accrue to the Chela. The disciple should realise the supreme necessity of obeying the Guru's commands and behests and keeping his faith in him unsullied and staunch.

Lay bare to your Guru the secrets of your heart; and the more you do so, the greater the sympathy, which means an accession of strength to you in the struggle against sin and temptation.

SAKTI-SANCHARA OR TRANSMISSION OF SPIRITUAL POWER

Just as you can give an orange to a man and take it back, so also spiritual power can be transmitted by one to another and taken back also. This method of transmitting spiritual power is termed Sakti-Sanchara. Like birds, fish and tortoise, the transmitting of spiritual power can be done by the Guru through touch or sight or willing, and thinking. The transmitter sometimes enters the astral body of the student and elevates his mind through his power. The operator makes the subject sit in front of him and asks him to close his eyes and then transmits his spiritual power. The subject feels the electric current actually passing from Muladhara Chakra higher up to the neck and top of the head. He does various Hatha Yogic Kriyas, Asanas, Pranayama, Bandhas, Mudras, etc., by himself without any instruction, through inspiration. Here Prakriti works herself. The student must not restrain his Iccha-Sakti. He must act according to the inner light. The mind is highly elevated. The moment the aspirant closes his eyes, meditation comes by itself. Through Sakti-Sanchara, Kundalini is awakened by the grace of the Guru in the disciple.

A spiritual teacher actually transmits his spiritual power to his disciple. A certain spiritual vibration of the Satguru is actually transferred to the mind of the disciple. Sri Ramakrishna Paramahamsa actually transmitted his spiritual power to Swami Vivekananda. Lord Jesus did the same to his disciples. This is Master's spiritual touch. A disciple of Samartha Ramdas transmitted his power to that dancing girl's daughter who was very passionate towards him. The disciple gazed at her and gave her Samadhi. Her passion vanished. She became very religious and spiritual. Mukund Rai, a Maharashtra saint, put the Badshah in Samadhi.

By the Guru's Grace, the devotee attains the eight-stepped Yoga (Ashtanga Yoga); by the Grace of Lord Siva, he attains perfection in Yoga which is eternal.

CHAPTER 41

HINTS TO ASPIRANTS

Aspirants to Yoga are classified into three degrees: (1) Arurukshu, one who is attempting to climb the steps of Yoga, (2) Yunjana, one who is busily engaged in the practice of Yoga and (3) Yogarudha, one who has already reached the height of Yoga.

INDISPENSABILITY OF INNER PURITY

Aspirants are very eager for realisation. But, when that realisation actually comes, they begin to tremble, to quiver. They cannot bear the illuminating blaze of God. They are so puny, impure and weak that they cannot face the mighty brilliance and divine splendour. They have not prepared the vessel to hold on the Divine Light. Mark how Arjuna trembled with fear at the huge cosmic vision of Virat and prayed to Lord Krishna to show him again the usual form with four hands which represents harmony, perfection, power and wisdom.

It is difficult to speak about Brahman. It is still more difficult to understand. It is yet still more difficult to practise spiritual Sadhana. This corresponds to the Gita's teaching, Chapter II-29:

"As marvellous one regardeth Him, as marvellous one speaketh thereof, as marvellous one heareth thereof; yet, having heard, none indeed understood."

It demands a subtle, pure, clear mind, determined will, patience, perseverance and Utsaha (cheerfulness) for the realisation of Brahman.

VITAL NEED FOR MORAL STRENGTH AND COURAGE

A spiritual aspirant will have to face boldly misrepresentation, calumny and misunderstanding. That has always been the lot of those who tried to raise themselves above their fellows. Moral strength and courage are necessary to meet that and to enable that man to maintain his position and what he thinks right, whatever those around him may think or say or do. People will despise and persecute you. You will have to stand boldly on your moral footing to live for your own convictions. As aspirant who has outgrown the rules of society should act according to the dictates of his pure conscience and pure reason. Then alone he can grow spiritually.

When anyone rises to fame and power, enemies come in by themselves. Even Sri Sankaracharya had many enemies. Even Sannyasins who live in forests have enemies. Jealous and petty-minded men create various sorts of mischief against people who are prosperous and famous. Have Sakshi-Bhava (feeling of witness) and rise above the idea of friend or foe. Become an Udasina (indifferent man). Develop the power of endurance. Bear insult, injury with a cool mind. Then only you can be happy in this world.

There are as many spiritual Sadhanas as there are individual minds. What suits one mind may not suit another. Raja Yoga will be easy for one mind, while Jnana Yoga will be easy for another. One form of Tapas may suit one mind. A different kind of Tapas will suit another.

DAILY SPIRITUAL ROUTINE

Here is a daily spiritual routine for whole-time aspirants. Those who work in offices and business-houses can adjust and make necessary alterations according to their convenience and time at their disposal.

Japa and Meditation	Morning	...	4 hours
	Night	...	4 hrs
Svadhyaya (study)		...	3 hrs
Interview (if need be)		...	1 hr
Asana and Pranayama	Morning	...	1 hr
	Night	...	1 hr
Walking		...	1 hr
Sleep		...	5 hrs
Service		...	$1\frac{1}{2}$ hrs
Bath, etc.		...	1 hr
Food		...	1 hr
Rest		...	$\frac{1}{2}$ hr
			24 hrs

A SLIGHTLY DIFFERENT SCHEDULE

It is difficult in the beginning to fix the mind on God all the twenty-four hours. As soon as meditation is over, the mind will begin to wander, will try its level best to have its old habits. What are you going to do to check its habits? You must give another Sattvic object for its grasp. It wants variety. Now, study philosophical books for some hours. As soon as study is over, take down notes on what you have studied. You can devote some time in this direction. This will serve to relax the mind. This will form a mental recreation. You can spend some time in serving poor, sick persons, according to your capacity. I give below a time-table for your daily routine:

Meditation	...	8 hrs
Study	...	4 hrs
Writing	...	2 hrs
Service	...	2 hrs
Food, bath, exercise	...	2 hrs
Sleep	...	6 hrs
		24 hrs

The most impious of men can, by earnestly devoting himself to God, reach the highest Bliss. "Even if the most sinful worship Me, with undivided heart, he too must be accounted righteous, for he hath rightly resolved" (Gita, IX-30). "*Pratijanihi na me bhaktah pranasyati*—Know thou for certain that My devotee perisheth not" (Gita, IX-31). What reason, then, is there for despair? Therefore, be up and doing. God will surely crown your efforts with success. Even the vilest of us shall obtain Moksha.

Om purnamadah purnamidam purnat purnamudachyate
Purnasya purnam-adaya purnam-eva-vasishyate

Om Santih Santih Santih

OM THAT IS FULL. THIS IS FULL. FROM THAT FULL, THIS FULL EMANATES,
TAKING AWAY THIS FULL FROM THAT FULL,
THE FULL STILL REMAINS BEHIND.
OM PEACE, PEACE, PEACE.

Hari Om Tat Sat

TO THE MIND

THY LIFE-HISTORY

O Mind; O Maya's child!
You always want a form
To lean upon;
You have two forms—
Suddha Manas, pure mind,
Asuddha Manas, impure mind.
Time, space and causation
Are thy categories.
You work through
The law of association;
You think, feel and know.

You are Atma-Sakti.
You are Manomaya Kosha.
You are like a mirror;
Brahman is reflected on you.
You are compared to a tree:
Ego is the seed of this tree,
Sankalpas are the branches,
Buddhi is the first sprout.

You have another three forms
The conscious mind,
The subconscious mind,
And the superconscious mind.
You are made up of
The subtlest form of food.
You are a bundle of habits,
Samskaras and Vasanas.

You are fourfold:
Manas does Sankalpa-Vikalpa,

Buddhi determines,
Chitta executes,
Ahankara self-arrogates.
Chitta comes under mind,
Buddhi comes under Ahankara.
It is all Vritti-Bheda.

THY BIRTH

Thy father, Supreme Brahman,
Felt loneliness once.
He was alone,
One without a second.
He wanted to multiply;
He thought,
"May I become many."
There was a vibration or Spandan
In thy mother, Maya,
The undifferentiated,
The unmanifested;
The equilibrium was disturbed.
You were born at once.
Thy body was made of pure Sattva;
You were known by the name 'Manas'.
The Lord ordained you to do four functions;
So you became fourfold—
Manas, Chitta, Buddhi, Ahankara.
You separated yourself from the Lord
Through self-arrogating 'I'.
You indulged in sensual objects
In company with the senses
And forgot thy divine origin.
You became attached to sons, wife,
Property, names, titles and honours;
You became quite worldly.
You identified yourself with the body,
Sons, wife, house and property
Through Avidya or ignorance.
This is the cause for your downfall

And all sorts of miseries and sufferings.
This is, in short, your life-history.
Give up attachments
And identification with the body.
Annihilate ignorance
By attaining Brahma-Jnana;
You can become one with Brahman
And regain thy divine nature.

THY ABODE

O wandering Mind!
You have three abodes.
In the waking state,
Your abode is the right eye
And the brain;
In the dreaming state,
You rest in the Hita Nadi
Of the throat;
In the deep sleep state
You rest in the Puritat Nadi
In the heart.
According to the Hatha Yogins,
Ajna Chakra is thy seat.
You can be easily controlled
If one concentrates on the Ajna.
Aspirants know now
Thy resting places;
They will surely attain you
And drive you out ruthlessly.
Vacate these dwelling houses
And go back to your original home,
The "Omkar Bhavan"
In the limitless Brahmapuri.

THY NATURE

You are compared to quicksilver,
Because your rays are scattered.

You are compared to a deer,
Because you are unsteady.

You are compared to a monkey,
Because you jump from
One object to another.
You are compared to a bird,
Because you fly like a bird.

You are compared to a ghost,
Because you behave like a devil.
You are compared to wind
Because you are impetuous
Like the wind.

You are compared to an engine,
Because you work
When the food-fuel is supplied.

You are compared to a child,
Because you need caning.
You are compared to the reins
In the Kathopanishad;
He who holds the mind-reins tight
Can reach the Abode of Bliss.

You are compared to a dog
That strolls in the streets.
You are compared to a flower,
Because a devotee offers you to the Lord;
This is the only good compliment for you.

THY THICK FRIENDS

O Mind! O Enemy of Peace!
Thy friends are many.
They help you
In a variety of ways.
So you are very strong.
Ahankara is your best friend;
He is very powerful too;
He is thy commander general.

Lust is your thick chum;
He is your right hand;
He lives with you always;
He is your constant companion;
You are attached to him.
Anger is your amiable friend;
He is your war-minister;
He is your left hand;
He assists you very much.
Raga-Dvesha are your
Intimate acquaintances;
They are very dear to you;
They render you great service.
Greed is your best friend;
He follows you
Like your shadow;
He is your obedient servant.
Pride feeds you;
Hypocrisy ministers you;
Moha counsels you;
Jealousy inspires you;
Cunningness vivifies you;
He is thy propaganda minister.
Crookedness energises you;
Arrogance fattens you;
Deceit rejuvenates you.

THY ENEMIES

O Mind, why do you tremble?
Show your strength now.
You cannot stand now.
Surrender yourself
Or you will be killed.
You shudder
When you hear the words
"Vairagya," "Tyaga," "Sannyasa,"
"Satsanga," "Sadhana," "Yoga."
Vairagya is your dire enemy;

It is an axe to cut you.
Renunciation is a sword
To cut your throat.
Sannyasa is an atom bomb
To reduce you to ashes.
Meditation will roast you.
Samadhi will fry you.
Take to your heels, O Mind;
Run away at once,
Get thee gone.
Tarry not; stop thy havoc.
You will be crushed now.
Your teeth will be extracted.
You will be blown out.
You will be smashed.
Japa and Kirtan also
Have joined the forces.
Pranayama is working hard.
Vichara is fiery.
Viveka is persevering.
There is not the least hope for you.
Go back to your original home
And rest peacefully.

THY TRICKS

O Mind! O Wanderer!
In this dire Samsara,
I have found out thy tricks;
You cannot delude me now.
You tempt the worldlings
Through imagination.
You produce intoxication
And turbulence of the mind.
You put on a veil also.
There is nothing in the objects;
And yet you make the people
Believe there is great pleasure
In the sensual objects.

You cause forgetfulness in people.
You cause perversions
Of the intellect.
You tantalise, tempt and enchant.
You cause disgust in monotony.
You always want variety.
You excite the emotions.
You play through instincts.
You agitate the senses.
You destroy discrimination.
Attachment, affection,
Praise, respect, name and fame
Are thy tempting baits.
O Mind! I cannot live with you;
I cannot tolerate now your company.
You are a traitor, diplomat.
You are treacherous.
You cannot play with me now.
Enough, enough of thy tricks.
I am a Viveki.
I will rest in Brahman.
I will ever be blissful.

THY SECRETS

O Mind! O Slayer of Atman!
I know thy secrets now.
You have no real existence.
You appear like a mirage.
You borrow your power
From the Brahman, the substratum.
You are only Jada,
But appear to be intelligent.
You lurk like a thief,
When thy nature is found out;
You are definitely pleased,
When you are coaxed;
You hiss and raise your hood,
When you are directly attacked.

You can be easily attacked
Through Pratipaksha-Bhavana method.
You keep the Samskaras
In the subconscious;
This is your strength,
This is your strong fortress.
You emerge out of your fort
And attack the Jiva again and again
And then hide yourself
In the subconscious.

You play with the Gunas.
You have three colours—
White, red and black.
When you are Sattvic,
You are white;
When you are Rajasic,
You are red;
When you are Tamasic,
You are black.

Vasanas and Sankalpas
Are your vital forces;
You exist
On account of them.
You are nowhere
If these are destroyed;
I will subdue you now
And attain Eternal Bliss.

THY BLUNDER

O Mind! Thy glory is indescribable.
Thy essential nature is all-bliss.
Thou art born of Sattva.
Thou art pure like crystal and snow.
Thy powers are ineffable.
Thou canst do anything.
Thou canst do and undo things.

Thou hast spoiled thyself

In company with Rajas and Tamas,
In friendship with the senses and objects.
Thou hast forgotten all about thy divine nature.
Bad company has tainted you.
The evil Vrittis have degraded you.

You were tempted once by lust;
You have become a slave of lust now.
You were very quiet, calm and serene;
Desires have made you restless now.
You were very near the Supreme Lord once;
Worldliness has blinded thy heart
And taken you away from the Lord.

Keep company with saints and sages;
Shun the company of Rajas, Tamas and senses.
Free yourself from the taint of desires.
You can regain your original position;
You can reach your original sweet home.

THY WEAKNESS

O Mind! You are the greatest fool on this earth!
You are dull, stupid and obstinate;
You never heard the words of the wise;
You have your own foolish ways;
You do not wish to attend Satsanga of saints;
You dislike, hate, speak ill of Mahatmas;
You belong to the dregs of the society;
You always like to revel in filth.

You never find out your own faults,
But you magnify the faults of others;
You even superimpose Doshas on them.
You never like to hear the praise of others;
You want to glorify yourself only;
You hide cleverly your own faults.
You never think of the glorious feet of the Lord,
But you think of all sorts of rubbish things.

You know you can get Supreme Bliss

Through meditation on the Supreme Lord;
And yet you wander here and there
Like the strolling street-dog.
I rebuked you, scolded you;
I reprimanded you;
I gave you admonitions;
And yet you stick to your own ways.

THY POWERS

O Mind! you are not weak.
You are not impotent
You are not a beggar.
You are not a slave of objects.
You are not impure.
You are not a clerk.
You are not poor.

You are omnipotent.
You are Light of lights.
You are Sun of suns.
You are King of kings.
The whole wealth of the Lord belongs to you.
You are the nectar's son.
You are the child of Immortality.
You are Amrita Putra.

You are purity itself.
You are strength itself.
You are fountain of joy.

You are ocean of bliss.
You are pool of immortality.
You are river of felicity.
You are the abode of peace.
You are sweet harmony.
Restlessness is not thy nature.
You have clairvoyance.
Ashta Siddhis are yours.
Nava Riddhis are thine.
Powers of judgment,

Discrimination, Vichara,
Reflection, meditation,
Thought-reading, telepathy,
Trikala-Jnana
Are all yours only.

Brahmakara Vritti
Rises from you alone.
The door of intuition is in you.
The key of knowledge is with you.
Thou art the Lord of lords.

WAY TO BLISS

O Mind!
I shall show you the way
To Eternal Bliss.
March in the way boldly
And go direct to the abode.

Do not think of objects any more.
Do not keep company with the senses.
Free yourself from Rajas and Tamas.
Kill Vasanas and cravings.
Give up 'mine-ness' and 'I-ness'.
Let thy conduct be pure.
Let thy behaviour be noble.
Let thy Nishtha be steady.

Be firm in your resolves.
Cultivate virtuous qualities.
Stick to daily spiritual routine.
Keep daily spiritual diary.
Follow the "Twenty Instructions."
Write Mantra for two hours daily.
Be truthful and non-violent.
Do 200 Malas of Japa.
Do Kirtan daily for one hour.
Study Gita and Bhagavata,
Upanishads and Yoga Vasishtha.
Fast on Ekadasi.

Take simple, Sattvic diet.
Be moderate in everything.

Have Saguna realisation first.
This will enable you
To equip yourself with the "Four Means"
And to attain Nirguna realisation.
Bhakti alone will give you Jnana.

GLORY OF DIVINE LIFE

O Mind! Just hear
The glory of the Divine Life.
You will love it immensely;
You will rejoice and dance.
The glory of Divine Life
Is the glory of the father,
Thy creator, thy master,
Thy source and support.
You will be ever peaceful.
You will be always blissful.
You will be one with the Lord.
No cares, worries and anxieties
Will affect you.
You will not be touched
By hunger and thirst.

You will be free from fear,
Fatigue and disease.
No enemies will attack you.
Atomic bomb cannot touch you.
Heat will not torment you.
Cold will not benumb you.
You will sleep soundly.
You will enjoy sleepless sleep.
You will experience Samadhi.
No bugs, no scorpions, no snakes,
No mosquitoes are there.
You will drink the nectar
Of Immortality.

No floods, no earthquake,
No epidemics are there.
There is no communal strife there.
There is no hooliganism.
There is no riot or strike there.

Rivers of honey flow there.
You will enjoy the celestial manna
And all divine Aisvarya.
You will feel oneness
With the Supreme Lord.
You will never be reborn
In the terrestrial plane.
You will become Immortal.

DRINK THE NECTAR OF NAME

O dull Mind!
Throw away laziness.
Meditate upon Lord Hari.
Drink, O Mind,
That immortal Elixir
Of Lord Hari's Name,
The joy of the devotees,
The medicine that destroys
The fear of Samsara
And all delusion in man.

Drink, O Mind,
The Divine Medicine
Of Sri Krishna's Name,
That excites the flow
Of divine ecstasy,
That awakens Kundalini
And makes it rise
In the Sushumna Nadi,
That helps the flow of nectar
From the Sahasrara.
Drink, O Mind,
The Amrita of Vishnu's Name.

There is no better Elixir
Than the nectar of
The remembrance of Lord's Name.
The Name will take you
To the other shore—
Of fearlessness and immortality.

MANO-MANDIR

O Mind! Drink thou
The nectar of Lord's holy Name.
Shun evil company.
Abandon tea, liquor and smoking.
Give up tobacco, costly dress.
Wear simple clothing.
Have plain living
And high thinking.
Associate with the saints,
Devotees and sages.
Hear thou Lord's discourses.
Drive lust, anger and greed.
Keep thy abode holy.
Then only the Lord
Will dwell in 'Mano-Mandir',
Temple of Mind.
A pure mind
Is the house of love.
Remove the seeds
Of jealousy and pride
Then only my King
Will dwell in you,
Light the light of love
And illumine His palace.

SERVE THE SAINTS

O Murkha Mind!
You can't expect
An iota of happiness
In sensual objects.

Give up all vain hopes
If you still hope.
It is like trying
To get butter
By churning water.
It is like the attempt
Of the Chatak bird
To get water from the smoke;
Its eyes will be spoiled.
It is like the attempt
To drink water
In the mirage;
Or to get silver
From the mother of pearl.
Think of the feet of Hari.
Recite His Name.
Live in the company
Of saints and Bhaktas.
Do regular Kirtan.
Meditate on His form.
Serve the saints.
You will enjoy bliss.

ADMONITION

O Mind! Devotion's path and devotees' company take;
Then Sri Hari will in thy inner Self, His sacred abode make.
Give up forever all abuse of man or beast;
Love and praise all, greatest as well as least.
At early dawn, O Mind, think intently on Ram;
Then soft, yet audible, chant Ram's sweet Name.
Right conduct, the supreme good, never a moment renounce;
The righteous one, all mankind on earth,
                                    most blessed pronounce.
O Mind! Vasanas wicked do thou never have.
Likewise, O Mind, sinful mentality never have.
O Mind! Ethics and morality, never leave;
And ever inwardly the essence of truth perceive.
O Mind! thou shouldst all sinful intent abandon;

Cling throughout life to pure and sincere intention.
Give up imagination vain of sensual pleasure;
Such indulgence brings on life-long shame and
                                    endless censure.
Never have, O Mind, this anger, so fraught with untold harm;
Never foul desire with all its variegated charm.
Never into thyself, the least access give,
To pride and to jealousy as long as you live.
A lofty ideal in life you shouldst conceive,
All the abuse of the world with forbearance receive.
Thyself shouldst always observe sweetness of speech,
For sweetness, the inmost heart of mankind doth reach.
Perform, O Mind, such actions just, noble and pure,
That, after demise, tend forever to make thy fame endure.
In selfless service wear thyself like sandal-wood;
In inmost heart do thou pray for universal good.
O Mind! Earthly wealth and treasures do not covet;
Selfishness of nature, O Mind, most ruthlessly reject.
Greed of mind, when unfulfilled, great sorrow brings;
Sinful acts, the heart later on with sharp remorse wrings.
Ever and anon on the Divine Lord let pour thy love,
To vicissitudes of life calmly and fearlessly bow.
Pains of physical form as mere trifles regard,
For, in essential nature, thou art nature's overlord.

REST AT THE FEET OF HARI

O Mind! You have all along been
In the habit of thinking
That wife, children and bungalows
Are your great possessions.
You have failed to bow
Before the Supreme Lord and saints.
Rest, my Mind, rest at the feet of Hari.
O Mind! Surely this body will drop down.
Every moment life is shortening;
The Serpent of Time is swallowing.
The Prana will depart at any moment.
You are happy-go-lucky and playful.

You are silly and stupid.
O Mind! Thou art blind.
You see only this vanity of things.
You do not see the great end drawing near.
Death is creeping in silently.
Wake up, O Mind,
From thy slumber of ignorance
And think of the all-merciful Hari.
There is no hope for thee
Except through the glorious Hari.
Break through the illusion
And take refuge in Hari.
Then alone you are blessed.
Thus sayeth Sivananda.

WHY DO YOU FORGET?

O Mind! You are still under delusion,
Even after doing some Sadhana
And enjoying the Satsanga of great souls.
Why do you, O Mind, forget
That this world is a manifestation of Lord Hari?
Why do you become angry,
Although you know
That all are forms of Lord Hari?
Why do you offer stale plantains to Hari,
Who feeds the whole world
With all kinds of food?
How vainly do you offer to the Lord
Sweetmeats, fruits and Shundal!
Feed Him with the nectar of devotion
And be happy forever.

SACRIFICE THE PASSIONS

O Mind, why art thou so anxious?
Abandon all anxieties.
Repeat Lord Hari's Name.
Sit in meditation in a quiet place.
Worship the Lord in secret

So that none may know.
You will become proud
From all pomp of worship.
Why do you sacrifice animals?
Sacrifice egoism, Raga-Dvesha
And the sex-passions.
What need is there for drums,
Bells and tom-toms?
Clap your hands
And lay your mind at His feet.
Why do you endeavour to illumine Him
With lamp, petromax and candle?
Light the jewelled lamp of the Mind.
Let it flash its lustre day and night.

TO THE MIND AND SENSES—I

O Mind! You are a fool. You have dragged me in the avenues of senses and brought disgrace on me.

I will not keep company with you in future.

You are playing truant. You are a mischievous monkey. You are a strolling street-dog. You are a pig who revels in filth. You are a vile wretch. You are a vagabond.

You are born of Ananda (bliss). Your parentage is very high. Your father is Brahman or the Absolute. You are born in a very exalted, reputed and cultured family and yet you have degraded yourself and me also by your useless company. Your mother Maya also is born in a very high family. She is the wife of Brahman.

Your very Svabhava is to run towards external, sensual objects. Just as the water runs downwards without any effort by its very nature, so also you run by your very nature towards perishable mundane things. You get knocks, blows and kicks and yet you repeat the same old things. You have become like a habitual, old criminal. Any amount of advice and admonition has not done you any good nor reformed your nature and character. Fie on thee!

Now I will totally disconnect myself from you. I will leave you alone. You can do just as you please. Good-bye unto you! I am going back to my original Supreme Abode of Immortality and Eternal Bliss (Param Dhama).

O Ear! You also have been spoiled by your company with the mind. You do take immense delight in hearing the censure of others and all sorts of news of the world, but you do not take so much delight in hearing the Lilas of the Lord and the Kirtan, religious discourses and sermons.

O Eye! You have no interest in looking at the picture of the Lord, images of God in temples, saints and Mahatmas; but you are wholly absorbed in looking at women.

O Nose! You are highly pleased in smelling the odour of scents, lavender, etc.; but you do not evince any interest in smelling the sweet fragrance of the flowers etc., offered.to the Lord.

O Tongue! You dance in joy in eating sweet-meats, fruits and all other palatable dishes; but there is no joy for you in taking Charanamrita and Prasad of the Lord in temples.

O Skin! You rejoice in touching women and other soft things; but you do not experience happiness in touching the feet of the Lord and the saints.

O Vak-Indriya! You daily talk all sorts of non-sense. You take delight in abusing others, in scandal-mongering and back-biting; but you do not feel any joy in singing Lord's Name and doing Japa and studying the Gita and other holy scriptures.

O Hands! You are highly pleased in taking bribes, in beating others, in stealing others' properties, in touching women; but you do not rejoice in doing charity, in serving the poor people and Sadhus, in doing worship of the Lord and offering flowers to Him.

O Feet! You take delight in going to cinemas, clubs, restaurants, hotels; but you do not find happiness in going to places of pilgrimage, temples and Ashrams.

O Senses! Behave properly in future. This is the last chance for you. Improve yourselves and get a good name. If you live for the Lord and serve Him, you will be ever happy. All miseries will come to an end.

Good-bye unto you all!

TO THE MIND AND SENSES—II

O Mind!
Always think of Lord Narayana.
Repeat Hari's Name.

Meditate on His form with four hands.
Fix yourself at His lotus-feet.

O Tongue!
Always sing Achyuta's Name and glory.
Do Kirtan and Bhajan.
Take His Prasad and Charanamrita.

O Ears!
Hear the Lilas of Kesava
And Hari Kirtan.

O Eyes!
Behold the image of Mukunda.

O Nose!
Smell the Tulasi leaves and flowers
That have been used in the worship of
Sri Krishna.

O Hands!
Offer flowers to Govinda.
Wave lights to Sri Rama.
Sweep the temple.
Clean the lights in the temple.
Bring flowers and Tulasi for worship.
Do charity and do service,
In worship of Panduranga.

O Feet!
Do Pradakshina around the temple.
Go on pilgrimage to temples of Vishnu.

O Body!
Serve the Bhaktas, saints and the Guru.
Serve the poor and the sick.

PRAYER TO THE LORD

O Lord of compassion!
Just hear my prayer.
The mind is very mischievous.
It is very turbulent.

It is disobedient.
I scolded the mind.
I gave him admonitions.
I gave him good counsels.
But he has his own ways.
I told the mind clearly
Not to take Laddu
When there is diarrhoea.
He said, 'Very well'
Like the lady in labour pains.
But he eats Laddu again!
I told the mind
Not to speak ill of others.
But he never leaves this habit!
I again and again told the mind
Not to become angry.
But he becomes annoyed
For trifling things!
I cannot control the mind.
Thou art the Indweller
And prompter of the mind.
You alone can control him,
Please do this for me.

PSYCHIC INFLUENCE

PERSONALITY

In common parlance when one says that Dr. Tagore has a good personality, he means that Dr. Tagore has a strong, stalwart, tall figure, a beautiful complexion, a fine nose, sharp and lustrous eyes, broad chest, a muscular body, symmetrical limbs, curly hair and so on. That which distinguishes one man from another is personality. In reality, personality is something more than this. It includes a man's character, intelligence, noble qualities, moral conduct, intellectual attainments, certain striking faculties, special traits or characteristics, sweet powerful voice, etc. All these things put together constitute the personality of Mr. So and so. The sum total of all these things makes up the personality of a man. Mere physical characteristics cannot make up the personality.

What you call an umbrella is really a long stick plus a black cloth and some thin iron pieces. Similarly, what you call 'personality' is really the external physical body, plus brain and the nervous system and the mind which has its seat in the brain.

If one man is able to influence many people, we say that such and such a man has a magnetic personality. A full-blown Yogi or Jnani is the greatest personality in the world. He may be of a small stature. He may be ugly also. He may be clad in rags. And yet he is a mighty personality, a great Mahatma. People flock to him in thousands and pay homage to him. A man who has attained ethical perfection by the continued practice of right conduct or Yama and Niyama has also got a magnetic personality. He can influence millions. But he is inferior to a Jnani or a Yogi who has got full knowledge of the Self.

Dr. Samuel Johnson had an awkward figure, a pot belly and unsymmetrical limbs. But he was the greatest personality of the age. He was neither a Yogi nor a Jnani. But he had intellectual attainments. He was a great essayist. He had good command of the English language. He was famous for his bombastic style. It was called Johnsonian English. Just hear some of his lines: "Will you be kind enough to allow my digits into your odoriferous concavity and extract therefrom some of the pulverised atoms which, ascending my nasal promontory, cause a great titillation of all my olfactory nerves?"

Rich people also have some personality. This is due to the 'Money-power'. They may be licentious. Money has its own share in the making up of the personality of man. It infuses in him a sort of colouring. The charitable nature may cover up their licentious nature and may send some fragrance abroad. People flock to them. Lord Jesus says: "Charity covereth a multitude of sins."

Character gives a strong personality to man. People respect a man who has a good character. Moral people command respect everywhere. He who is honest, sincere, truthful, kind and liberal-hearted always commands respect and influence at the hands of people. Sattvic virtues make a man divine. He who speaks truth and practises Brahmacharya becomes a great and dynamic personality. Even if he speaks a word, there is power in it and people are magnetised. Character-building is of paramount importance if a man wants to develop his personality. Brahmacharya is the root of a magnetic personality. No development of a strong personality is possible without celibacy.

Personality can be developed. Practice of virtues is indispensable. One should try to be always cheerful. A morose, gloomy man cannot attract and influence people. He is an infectious parasite amidst society. He spreads gloom everywhere. A man of a jolly nature with the spirit of service, with humility and obedience can influence millions. The law of "like attracts like" operates in the physical and mental planes. A man of strong personality need not send invitations to people. Just as bees come and perch as soon as flowers blossoms, so also people of lesser mind are attracted to men of strong personality, of their own accord.

A powerful, sweet voice, knowledge of music, knowledge of astrology, astronomy, palmistry, art, etc., add to the personality of man. One should know how to behave and adjust himself with other people. You must talk sweetly and gently. This produces a tremendous impression. You must be polite, civil, courteous. You must treat others with respect and consideration. He who gives respect to others gets respect. Humility brings respect by itself. Humility is a virtue that subdues the hearts of others. A man of humility is a powerful magnet or loadstone.

You must know the ways to approach people. You must know how to talk with them and how to behave towards them. Behaviour is most important. An arrogant, stubborn and self-willed man can never become a man of strong personality. He is disliked by all.

Develop joyful nature. Always keep a smiling and cheerful face. This will give you a good personality. People will like you much. Your superiors will be very much pleased. Have an amiable nature, a modest and unassuming temperament. You will succeed in your interviews with all big guns. Take down notes of what you want to speak with them in the course of the interview. Keep a small memorandum slip in your pocket. Remember the points well and talk slowly and gently. Then the man will patiently hear. Do not be agitated in your talks. Do not become nervous. Be bold. Pay respects with sincerity as soon as you see the person. Do not stand erect like the proverbial man who holds the gas-light in a marriage procession. Gently bow your head with feeling. The man will be immensely pleased. He will be glad to receive you with a depth of feeling and you will get success in your interview. Talk about the important points first and just review in your mind whether you have finished all the points you wanted to talk. In the West, people care for personality. In India, people care for individuality and assert: "Aham Asmi"—which means "I exist." They try to destroy the personality to realise the Self.

Endeavour to possess a magnetic personality. Try to possess that strange and mysterious power, personal magnetism which charms and fascinates people. Understand the secrets of personal influence. Develop your will-power. Conserve all leaking energy. Enjoy robust, blooming health and a high standard of vigour and vitality and achieve social and financial success in every walk of life. If you can understand the amazing secrets of personal influence, you can increase the earning capacity and can have a broader and happier life.

A strong personality is a very valuable asset for you. You can develop it if you will. "Where there is a will there is a way" is a maxim which is as true today as it was from the time of Adam. Win laurels of name and fame and attain success in life through a dynamic personality. You can do it. You must do it. You know the science now. I shall back you up.

POWER OF SUGGESTIONS

You should have a clear understanding of suggestions and their effects upon the mind. You should be careful in the use of suggestion. Never give wrong suggestion which will have destructive results to anybody. You will be doing a great harm and a disservice to him. Think well before you speak. Teachers and professors should have a thorough knowledge of the Science of Suggestion and Auto-suggestion. Then they can educate and elevate students in an efficient manner. In Southern India, when children cry out in houses, parents frighten them by saying: "Look here, Balu! Irendukannan has come. (The two-eyed man has come.) Keep quiet. Or I will hand you over to this man." "Puchandi (or ghost) has come" and suggestions of this sort are very destructive. The child becomes timid. The minds of children are elastic, tender and pliable. Samskaras are indelibly impressed at this age. Changing or obliterating the Samskaras becomes impossible when they grow. When the child grows into a man, he manifests timidity. Parents should infuse courage into the minds of their children. They should say: "Here is a lion. See the lion in this picture. Roar like a lion. Be courageous. See the picture of Shivaji, Arjuna or Clive. Become chivalrous." In the West, teachers show the pictures of battlefields to children and say: "Look here, James! See this picture of Napoleon. Look at his cavalry. Won't you like to become a Commander-in-Chief of the army or a Brigadier-General?" They infuse courage into the minds of children from their very childhood. When they grow, these Samskaras get strengthened by additional external stimuli.

Doctors should have a thorough knowledge of the science of suggestion. Sincere, sympathetic doctors are very rare. Doctors who have no knowledge of suggestion do more harm than good. They kill patients sometimes by unnecessarily frightening them. If there is a little cough of an ordinary nature, the doctor says: "Now, my friend, you have got T.B. You must go to Bhowali or Switzerland or Vienna. You must go in for a course of tuberculin injections." Poor patient is frightened. There is not at all any sign of consumption. The case is an ordinary one. It is simple catarrh of the chest from exposure to chills. The patient actually develops phthisis by fright and worry owing to the wrong destructive suggestion of the doctor. The doctor ought to have told him: "Oh, it is nothing. It is simple cold. You will be all right by tomorrow. Take a purgative and inhale a little oil of eucalyptus. Adjust your diet. It is better you fast today." Such a doctor is God Himself. He must be adored. A doctor may say now: "Well, sir, if I say so, I will lose my practice. I cannot pull on in this world." This is a mistake. Truth always gains victory. People will run to you as you are sympathetic and kind. You will have a roaring practice.

There is healing by suggestion. This is a drugless treatment. This is suggestive therapeutics. By good and powerful suggestion, you can cure any disease. You will have to learn this science and practise it. All doctors of Homoeopathic, Allopathic, Ayurvedic and Unani systems should know this science. They can combine this system along with their own systems. They will have a roaring practice by this happy combination.

Do not be easily influenced by the suggestions of others. Have your own sense of individuality. A strong suggestion, though it does not influence the subject immediately, will operate in due course. It will never go in vain.

We all live in a world of suggestions. Our character is daily modified unconsciously by association with others. We unconsciously imitate the actions of those whom we admire. We daily absorb the suggestions of those with whom we come in daily contact. We are acted upon by these suggestions. A man of weak mind yields to the suggestions of a man of strong mind.

The servant is always under the influence of the suggestions of his master. The wife is under the influence of the suggestions of her husband. The patient is under the influence of the suggestions of the doctor. The student is under the influence of the teacher. Custom is nothing but the product of suggestion. The dress that you put on, the manners, the behaviour and even the food that you eat are all the outcome of suggestions only. Nature suggests in various ways. The running rivers, the shining sun, fragrant flowers, the growing trees, are all incessantly sending you suggestions.

All the prophets of yore were hypnotists. They knew the science of suggestion fully well. Their words had tremendous powers. Every word they uttered had magic power and a peculiar charm. All the hearers remained spell-bound. A spiritual preacher produces a sort of hypnosis in the minds of others. The hearers come under the influence of his suggestions.

There is power in every word that is spoken. There are two kinds of Vrittis, viz., Sakti-Vritti and Lakshana-Vritti in words. In the Upanishads, the Lakshana-Vritti is taken. "Veda-svarupoham" does not mean "embodiment of Vedas." The Lakshana-Vritti does denote "Brahman" who can be reached by the study of the Upanishads alone: by the Sabda Pramana alone.

Mark here the power in the words. If anyone calls another "Sala" or "Badmash" or "fool," he is thrown into a state of fury immediately. Fight ensues. If you address anyone as "Bhagavan" or "Prabhu" or "Maharaj," he is immensely pleased.

HYPNOTISM AND MESMERISM

A greater mind can influence a smaller mind. This is mesmerism or hypnotism. This is not at all a new science. It is also Anadi. It has existed from beginningless time. It was only Mesmer and Braid who popularised this science in the West. Hindu Rishis knew this science in days long gone by. Demosthenes and Socrates, Visvamitra and Patanjali Maharshi used hypnotism and mesmerism in olden days. It was James Braid, the Manchester surgeon, who gave this name hypnotism to this science and who first founded this science in the West. The term 'hypnotism' has a Greek origin which means sleep.

Mesmer was a philosopher, physician and astrologer. He was born in 1784. He died in 1815. He brought in the theory of animal magnetism. He believed that man had a wonderful magnetic power by which he could heal and influence other people. He made use of this power in the treatment of various diseases. The system of mesmerism is known after his name.

All orators possess the power of hypnotism. Consciously or unconsciously they subdue the minds of hearers. The hearers are swayed by the powerful speech of orators. They are charmed, as it were, for the time being. All the religious preachers and prophets of the world possessed this power to a remarkable degree.

Suggestion is the master-key to hypnotism. The hypnotist

suggests and the operator acts implicitly. The lesser mind implicitly obeys the higher mind. Suggestion is an idea communicated by the operator to the subject. Suggestion is a science. One should be very clever in putting the suggestion in a skilful manner. We live in the world of suggestion and under the magic spell and influence of hypnotism. Hypnotism is a mighty power in the world. We are all hypnotised by the spell of Maya. We will have to dehypnotise ourselves to obtain a knowledge of the Self. Vedanta gives powerful suggestions to dehypnotise ourselves. Hypnotism is a state of mind in which suggestions, verbal and visual, are received as true whether they are true or not. There is an irresistible desire to carry out the suggestions. The power of will and the power of suggestion are very closely linked together.

The operator develops his power of hypnosis through the practice of crystal-gazing and other methods of concentration. Pranayama also helps a lot in the development of this power. Brahmacharya also is very essential. A man of loose character cannot become a powerful hypnotist.

A man can be hypnotised by gazing or suggestion or passes. The operator makes some 'passes' in front of the subject and the subject passes into a hypnotic state. The passes in the reverse direction will bring back the subject to normal consciousness. Sometimes, if the hypnotist is a powerful man, he can hypnotise several persons in a group or bunch. That man who resists the suggestions of the hypnotist cannot be hypnotised so easily. If one believes in the hypnotiser and thinks he can be hypnotised, he can rapidly come under his spell and operation.

There is also another variety of hypnotism called the stage hypnotism in which the hypnotist hypnotises the whole audience and shows several tricks. He puts a lady in a small tight box in standing posture, ties her hands and closes the box and then cuts the box with a saw. Afterwards he opens the broken box and the lady comes out without any injury. A famous Fakir ascended the platform in England with a red rope in his hand, threw it in the air and climbed up through the rope and then vanished in the air. This is stage-hypnotism. This is the famous 'rope-trick' of the Fakir. There was no impression in the plate of a camera. This is a trick only after all. A hypnotist hypnotises a boy and places his head and feet over two chairs. He then places a large weight over his body. The body does not bend. He asks the audience to clasp the fingers of both hands and makes a strong current of electricity to pass. They all actually feel the shock of the current. He first starts the current in his own hands and thinks strongly that the current should pass to the hands of others.

Hypnotism is very beneficial in the correction of bad habits of boys and in the treatment of hysteria and other nervous diseases. The opium habit and the drinking habit are also removed. The hypnotist should not misuse the power in wrong channels. He will get a hopeless downfall. Wherever there is power, there is side by side a chance for misuse. There are temptations also. One has to be very careful.

A hypnotist looks at the second-hand of a watch and the second-hand stops immediately. He asks a subject to look at the second-hand of a watch and stops his thinking. His eyes becomes listless. A hypnotist makes the body of a hypnotised subject to levitate and move in the air through a big iron ring. The hypnotised person is blindfolded. He is able to walk over a rope that is distributed on the ground in quite a zigzag manner. He is able to read the contents of a sealed letter and give proper answers to questions. Here the unconscious mind of the subject operates. He can see through an opaque wall. Marvellous are the mysteries of the science of hypnotism! Thanks to Mr. James Braid of happy memory!

TELEPATHY

Telepathy is thought-transference from one person to another. Just as sound moves in the ethereal space, so also thought moves in the mental space, Chidakasa. There is an ocean of ether all round. There is also an ocean of mind all round. Thought has shape, colour, weight and form. It is as much matter as this pencil. When you have some good thought of an elevating nature sometimes, it is very difficult to say whether it is your own thought or the thought of some other person. Thoughts of other persons enter your brain.

Telepathy was the first wireless telegraphy of the Yogis. Yogis send their messages through telepathy. Thought travels with electric speed that is unimaginable. Sometimes you think of a friend with such intensity in the evening that you get a letter from him early in the morning. This is unconscious telepathy.

Your powerful thought has travelled and reached the brain of your friend immediately and he has replied you then and there. So many interesting and wonderful things are going on in the thought-world. Ordinarily, people who have not developed the power of telepathy are groping in the darkness.

Telepathy is communication of mind with mind. The pineal gland which is considered by occultists as the seat of the soul plays an important part in telepathy. It is this pineal gland that actually receives messages. It is a small piece of nervous matter that is imbedded in the brain or hind-brain in the floor of the mind ventricle. It is an endocrine gland that is ductless. It has got an internal secretion which is directly poured into the blood.

Practise telepathy in the beginning from a short distance. It is better to practise at nights, to start with. Ask your friend to have the receptive attitude and concentration at ten o'clock. Ask him to sit on Virasana or Padmasana with closed eyes in a dark room. Try to send your message exactly at the appointed time. Concentrate on the thoughts that you want to send. Will strongly now. The thoughts will leave your brain and enter the brain of your friend. There may be some mistakes in the beginning here and there. When you advance in practice and know the technique well, you will always be correct in sending and receiving messages. Later on, you will be able to forward messages to different corners of the world. Thought-waves vary in intensity and force. The sender and receiver should practise great and intense concentration. Then there will be force in sending the messages, clarity and accuracy in receiving the messages. Practise in the beginning telepathy from one room to the next room in the same house. This science is very pleasant and interesting. It needs patient practice. Brahmacharya is very essential.

You can influence another man without any audible language. What is wanted is concentration of thought that is directed by the will. This is telepathy. Here is an exercise for your practice in telepathy. Think of your friend or cousin who is living in a distant land. Bring a clear-cut image of his face to your mind. If you have his photo look at it and speak to it audibly. When you retire to bed think of the picture with intense concentration. He will write to you the desired letter the following day or so. Try this yourself. Do not doubt. You will be quite surprised. You will get success and firm conviction in the science of telepathy. Sometimes, when you are writing something or reading a newspaper, suddenly you get a message from some one near and dear to you. You think of him suddenly. He has sent you a message. He has thought of you seriously. Thought-vibrations travel faster than light or electricity. In such instances, the subconscious mind receives the messages or impressions and transmits the same to the conscious mind.

Great adepts or Mahatmas who live in the Himalayan caves transmit their messages through telepathy to deserving aspirants or Yogis in the world. These Jijnasus or Yogis carry out their orders and disseminate their knowledge far and wide. It is not necessary that Mahatmas should come on the platform and preach. Whether they preach or not, it does not matter. Their very life is an embodiment of teaching. They are the living assurance for God-realisation. Preaching on the platform belongs to the second-class type of men who have no knowledge of telepathy. The hidden Yogis help the world through their spiritual vibrations and magnetic aura more than the Yogis of the platform. In these days, politicians expect even Sannyasins to work on the political platform. They even force them. As their minds are saturated with Karma Samskaras, they are not able to grasp and understand the grandeur, utility and magnanimity of pure Nivritti of Dhyana-Yogis. The field or domain of activity of Sannyasins is entirely different. They cannot become presidents of Sabhas or Mandalas. Their sphere is of a cosmic nature. Their field is Adhyatmic that relates to the science of the Self. Let me repeat the words of Bhagavan Sri Krishna:

"Lokesmin dvividha nishtha pura prokta mayanagha,
Jnanayogena samkhyanam karmayogena yoginam."

"In this world there is a twofold path, as I said before, O sinless one, that of Yoga by Knowledge, of the Sankhyas, and that of Yoga by action, of the Yogis" (Gita, III-3). The glory of Hinduism will be lost, if Sannyasins become extinct. They can never become extinct from India. The Samskaras of Tyaga and renunciation are ingrained in their cells, nerves and tissues. Buddhists have got monks. Mohammedans have their Fakirs. Christians have got their priests, clergymen and reverend fathers. Every religion has people in the world with the spirit of renunciation. There must be a set of people in every religion who are entirely devoted to divine contemplation. It is the duty of householders to attend to their wants. They will receive their blessings. It is these people who lead the life of Nivritti Marga, who can make researches in Yoga and give to the world new messages. It is these men who can really help the world at large and do Loka-Kalyana.

CLAIRVOYANCE

Clairvoyance is vision of distant objects through the inner astral eye or psychic eye. Just as you have physical sense in the physical body, there are astral counterparts of these Indriyas in the inner, subtle, astral body. The Yogi or the occultist develops these inner organs through practice of concentration. He develops clairvoyant vision. He can see objects in far-off climes. This Siddhi or power is called Dura Drishti.

Just as light rays penetrate a glass, just as X-rays penetrate solid, opaque objects, so also the Yogi can see the things through a solid wall, can see the contents of a sealed envelope and the contents of a hidden treasure underneath the ground through his inner psychic eye. This psychic eye is the eye of intuition or Divya Drishti or Jnana-Chakshus. One has to develop this inner eye through concentration. Just as the microscope magnifies the small cells, germs, etc., so also he can see things of the astral world very clearly through this inner eye and can magnify them also by special focussing of the inner astral lens.

He creates an astral tube by willing and the strong wishing and thinking and, through this astral tube, he sees things at a distance. The vision may not be very clear in the beginning. Just as the new-born baby learns, so also he learns in the beginning. As he advances in his practice, his inner vision becomes quite distinct. There is another method. The Yogi takes astral journey and sees things during his astral travelling unconsciously.

Just as light rays travel in space, so also astral light rays travel with tremendous velocity. They are caught up by the astral eye. Every one of you has got these astral senses. But few only consciously develop them. A clairvoyant can see the events of the past by looking into the Akasic records and have Trikala Jnana also. The degree of power varies in different individuals. Advanced clairvoyants are very rare.

CLAIRAUDIENCE

Clairaudience is the hearing of distant sounds in the astral plane by means of the astral ear. The process is similar to clair-voyance. The astral sound-vibrations are caught hold of by the astral sense of hearing. A clairvoyant need not necessarily be a clairaudient. These are two distinct powers.

Patanjali Maharshi gives the method to develop this power of distant hearing. *"Shrotrakasayoh"* (Patanjali Yoga Sutras, 3-41). By Samyama on the relation between the ear and Akasa, comes divine hearing. Samyama is concentration and meditation combined.

All the inhabitants of the Pitriloka possess this power. Where their descendants perform Sraaddha and Tarpana in this world, they hear these sounds through the power of clairaudience and they are highly pleased.

These psychic Siddhis are all by-products of concentration. Just as there are various coal-tar derivatives and various petroleum preparations, so also there are these Siddhis mani-fest in a Yogi when he concentrates. These are all obstacles in the path of spirituality. The aspirant should ignore them and de-velop Vairagya. Then only will he be able to reach the goal.

All the sound vibrations of the past are in the Akasic re-cords. The Yogi can hear these sounds nicely. He can hear the sounds of Shakespeare, Johnson, Valmiki, Visvamitra, etc. Just as you can hear now the music and song of a songster who died fifty years ago in the gramophonic records, so also the Yogi can hear the sounds of those persons of the past by concentration connecting his astral hearing to the Akasic re-cords. Just as impressions of your boyhood remain in your brain and the subconscious mind, so also the impressions of old sounds remain in the Akasic records. One should know the Yogis' technique only. Just as the experienced record-keeper in the office can bring out in a short time any old record, so also the Yogi can hear the sound of good old days in the twinkling of an eye.

ANNIHILATION OF MIND

Mind is Atma-Sakti. Mind is a bundle of Vasanas (desires) and Sankalpas (thoughts, imaginations). Mind is a bundle of Raga-Dvesha (likes and dislikes). Annihilation of mind is Manonasa.

Manolaya is temporary absorption of the mind. This cannot give Moksha. The mind can come back again and wander in sensual objects. Manonasa alone can give release or Moksha.

VICHARA

How is the mind purified, brought under control and how are its activities stopped and how is it annihilated? Here are some useful and practical points. Mind can be controlled and annihilated by Vichara or enquiry of "Who am I?" This is the best and most effective method. This will annihilate the mind. This is the Vedantic method. Realise the unreality of the mind through philosophical thinking.

SLAY THE EGO

Eradicate the feeling of egoism. Ego is the seed of the tree of mind. "I" thought is the source of all thoughts. All thoughts are centred on the little "I." Find out what the little "I" is. This little "I" will dwindle into an airy nothing. It will be absorbed in the infinite "I" or Parabrahman, the source for the little "I" or Ahankara (egoism).

The Sun of Self-realisation is fully seen when the cloud of ego disappears.

VAIRAGYA

Vairagya (dispassion) is another method for annihilating mind. It is distaste for objects of sense-pleasures by finding out the defects in the sensual life. Objects are perishable. Sensual pleasure is momentary and illusory.

ABHYASA

Abhyasa or practice is another method. Concentrate the mind by fixing it on Brahman. Make it steady. Abhyasa is ceaseless meditation. This leads to Samadhi.

NON-ATTACHMENT

Asanga or non-attachment is a sword to destroy the mind. Take the mind away from objects. Detach. Attach. Detach it from the objects. And attach it to the Lord. Do this again and again. The essence of the seed of the sprout of world experience, which is desire, can be destroyed by the fire of non-attachment.

VASANA-KSHAYA

Vasana-Kshaya is another method. Vasana is desire. Renunciation of desires leads to Vasana-Kshaya. This will lead to annihilation of mind (Manonasa). Desire for objects of pleasure is bondage; giving it up is emancipation. Desire is the most essential nature of the mind. Mind and egoism are synonymous.

PRANAYAMA

Vibration of Prana causes movement of the mind. It gives life to the mind. Pranayama or control of Prana will stop the activities of the mind. But it cannot destroy the mind to its roots like Vichara.

CONTROL THE THOUGHTS

Control the thoughts or Sankalpas. Avoid imagination or day-dreaming. The mind will be annihilated. Extinction of Sankalpas alone is Moksha or release. The mind is destroyed when there is no imagination. The experience of the world illusion is due to your imagination. It vanishes away when imagination is completely stopped.

RENUNCIATION

Mental renunciation of possessions is another method. The absolute experience can also be realised if you learn to be in a state of thought-suspending Samadhi.

BE BALANCED

Attainment of equanimity is another method. Be balanced in pain and pleasure, heat and cold, etc.

He alone experiences everlasting peace and eternal bliss who has transcended the mind and rests in his own Satchidananda Atman.

DEVOTION AND SERVICE

Japa, Kirtan, prayer, devotion, service of Guru and study are also means to annihilate the mind.

GLOSSARY

A

ABHASA: reflection
ABHEDA: without difference
ABHIMANA: ego-centred attachment
ABHYASA: spiritual practice
ACHARYA: preceptor
ADAMBHITVA: unpretentiousness
ADHAMA-UDDHARAKA: uplifter of the downtrodden
ADHIBHAUTIC: elemental
ADHIDAIVIC: celestial
ADHYATMIC: spiritual
ADVAITA: non-duality
ADVAITA-NISHTHA: establishment in the state of non-duality
AGNI: fire
AGNI-ASTRA: fire-missile
AGNIHOTRA: a fire-offering
AHAM: "I" or the ego
AHAM BRAHMA ASMI: I am Brahman
AHANGRAHA UPASANA: meditation in which the
    aspirant identifies himself with Brahman
AHANKARA: egoism
AHIMSA: non-violence
AISVARYA: divine powers
AJNA CHAKRA: centre of spiritual energy between the
    two eyebrows
AJNANA: ignorance
AKHANDA EKARASA: the one undivided Essence
AKARTA: non-doer
AKASA: ether

AKASAMATRA: ether only
AKHANDA: indivisible
AKHANDAKARA: of the nature of indivisibility
AMALAKA: *phyllanthus emlica*, Indian gooseberry
AMRITA: nectar
AMRITA PUTRA: nectar's son
AMSA: part
ANADI: beginningless
ANAHATA: mystic sounds heard by Yogins
ANANDAGHANA: mass of bliss
ANANDAMAYA: full of bliss
ANANTA: infinite
ANANYA BHAKTI: exclusive devotion to the Lord
ANASAKTA: unattched
ANATMA: not-Self
ANITYA: transitory
ANNAMAYA KOSHA: food sheath, the gross physical body
ANTARGATA: immanent
ANTARIKA: internal
ANTAR-INDRIYA: internal sense-organ
ANTARJYOTIS: inner Light
ANTARMUKHA VRITTI: introspective thought-current
ANTARVAHA SARIRA: the subtle body of a Yogi by
      which he accomplishes entry into the bodies of others
ANUBHAVA: spiritual realisation
ANUBHAVA-GURU: preceptor who has had pesonal
      spiritual realisation
ANUSANDHANA: enquiry into the nature of Brahman
ANVAYA: the positive aspect
APANA: the down-going breath
APANCHIKRITA: non-quintuplicated
APAS: water
APAVADA-YUKTI: employment of the logical
      method of negation
ASABDA: soundless
ASAMPRAJNATA SAMADHI: superconscious state
      where the mind is totally annihilated
ASANA: bodily pose

ASANGA: unattached
ASHRAMA: hermitage
ASHTA: eight
ASHTAVADHANA: doing eight things at a time
ASTI-BHATI-PRIYA: same as Satchidananda, the eternal
    qualities inherent in Brahman
ASTRA: a missile invoked with a Mantra
ASUBHA: inauspicious
ASUDDHA: impure
ASUDDHA MANAS: impure mind
ASVANI MUDRA: a Hatha Yogic Kriya
ATMA(N): the Self
ATMA-DRISHTI: the vision of seeing everything as the Self
ATMA-JNANA: Knowledge of the Self
ATMAKARA: pertaining to Atman
ATMA-SAKSHATKARA: Self-realisation
ATMA-SAKTI: Soul-power
AVASTHA: state
AVICHHINNA: continuous
AVIDYA: nescience
AVINASI: imperishable
AVYAKTA: unmanifest

B

BAHIRMUKHA VRITTI: the outgoing thought-current
BAHIR-VRITTI: same as above
BAHIR-VRITTI-NIGRAHA: restraint of the outgoing
thought-current
BAHYA-VRITTI-NIGRAHA: ṣame as above
BHAJANA: devotional singing
BHAKTA: devotee
BHAKTI YOGA: the Yoga of devotion
BHASTRIKA PRANAYAMA: a type of breathing exercise
BHAVA(NA): attitudinal feeling
BHAVA-SAMADHI: superconscious state attained by
    devotees through intense divine emotion
BHEDA BUDDHI: the intellect which divides
BHOGA: enjoyment
BHOKTRITVA: the stage of being an enjoyer

BHRANTIMATRA: mere illusion
BHUTAJAYA: control over the elements
BHUTA-SAKTI: the power of the element
BRAHMACHARI(N): celibate
BRAHMACHARYA: celibacy
BRAHMAKARA VRITTI: thought of Brahman
BRAHMA LOKA: the world of Brahma,
    the four-headed Creator
BRAHMAN: the Absolute Reality
BRAHMANA: member belonging to the priestly caste
BRAHMA NADI: same as Sushumna
BRAHMA-NISHTHA: one who is established in the
    Knowledge of Brahman
BRAHMANUBHAVA: Self-realisation
BRAHMIN: Same as Brahmana
BUDDHI: intellect

C

CHAITANYA: pure consciousness
CHAKRA: centre of spiritual energy
CHANCHALA: wavering
CHANCHALATA: tossing of the mind
CHARANAMRITA: water sanctified by the feet of a
    Deity or of a holy man
CHATAK: a bird
CHELA (Hindi): Disciple
CHIDGHANA: mass of consciousness
CHINMAYA: full of consciousness
CHINTANA: thinking
CHIRANJIVI: one who has gained eternal life
CHIT-MATRA: consciousness alone
CHIT-SVARUPA: of the very form of consciousness
CHITTA: subconscious mind
CHITTA-SUDDHI: purity of mind

D

DAMA: restraint of the sense-organs
DAMBHA: hypocrisy
DANA: charity

DARPA: vanity
DARSANA: vision
DEHADHYASA: attachment to the body, identification
    with the body
DEHATMA-BUDDHI: the intellect that makes one identify
    with the body
DEVA: a celestial being
DEVATA: a Deity, also the Lord
DHAIRYA: courage
DHARANA: concentration
DHARMA: righteous conduct; characteristic
DHRITI: spiritual patience
DHYANA: meditation
DHYANA YOGA: the Yoga of meditation
DINABANDHU: friend of the poor and the helpless, God
DOSHA: defect
DOSHA-DHRISHTI: the vision that perceives defects
DRISHTI: vision
DRISHTI-SRISHTI VADA: the theory that the world
    exists only so long as it is perceived
DURA-DRISHTI: distant vision
DVAITA: dualism

E

EKADASI: the eleventh day of the Hindu lunar fortnight
EKAGRA: one-pointed
EKAGRATA: one-pointedness of mind

G

GANIKA: prostitute
GHRINA: ill-will
GUNA: quality
GURU: preceptor

H

HATHA YOGA: the Yoga of physical perfection
HIRANYAGARBHA: Cosmic mind
HITA: astral tubes near the heart

I

IDA NADI: the psychic nerve-current which
flows in the left nostril
INDRIYA: sense-organ
ISVARA: Lord, God

J

JAALA: jugglery, illusion
JAGADGURU: world-preceptor
JAGAT: world
JAGRAT: waking state
JALANDHARA BANDHA: a Hatha Yogic exercise
JAPA: repetition of the Name of the Lord
JIVA: the individual soul
JIVANMUKTA: one who is liberated in this life
JIVASRISHTI: creations of the individual soul such as egoism,
mine-ness, etc.
JIVATMA(N): the individual soul
JNANA: knowledge of the Self
JNANA-BHUMIKA: plane of knowledge
JNANAGNI: fire of spiritual knowledge
JNANA-INDRIYAS: organs of knowledge or perception
JNANA YOGA: the Yoga of knowledge
JNANA YOGI(N): one who practises the
Yoga of Knowledge
JNANI(N): the sage of wisdom

K

KALA-SAKTI: Divine Mother manifesting as Time
KALPA: a period of 432,00,00,000 years
KALPANAMATRA: lying only in imagination
KAMA: desire, lust
KAMANA: longing
KANDAMULA: roots and tubers
KARANA SARIRA: the causal body or the seed body
KARIKA: commentary
KARMA: action operating through the Law of
Cause and Effect
KARMA-INDRIYAS: organs of action

KARMA YOGI(N): one who practises the Yoga of
    selfless service
KASHAYA: a subtle influence in the mind produced
    by enjoyment, hidden Vasana
KEVALA ASTI: pure Existence
KIRTAN: singing the Lord's Name
KRIYA: Hatha Yogic exercise
KRODHA: anger
KSHAMA: forgiveness
KSHATRIYA: member belonging to the ruling caste
KULA-KUNDALINI: same as Kundalini
KUMBHAKA: retention of breath
KUNDALINI: the primordial cosmic energy located in the
    individual
KUTASTHA: the rock-seated, unchanging Brahman

L

LAKSHANA: characteristic
LAKSHYA: goal
LAYA: absorption
LILA: divine sport
LILA-VILASA: the splendour of divine sport
LINGA SARIRA: the subtle body, the astral body
LOBHA: covetousness
LOKA-KALYAN(A): good of the world

M

MADA: pride
MADHUKARI BHIKSHA: alms collected from door to
    door like a bee collecting honey from flower to flower
MAHABHEDA: a Hatha Yogic Kriya
MAHARAJA: emperor
MAHARSHI: great sage
MAHATMA: great soul
MAHAVAKYA: (Lit.) Great sentence; Upanishadic
    declarations, four in number, expressing the identity
    between the individual soul and the Supreme Soul
MAHAVAKYANUSANDHANA: enquiry into the truth of
    the Mahavakyas

MALA-VASANA-RAHITA: free from impurities and
     subtle desires
MANO-MANDIR: temple of mind
MANAS: mind
MANDALA: region, sphere
MANIPURA CHAKRA: centre of spiritual energy in the region
of the navel
MANONASA: annihilation of the mind
MANTRA: incantation
MANTRA SIDDHI: psychic power acquired through
     repetition of Mantra
MARGA: path
MATRA: unit; alone
MATSARYA: jealousy
MAUJA (Urdu): sweet will
MOUNA: silence
MAYA: the illusory power of Brahman
MAYURASANA: the peacock pose
MITHYA-DRISHTI: the vision that the universe is unreal
MITHYATVA-BUDDHI: the intellect that considers this
     world as unreal
MOHA: delusion
MOKSHA: liberation
MUDRA: a type of exercise in Hatha Yoga
MUKTI: liberation
MULA AVIDYA: primal ignorance
MULA BANDHA: a Hatha Yogic exercise
MULADHARA CHAKRA: centre of spiritual energy
     located at the base of the spinal column
MUNI: an ascetic
MURKHA: foolish

N

NADA: a mystic sound
NAIYAYIKAS: followers of the Nyaya school of
     Indian philosophy
NAMA: name
NAVA RIDDHIS: the nine minor spiritual powers
NETI, NETI: not this, not this

NIDIDHYASANA: profound meditation
NIRABHIMANATA: free from ego-centred attachment
NIRABHIMANI: one who is devoid of Abhimana
NIRAKARA: formless
NIRAVAYAVA: without limbs
NIRBIJA-SAMADHI: Samadhi wherein the Bija or seeds
    of Samskaras are fried by Jnana
NIRGUNA: without attributes
NIRGUNA BRAHMAN: the impersonal, attributeless
    Absolute
NIRODHA: suppression
NIRVANA: liberation
NIRVIKALPA: without the modifications of the mind
NIRVIKARA: unchanging
NIRVISHAYA: without object
NISCHAYATMIKA: with firm conviction
NISHKAMA: without desire
NISHKRIYA: without action
NISHTHA: meditation, establishment (in a certain state)
NISSANKALPA: devoid of thought or imagination
NIVRITTI: renunciation
NIYAMA: observances
NYAYA: logic

O

OM(KARA): the sacred syllable symbolising Brahman
OM TAT SAT: a benediction, a solemn invocation of the
    Divine blessing

P

PADMASANA: the lotus pose
PARAMAHAMSA: the fourth or the highest class of
    Sannyasins
PARAMANANDA: supreme bliss
PARAMATMA(N): the Supreme Soul
PARAM DHAMA: the Supreme Abode (Brahman)
PINGALA NADI: the psychic nerve-current which flows
    in the right nostril
PITRILOKA: the world of manes

PRABHU: Lord
PRACHARANA: A Hatha Yogic Kriya
PRADAKSHINA: circumambulation
PRAJNA: Chaitanya associated with the causal body
    in the deep sleep state
PRAJNANAGHANA: mass of consciousness
PRAJNA-SAKTI: power of consciousness
PRAKAMYA: unhampered will
PRAKASA: luminosity
PRAKRITI: Nature, the primitive non-intelligent principle
PRAMANA: proof
PRANA: the vital force, the life-current
PRANAVA: same as OM
PRANAVA DHVANI: the cosmic sound of OM
PRANAYAMA: control of breath
PRAPANCHA VISHAYA: worldly objects
PRARABDHA: destiny
PRASAD: anything consecrated by being offered to
    God or to a saint
PRATIPAKSHA BHAVANA: entertaining a counter-idea
PRATISHTA: reputation, fame
PRATYAGATMA: Inner Self, Brahman
PRATYAHARA: abstraction or withdrawal of the
    senses from their objects
PRATYAKSHA: direct perception
PRAVAHA: flood-tide
PREMA: affection
PRITHVI: earth
PUJA: worship
PUNDIT: a learned man
PURITAT NADI: one of the astral tubes or subtle
    passages in the body

R

RAGA-DVESHA: attraction and repulsion, like and dislike,
    love and hatred
RAGA-RAGINIS: melodic structures in music
RAJA: king
RAJASIC: passionate, active

RAJA YOGA: the Yoga of meditation
RIDDHIS: minor spiritual powers
RISHI: a seer of Truth
RUPA: form

S

SABDA: sound
SABDA-BHEDA: difference in sound
SABDA BRAHMAN: sound-form of Brahman
SABDA-JAALA: jugglery of words
SABHA: assembly
SADHAKA: spiritual aspirant
SADHANA: spiritual discipline
SADHU: a righteous man; a Sannyasin
SAGUNA: with attributes
SAHAJA: natural
SAHAJANANDA: state of bliss that has become natural
SAHAJA PARAMANANDA: state of absolute bliss that
        has become natural
SAHAJAVASTHA: superconscious state that has become
        natural and continuous
SAHASRARA: centre of spiritual energy at the
        crown of the head
SAKSHI: witness
SAKTI: power, potency
SAKTI-CHALANA: a Hatha Yogic Kriya
SAMA: calmness of mind induced by eradication of Vasanas
SAMA-BHAVA: feeling of equality
SAMADHANA: mental balance
SAMADHI: the state of superconsciousness where
        Absoluteness is experienced
SAMA-DRISHTI: equal vision
SAMANYA: ordinary
SAMBHAVI MUDRA: a Hatha Yogic Kriya
SAMSARA: the wheel of transmigration, cycle of birth
        and death
SAMSKARA: impression in the subconscious mind
SAMYAG-DARSANA: unclouded vision
SAMYAG-JNANA: Supreme knowledge

SAMYAMA: concentration, meditation and Samadhi
SAMYAVASTHA: the state of equanimity
SANDHYA: the daily worship of offering oblations to the
    Sun-God thrice a day—at sunrise, noon and sunset
SANGRAHA BUDDHI: the intellect that wants to
    accumulate and possess
SANKALPA: thought, imagination
SANKALPAMATRA: existing in thought only
SANKHYA: system of Indian philosophy founded by
    Kapila Muni
SANNYASI(N): renunciate, monk
SANTA-SIVA-ADVAITA: peaceful, auspicious, non-dual
    Brahman
SANTI: peace
SAPTA SVARA: the seven notes of the Indian
    scale of music
SARA VASTU: true substance, real entity
SARVA: all, everything
SARVANGASANA: a Yogic pose
SARVATMA BHAVA: feeling the one Self in all
SASTRAS: scriptures
SATAVADHANA: doing hundred things at a time
SATCHIDANANDA: Existence-Absolute, Knowledge-
    Absolute, Bliss-Absolute; Brahman
SATGURU: a true preceptor
SATSANGA: company of the wise
SAT SANKALPA: pure will
SATTVIC: pure
SATYA: truth
SAVIKALPA: with modifications
SAVITARKA SAMADHI: Samadhi with argumentation
SEVA: service
SIDDHANTA: established doctrine
SIDDHASANA: a meditative pose
SIDDHI: major psychic power; perfection
SIRSHASANA: the topsy-turvy pose
SIVOHAM: a Vedantic assertion meaning "I am Siva
    (the Absolute)"

SLOKA: verse
SMRITI: memory
SOHAM: a Vedantic assertion meaning "I am He
    (Brahman)"
SPHURANA: vibration, bursting forth
SRAADDHA: an annual ceremony when oblations are
    offered to the manes
SRADDHA: faith
SRUTI: musical refrain
STHULA AVIDYA: gross ignorance
STOTRAS: verses of praise
SUBHA: auspicious
SUDDHA: pure
SUDDHA MANAS: the pure mind
SUDDHA SANKALPA: pure will
SUDDHI: purity
SUKHA: happiness
SUKHASANA: the comfortable pose
SUKSHMA: subtle
SUKSHMA SARIRA: the subtle body, the astral body
SUSHUMNA: the psychic nerve-current that passes through
    the spinal column and through which the Kundalini is
    made to rise through the practice of Yoga
SUSHUPTI: the deep sleep state
SUTRADHARA: the wire-puller, God
SVABHAVA: innate nature
SVADHYAYA: reading of scriptures
SVAPNA: dreaming state
SVARA-SADHANA: science of breath
SVARODAYA: same as above
SVARUPA: essential nature
SVARUPA-LAKSHANA: distinguishing marks of the
    essential nature of Brahman

T

TADANA: a Hatha Yogic Kriya
TAIJASA: Chaitanya associated with the astral body
    in the dream state
TAMASIC: dull

TANMATRAS: subtle elements
TAPA: burning
TAPAS: penance
TAPASYA: practice of penance
TARPANA: libation of water for gratifying the manes
TATTVA: principle, Reality
TATTVA-JNANA: knowledge of Brahman
TAT TVAM ASI: That Thou Art
TIRTHA: place of pilgrimage usually containing a
      bathing place
TIRTHA-YATRA: pilgrimage
TITIKSHA: endurance
TRATAK(A): steady gazing
TRIKALA JNANA: knowledge of the three periods of time
TRIPHALA: three fruits used in the Ayurvedic
      system of medicine
TRIVENI: the place where three holy rivers meet
TUL(A)SI: the Indian holy basil plant
TURIYA: superconscious state
TUSHNIMBHUTA AVASTHA: a neutral state of the mind
TYAGA: renunciation

U

UDBODHAKA: stimulus, awakener
UDDIYANA: a Hatha Yogic exercise for raising the
      diaphragm
UDDIYANA BANDHA: same as above
UDGITHA: sonorous prayer prescribed in the Chhandogya
      Upanishad to be sung aloud
UNMANI AVASTHA: mindless state of Yogins
UPADHI: limiting adjunct
UPAHITA CHAITANYA: pure consciousness associated
      with Upadhis, the individual soul
UPASAKA: worshipper
UPASANA: worship
URDHVARETAS: a Yogi in whom the seminal energy
      flows upwards to the brain and is stored up as Ojas
      Sakti or spiritual energy
UTSAHA: cheerfulness, enthusiam

V

VAIRA-BHAKTI: constant and intense thought of God induced by hatred and enmity

VAIRAGYA: dispassion

VAISESHIKA: system of Indian philosophy founded by Kanada Rishi

VAK-INDRIYA: the organ of speech

VAKYA: sentence

VARUNA-ASTRA: water-missile

VASANA: latent subtle desire

VASTU: substance, entity

VAYU: air

VEDA: the revealed scripture of the Hindus containing the Upanishads

VEDANTA: (Lit.) end of the Vedas; the school of thought based primarily on the Vedic Upanishads

VIBHU: all-pervading

VICHARA: enquiry

VIDEHAMUKTA: one who has attained disembodied Salvation

VIJATIYA-VRITTI-TIRASKARA: casting aside of alien thoughts, i.e., thoughts other than those of God

VIJNANAMAYA KOSHA: the intellectual sheath

VIJNANAVADA: subjective idealism

VIKALPA: fancy

VIKARA: modifications or change

VIKSHEPA: tossing of mind

VIRAT: macrocosm; the Lord in His form as the manifested universe

VIRAT-VISVARUPA-DARSANA: the vision of the Lord's cosmic form

VISESHA: special

VISHAYA: sense-object

VISHAYAKARA-VRITTI: the flow of objective thinking

VISHAYA-VRITTI-PRAVAHA: the continuous thought-current of worldly objects

VISISHTADVAITA: the doctrine of conditioned non-dualism

VISTARA: expansion

VISVA: Chaitanya associated with the gross body
    in the waking state
VIVARTA: illusory appearance, apparent variation,
    superimposition
VIVEKA: discrimination
VRATA: religious vow
VRITTI: a wave of thought, a modification of the mind
VYAKARANATMAKA: grammatical
VYANJAKA: indicative, manifesting
VYAPAKA: all-pervading
VYAVAHARA-RAHITA: devoid of worldly activity
VYAVAHARIC: worldly
VYAVASAYATMIKA: with resolution and determination

Y

YAJNA: sacrifice
YAMA: self-restraint
YOGA: (Lit.) union; union of the individual soul with the
    Supreme Soul; any course which makes for such union
YOGABHRASHTA: one who has fallen from the high
    state of Yoga
YOGAMAYA: the power of divine illusion
YOGA SADHANA: the spiritual discipline of Yoga
YOGI(N): one who practises Yoga; one who is established
    in Yoga
YONI-MUDRA: the Mudra in which one closes the ears,
    eyes, nose and mouth with the thumbs and fingers of
    the hands to enable one to hear the Anahata sounds